Volpone

KU-451-704

Longman Study Texts

General editor: Richard Adams

Titles in the series:

Ben Jonson

Volpone

edited by
Peter Hollindale

with a personal essay by
Leo McKern

Longman

LONGMAN GROUP LIMITED
Longman House
Burnt Mill, Harlow, Essex, CM20 2JE, England
and Associated Companies throughout the world

© Longman Group Limited 1985
All rights reserved. No part of this publication
may be reproduced, stored in a retrieval system,
or transmitted in any form or by any means, electronic,
mechanical, photocopying, recording or otherwise,
without the prior written permission of the Publishers.

First published 1985
ISBN 0 582 35447 1

Set in 10/12 pt Baskerville, Linotron 202

Printed in Hong Kong by
Wing King Tong Co Ltd

Acknowledgements

The editor and publishers are grateful to Hodder and Stoughton for the use of their text of *Volpone*, to which some small alterations have been made for the purposes of an educational edition.

Leo McKern acknowledges Michael Jamieson's introduction to *Ben Jonson: Three Comedies* published by Penguin in 1966 in the writing of his personal essay.

The photographs by Bob Johnson were supplied by Leo McKern.

Contents

A personal essay

by Leo McKern

Playing 'The Great Fox'

As an actor, I shall always be grateful for having had the opportunity to experience the delights of playing Volpone, 'The Great Fox' as I privately call him. What observations I make must of necessity be those of someone whose reactions to a part or a play come from somewhere below the neck and not above it; more from the gut than from the brain.

Whatever other ends he may hope to achieve with an audience, let there be no doubt whatever that the primary function of a playwright is that of entertainment. Whatever instruction, comment, message or moral he may wish to implant, none will take root without a stimulating compost of emotional appeal; laughter or tears in one form or another. Although the modern usage of the word usually implies simply being amused, I use the word in its complete sense; entertainment contains King Lear's mountainous grief as well as Laurel and Hardy's pratfalls.

I am an Australian born but only (theatrically) half-bred, for it was only after arriving in this country in 1946 that the major part of my professional education began. At school in Australia I was introduced to Shakespeare's plays in a manner which resulted in my thorough detestation of the subject; parsing and analysing is hardly the means of attaining a happy and enthusiastic relationship with the works of a genius. I suspect that there may be many like me in this respect, whose potential appreciation and enjoyment of great literature is stifled at birth.

And herein lies the main reason of why the writing of this

introduction is important to me; for it was not until I was twenty-seven years old, when I was able to see and hear the realizations of the greatest English plays, that the door of a treasure-house opened for me, and I realized what I had missed for so many years. So that if I can help to provoke sufficient interest in your young and therefore receptive minds to at least try the handle of that door, I will be more than pleased.

Ben Jonson's admiration of his contemporary was tremendous; after Shakespeare's death Jonson wrote 'TO THE MEMORY OF MY BELOVED MR WILLIAM SHAKE-SPEARE' –

"I, therefore, will begin. Soul of the Age!
The applause, delight, and wonder of our Stage!. . . . . .
. . . . . . Thou art a Monument without a Tomb,
And art alive still, whole thy book doth live,
And we have wits to read and praise to give . . . . . ."

Jonson was 'brought up poorly' somewhere near Charing Cross. He may have left school before his fifth-form year. He was a volunteer and fought in the Low Countries and killed an opponent in single combat and stripped him of his armour, an event witnessed by both sides. He was quarrelsome and self-confessedly promiscuous ('given to venery'), a flamboyant, un-domesticated, not-too-happily-married man. He was certainly a strolling player. He was arrested for sedition, though released after a short time with charges unproven. He killed an actor in a duel in Hoxton fields, was arrested for felony, became a Roman Catholic in prison, and only escaped hanging by claiming rights of clergy; but all his possessions were confiscated and the mark of Tyburn, 'T', branded on his left thumb. By his own efforts he became a scholar admired by scholars and a favourite of the King.

I give these brief extracts of some of the events of his life simply as an indication of the kind of man whose writings could hardly be dull, dry or dreary.

Jonson wrote *Volpone* in five weeks of 1606. Together with *The Alchemist, Bartholomew Fair* and two others, it is one of his most important plays. They are all very good theatre. His dialogue is as robust, as his characterizations; his plots are intricate and disciplined, and his splendid satire, consistently instructive, runs from stringency to ludicrous hilarity and sheer fun. His presentation of characters dominated by their obsessions is masterly.

I missed seeing the late Sir Donald Wolfit play Volpone, a part for which, among others, he became famous. Touring the country in what was usually a very poor company (he was probably the last actor-manager), he nevertheless presented school audiences with productions of plays which would perhaps not otherwise be seen; I would have been glad, when at school in Australia, to have been able to see such performances. When I was asked to play the part at the Oxford Playhouse I was delighted. I had worked with Frank Hauser, the director, many times; always in interesting plays, some of them first British presentations of foreign plays by such authors as Montherlant and Betti. There were always special school matinees, with the actors and director appearing after the performance to be quizzed by the students. Hauser almost invariably presented the plays being studied at the time for 'O' and 'A' levels; they were faithful and straightforward productions without experimental or sophistical slants indulged in so often now, and so often of but superficial interest.

It is only fairly recently that interest in Jonson's work has revived, his acknowledged great learning helping to contribute to his reputation as an academician's playwright. T.S. Eliot wrote an appreciative essay and re-kindled some interest in the man who has been described as the greatest unread English author, studied only by 'antiquarians and historians'. It can indeed be off-putting to contemplate the study of the works of someone with a reputation for monumental learning; my own immediate reaction is one of doubt of my capacity to understand what such a mental giant was on about. Let me therefore set your minds at rest on this score with the assurance that *Volpone* contains as much fun as a Feydeau farce. In 1976 a production based on *Volpone*, a version by Larry Gelbart set in nineteenth-century San Francisco, was presented on Broadway with much acclaim; it was called *Sly Fox*.

Let me also beg you not to be led into despair by unfamiliar language. I have had the good fortune of playing the title role in Jonson's *The Alchemist* at the Old Vic in a production by Sir Tyrone Guthrie, a great director. He was merciless in his treatment of Jonson's text when he believed that the author's intention would be lost or misunderstood by a modern audience; purist and academic condemnation apart, I cannot but believe that Jonson himself would have been delighted by the full-blooded and enthusiastic reception by the fully-comprehending audiences of this famous production, 358 years after he wrote it. Guthrie was one of the few innovators whose production treatment of classical plays was nearly always successful, clarifying the author's intentions for present-day playgoers. I remember him addressing us at the first reading of his production of *Coriolanus* at the newly-opened Nottingham Playhouse, and remarking how dreary it would be to see actors traipsing around in bed-sheets. He dressed the play in French Empire costume, and the function of a revolutionary mob, a patrician class, and the arrogance and pride of the military became at once clearer and about eighteen hundred years closer. But to revert to *The Alchemist*; there is a similarity of theme and character with *Volpone*, for both the leading characters are 'con-men' – confidence-tricksters, both exploiting human frailty and both eventually receiving their just punishment.

Volpone is a savage satire on human greed, unsoftened by sentiment or compassion. There is a sense of strong morality throughout and a harsh inexorable justice meted out to the 'baddies'; even the unfortunate dupes are contemptuously derided, without sympathy. As Professor Coghill has observed, no one is loving or loved. It is interesting to note the play's setting:

Venice, the home of Shakespeare's Shylock, a Renaissance Chicago, rich, powerful, dazzling and corrupt. The characters have names that read like extracts from an Italian bestiary, and each exhibits the qualities attributed to his or her animalistic namesake; while others' names are simply Italian nouns; Servitore is a servant, Castrone a eunuch, etc., and in our Oxford production this was further enhanced by make-up, costume, and even physical mannerisms in the actors emphasizing the animal; Voltore had a nose like a vulture's beak and Corvino's bird-strut was assisted by flapping elbows.

The enjoyment of playing The Great Fox is as enormous as the character himself. It is an actor's delight, for it entails parts within a part. As a supposed invalid at death's door, he hoodwinks a succession of greedy gulls into competing with each other in the munificence of their gifts to him, each hoping to become his sole heir on the occasion of his imminent demise. His depravity and lust are villainous (but villains are immensely attractive to this particular actor, being so often much more interesting!), but he is at the same time a sort of nemesis for his victims, exulting in his power over them and regarding with savage satisfaction the torments into which, at his instigation, their own cupidity and avarice leads them.

The action of the play is contained within the space of a single day, from Volpone's rising in the morning with his almost blasphemous speech of adoration –

Good morning to the day; and, next, my gold!
Open the shrine, that I may see my saint.

(MOSCA *reveals the treasure*)

to his arrest in the evening, his treasures confiscated and given to the Hospital for Incurables; and as he has feigned

. . . . . .lame, gout, palsy, and such diseases,
Thou art to lie in prison, cramped with irons,
Till thou be'st sick and lame indeed. . . . . . .

and there can scarcely be a more action-packed day in the history of theatre! His servant Mosca (a fly), apparently loyal and brilliantly stage-managing his master's schemes of fraud or seduction of a young and beautiful wife, is eventually shown to be as much of a gold-glutton as Volpone himself, and attempts to blackmail him with threats of exposure. Volpone defeats this, his fury driving him to confession so as to drag Mosca down with him. All the characters receive the punishment poetically fitting their particular circumstance. The action is wonderfully fast; the successive scenes in that bizarre household, from private entertainment by his grotesques (eunuch, dwarf and hermaphrodite), to the visits, each upon the other's heels, of his greedy and hopeful heirs, follow each other with mounting complexity and excitement.

In the Oxford Playhouse production, which transferred to The Garrick Theatre in London for a limited season, the whole of the part of Sir Politic Would-be was cut from the play, although we retained his wife as a necessary part of the procession of characters through the bedroom. Sir Politic – Sir Pol, a parrot – has nevertheless been played with great success (by Michael Hordern, for example, at Stratford-upon Avon), and it may be argued that he is not expendable. He is an absurd figure, an English eccentric in a foreign city, obsessed with intrigue and with a paranoid distrust for anything not English; a character one might expect to find in an Italian or French comedy, and his introduction by Jonson invites the audience to laugh at one of themselves, the ludicrous English tourist abroad.

Cutting a play is a matter of compromise throughout. It is done for a number of different reasons, but generally because the play is too long. In this case the removal of Sir Pol has two advantages, if the play is to be cut at all; it is the simplest way to shorten the play, and it does not materially affect the mainstream of the plot. The cutting of plays from this period is by no means a recent practice; apart from obscurities in the text, audience tastes and demands change, as do the means of presentation (lighting, back-projection, audience participation, etc.), and it is generally accepted that the plays are too long for present-day theatre-goers. Occasionally full texts of classics are presented; the National Theatre's production of Marlowe's *Tamburlaine*, and the marathon of *The Greeks*, but they do not seem to enjoy long runs on the whole; they are 'kudos' productions, and by no means the norm. And the demands on the actor are enormous; it is well to remember also that such plays were contemporaneously presented in daylight, in public theatres open to the sky, and there were also far fewer performances; certainly not eight per week, with two twice-daily matinee-days, month after month, as is the case now. Even in an eighteenth-century production of *The Alchemist* by Garrick, that actor made (according to the stage-historian Robert Gale Noyes), '. . . . . . one hundred and fifty-four cuts, varying from one line to three pages'. One part, that of Sir Epicure Mammon, suffered to the extent of two hundred and fifty lines. It seems almost certain that this was done to amplify the part Garrick played, a minor supporting character which presumably assumed the importance of the lead. This would be unsupportable in a modern production, but Garrick was a public figure of fame of gigantic popularity.

The usual and acceptable length of a modern production is from one and three-quarter to two-and-a-half hours, perhaps three at the most. In our Old Vic production of *Peer Gynt* in 1982 the full text played ran nearly four hours and even Tyrone Guthrie, while acknowledging it as one of his most exciting nights in the theatre, also admitted that after three hours his '. . . . . . head was bursting'. So it seems that modern audiences are content with a briefer time in the theatre that those of the sixteenth century, and although Sir Pol earns his part in *Volpone*, I do not consider that the play suffers greatly by his excision.

It was immediately clear to me, on reading the play, that the basic requirements for the actor (apart from what one hopes is an underlying talent) were voice, energy and stamina. All these Wolfit undoubtedly possessed, and so, fortunately, did I. Also fortunately for me, Volpone may be played by an actor who does not necessarily possess the qualities of a conventional leading man as far as good looks are concerned (Guthrie once described me as '. . . . . . a bun-faced person . . . . . .', but he said some pleasant things as well). However, the playing of an important leading part demands many things from an actor apart from those mentioned; I find that the concentration I consider necessary for a performance entails the expenditure of energy equivalent to that used in a day's work. A good performance ends with true tiredness, but elation as well. There is, of course, especially in a long run, the temptation to achieve the lowest common denominator of effort, and these sort of performances may be often seen; the actor is 'walking through', devoid of passion or perspiration, and probably thinking about what to have for supper. Of course, some parts are more demanding than others, but there is a level of energy expenditure which is necessary in even the least demanding part.

A mysterious part of an actor's equipment is personality. It is the rare quality that made household names of many film stars whose acting abilities were minimal; they were not so much 'do-ers' as 'be-ers' but for their millions of fans this was more than sufficient; however, when such a personality is augmented by a similarly large talent, the result, in a performance, is as remarkable as it is rare. I believe that Edmund Kean was such an actor; of whom a comtemporary critic said that when watching him perform, it was '. . . . . . like reading Shakespeare by flashes of lightning'. He it is who I would most liked to have seen; the man who, in a performance of a melodramatic villain, Sir Giles Overreach, caused '. . . . . . women to faint, and strong men turn pale'.

Alas, it is not possible to be taught talent, or to learn to have personality, a sense of timing, or a sense of humour; such as possess them are rightly called 'gifted'.

The approach of an actor to a part is as varied as the actors themselves. I had not read *Volpone*. When the part was offered me, I read the play once, as is my practice, at one sitting, and accepted it; as with every other job, it is accepted or rejected on that basis, and I do not have to 'think about it' or be 'talked into it'; its virtues or drawbacks have an immediate impact. I do not then read the play until the first reading-rehearsal, because (a) I have to discover what the director intends and (b) studying a part before rehearsal inevitably leads to ideas, convictions and decisions about it which one may have to discard or which may conflict with the director's. Rehearsal is for me more satisfying (though in a different way) than performance, for it is the time of discovery and enlightenment, and I am being instructed and inspired, which I enjoy, rather than being taught, which I don't. Put in another way, rehearsal is the education, performance the exam, and the audience the markers.

I have been asked to play Volpone since the Oxford production, but have declined; I have explored the play as far as it is possible for me to do so, and I feel somehow a waste of my finite working life to go over ground already explored.

In the playing of it, I found that pace is essential, as in all comedy, but speed of production is not to be obtained simply by speaking quickly, for meaning and clarity must not be lost. The secret of pace is in the immediate picking up of cues; nothing will dull a comedy so much as actors reacting before they speak instead of responding at once and combining reaction *with* speech. A pause after each cue-line while the actor demonstrates a reaction can add minutes to a scene and destroy the pace. There are, of course, moments when the right pause in the right place (a double-take, for instance) can be as fruitful as the best gag-line; one is reminded of Oliver Hardy's slow burns, redolent with disgust, straight into camera, in response to one of Laurel's particular idiocies; and even the memory provokes a smile.

Volpone is a wonderfully full-blooded and rewarding part to play, and the play is one of our greatest satirical comedies; only one of the vast number that has established English playwrights and theatre in the forefront of world drama for centuries, a great heritage for our great enjoyment. It deals with aspects of the human condition that are as readily recognizable now as when the play was written, for though customs and manners may change human beings essentially do not. In your study of it, I only hope that you can achieve even a small part of the kind of enjoyment that I have received from it.

Above all, it is to be remembered while in the reading of them, that plays were written to be seen and heard; do not, I beg, miss an opportunity of seeing this one, for as The Great Fox himself says in the epilogue –

The seasoning of a play is the applause.

Androgyno and Nano entertain Volpone. (Act I Scene ii)

Celia looks down from her window at Volpone disguised as a
mountebank.
(Act II Scene ii)

Volpone and Lady Would-Be Politic (Act III Scene iv)

One of the freaks provides an audience for Volpone's wooing of Celia (Act III Scene vii)

The trial, from left to right, Corvino, Volpone, Corbaccio, Mosca and Voltore (Act V Scene vii)

Introduction

Ben Jonson and Volpone

Ben Jonson is a unique and memorable dramatist. *Volpone* is a unique and memorable play. The qualities which set *Volpone* apart from other plays, including the rest of Jonson's own, are a strangely appropriate expression of the qualities in Jonson's mind, personality and life which set him apart from other men. There is of course nothing 'autobiographical' about *Volpone*, yet few writers have managed to leave such a vivid testament behind them.

The Man

Jonson was a man of letters, a classical scholar, familiar with a prodigious range of Greek and Latin literature and fiercely insistent on the authority of classical rules for literary composition. He was also a strict and orthodox moralist. The Epistle which precedes *Volpone* is an eloquent statement of his intellectual loyalties. It is a bold attack on what Jonson considered the profane and debased drama of his time – drama which violated the laws of content, style, moral doctrine and didactic purpose which Jonson believed essential to dramatic writing. In the Epistle he makes high claims for poetry: it is 'to inform men in the best reason of living'. He makes high personal demands on the poet, affirming 'the impossibility of any man's being the good poet, without first being a good man'. He castigates the misuse of poetry and drama for spreading personal abuse and slanders, denying that he himself has offended in such ways. Even though he is forced to admit that the end of *Volpone* may seem to break the rules of comedy a little, he reaffirms his belief in 'the strict rigour of comic law', which required comedy to respect its classical ancestry. If *Vol-*

pone does indeed bend the rules, Jonson argues, it was with the higher purpose of discrediting those critics who attacked comedy for not showing justice done. It is, after all, 'the office of a comic poet to imitate justice and instruct to life, as well as purity of language, or stir up gentle affections'. The visible exercise of comic justice in *Volpone* is Jonson's excuse for having written a comedy which denies its audience the conventional happy ending. His tone is that of a man wedded to classical learning and the critical doctrines which the classics exemplified and taught; that of an orthodox Christian devoted to strict morality and its exercise through public and dramatic justice; and that of an austere, disciplined writer with an exalted view of poetry and contempt for filth, vulgarity and muck-raking. Significantly, his tone is also highly pugnacious.

Whether this high-minded notion of comedy actually fits *Volpone* is a question I shall ask in a moment. Whether this high-minded view of the poet fits Ben Jonson is a more immediate question. The short answer is that it does. He was indeed the classicist, the Christian, the disciplined writer, the strict moralist. And yet it doesn't. For Ben Jonson was also the turbulent, quarrelsome, aggressive figure whose combative nature and constant brushes with the law made his lifetime so eventful. His background was a humble one; he was the stepson of a Westminster bricklayer, and in his youth became a bricklayer himself. He served in the wars and killed an enemy in single combat – to his lasting pride and satisfaction. At the very beginning of his career as a playwright he was in hot water with the authorities for writing a seditious play, and spent some time in prison. In 1603, with *Sejanus*, and in 1605, with *Eastward Ho!* his plays landed him in custody yet again because of their supposed seditious content or their injudicious satire. These 'professional' spells behind bars were mixed with others, some of them more serious still. In 1598 he killed a fellow-actor, Gabriel Spencer, in a duel, and narrowly escaped the hangman. Some years later he was interestingly close to important conspirators in the Gunpowder Plot, and in 1606 was risking the death penalty again when charged with being 'by fame a seducer of youth to the Popish religion'. His life in these years, within the theatre and outside it, was a chequered story of quarrelsome energies and constant risk. As for his aversion to dramatized slanders, this is expressed with such fervour by one who only a few years earlier had been a principal fighter in the 'war of the theatres', swapping abusive play for abusive play with his fellow dramatists Marston and Dekker.

Naturally this rash and turbulent career was not sustained at such a pitch all his life. He enjoyed years of prosperity, royal favour, and high critical renown. Yet the end was far from happy. He died in 1637, after some years of illness, poverty and dwindling achievement, leaving only his work behind as his memorial. All his children were long dead, none having survived to adult life.

The Play

More than any other play, *Volpone* reveals the same pattern of qualities and seeming contradictions as its author. Here is a play which largely obeys the classical 'rules' for comedy, but gives the rules short shrift when they interfere with moral necessity or the energies of dramatic art. It is a play which respects the processes of law and the demands of justice, yet also satirizes the law and its official ministers, and casts a long last shadow on the operations of justice itself. Its close leaves us firmly committed to belief in the necessity of justice and yet uneasily doubtful whether we have seen it done. It is a play governed by moral clarity and rigour, unsparing in its exposure of repulsive immorality, yet one which voices its moral insights through the mouths of two perverse and self-regarding rogues. It is a play filled with classical learning and religious terminology, yet showing us religious language and devotion misapplied to gold, and classical allusions grotesquely misused and misunderstood. It is a play which celebrates intellectual vigour, quick-wittedness, ingenuity and imagination, yet shows them flourishing in the ruthless conduct of a fraud. It is a play which stirs our delight in zest and energy, as expressions of a fuller, more intense existence, yet shows that seductive energy at work most powerfully in knaves. It is a comedy which concludes with elements of tragedy, a play which is full of laughter and yet deeply serious.

Volpone is the work of a highly disciplined intelligence driven by imaginative zest. Neither its intellectual clarity nor its moral certainty are ever in danger; they are central to the play's effect. Yet it achieves its moral and didactic purposes in some curious and unexpected ways, leading our sympathies in strange directions, leaving our moral insight strengthened but our human judgement troubled and disturbed. Jonson's own life *seems* at first sight paradoxical and inconsistent, but when his intellect is married to his energy it falls into place. The same is true of *Volpone*. It is the matching of strict intellectual discipline with generous energy that gives it unity, coherence and power. It is a complex play, marvellously attuned to its author's complex personality and life.

Discipline: Volpone as a classical comedy

I have already said that Jonson showed greater regard for the 'rules' of classical comedy, which English writers derived from the neo-classical critics of the Italian Renaissance, than most of his contemporaries did. On the other hand, he did not hesitate to break the rules when it suited him. One of the principles of 'classical' comedy remains fundamentally true for Jonson, however, no matter what variation he is playing on it. For him, comedy is a serious dramatic form. Its main purpose is not just to make us laugh. Laughter is almost certain to be an important way for it to achieve its effects, but laughter is a means to an end. The purpose of comedy is didactic. It sets out to educate its audience. Its nature and objective in classical thinking were clearly summarized in this way by Sir Philip Sidney in his *Apologie for Poetry*: 'Comedy is an imitation of the common errors of our life, which he (the dramatist) representeth in the most ridiculous and scornful sort that may be, so as it is impossible that any beholder can be content to be such a one.' Jonson in *Volpone* certainly does this, but it is by no means *all* he does, so that the play has a didactic moral design which satisfies 'classical' requirements but is complicated by some special and less orthodox effects. In this section I shall be considering the disciplined classical design of *Volpone*, and in the next section the special events and presences which make it complex and unique.

The Characters

Certainly the world of *Volpone* is full of people of whom it can be said that we would not 'be content to be such a one'. Almost everyone in the play is a fool or a knave, while the characters we could call innocent or virtuous are mostly low-key and uninteresting. The Venice of Jonson's imagination is dominated above all by avarice and greed. In this hideous world of unscrupulous and grasping misers, it is important always for us to notice how Volpone himself is set apart from other characters. After all, he too is in search of wealth. Yet from the very first speech of the play it is clear that his motives are different. He glories more in the 'cunning purchase' of his wealth than in the 'glad possession'. Volpone himself is not a miser. He is generous with his gold, notably in his offerings to Mosca and to Celia. Nor is wealth his sole interest. His greatest joy is to fool and torment his victims by turning their own greed and miserliness against them. His other dominant passion is lust, and his attempted seduction of Celia is filled with ravishing images of material and sexual wealth. For Volpone, gold is the means to two kinds of intense sensual pleasure – gratified sexual lust and gleeful scorn for the vicious idiots he exploits.

In talking even thus far about Volpone, we seem to be discussing a 'character' – and about Volpone there is much more to be said. But the other characters, especially the legacy-hunters, are often described as 'caricatures' – two-dimensional beings with little reality or convincing psychological depth. They seem to exist as embodiments of a single obsessive vice.

It is certainly true that the characters are concentrated and distorted inhabitants of a highly concentrated and distorted world. Jonson's Venice is a closed and sealed society, uniquely powerful in its avaricious driving force and not transferable to everyday reality. Likewise, the group of vicious fools exploited by Volpone draw their reality from the perverted world they live in, and we cannot see them as rounded, psychological creations with a possible life elsewhere. Jonson differentiates one from another by giving separate 'points of concentration' to their shared avaricious scheming. Voltore's 'gold-tipped' tongue is his distinguishing mark: as a corrupt lawyer he has a brilliantly persuasive, smooth eloquence which is quite devoid of personal substance. Except when performing, he slides into foolish triviality, incoherent passion, or stunned silence. In consequence, we are shown a man who is only alive either in avaricious folly or smooth and eloquent deceit. The rest of him is empty. Corbaccio is a more grotesque creature – old, senile and decrepit, and yet obsessed with avaricious scheming for the futile enrichment of his worn-out life. He is a moral, mental and physical imbecile, with avarice as the single residue of vitality in his collapsed existence. Corvino is a more complicated figure, but he too can be reduced to essentials, with his avarice offset by sexual jealousy and a strange fear of public humiliation which seeks masochistically to bring about the very thing it fears.

Viewed like this, the figures are something more than caricatures. Rather they are diverse, concentrated examples of an all-consuming shared obsession. All the same, the concentration and distortion of their portraits has the effect of distancing them from us, arousing in the audience not so much an involved emotional disgust but rather an objective moral repugnance. This is entirely in keeping with the didactic purposes of the play as classical comedy. It is deliberate on Jonson's part, and strongly reinforced by the bird and animal imagery of their names, so fully borne out by their carrion-hunting existences. Their animal associations dehumanize both them and their world, reducing mankind to a violent and predatory existence, diseased and seeking out disease, consuming and being consumed. In its potent animal simplicities, Jonson's comic world is deeply in debt to classical tradition. Watching its inhabitants, we are tutored by revulsion.

If the legacy-hunters are selective and intense versions of human vice, Celia and Bonario are wooden and largely silent representatives of human virtue. When they do speak out, the effect is one of stilted and self-conscious righteousness which excites little emotional sympathy. They are youthful, inexperienced, naive and inept. They are almost completely lacking in the force and vitality which drive even the dupes, let alone the massive and exhilarating vigour of Mosca and above all of Volpone himself. This is important, since their pallid natures are an essential part of the play's effect. If Celia and Bonario stirred our sympathies, we should find it intolerable to watch the prolonged viciousness of their treatment without being wholly alienated from Volpone. As it is, they allow the play to achieve an important double effect. We recognize and approve of Celia's and Bonario's virtues, and fully accept the moral necessity that their innocence should be established and the guilty punished. Formally, that is, they allow us to watch the triumph of virtue and the self-destructive force of evil: Jonson has fulfilled his pledge 'to imitate justice and instruct to life', and allowed his comedy its proper didactic function. But because Celia and Bonario are not strong or appealing enough to entangle our sympathies, they do not detach us from Volpone, or the subversive delight and complicity he arouses in us. Hence the complexity of the play's ending: we approve the spectacle of justice done, but we also question it and find it troubling. The formal design of comedy is both observed and flouted.

The Unities

Another requirement of neo-classical comedy is that the 'unities' – unity of time, unity of place, and unity of action – should be observed. These unities supposedly derived from Aristotle, though they are not in fact contained in any of his extant writings. Unity of time demanded that the action should be continuous, and events on stage should be consistent with the time they would need in real life. Unity of place dictated that the whole action should take place in one town or district. Unity of action called for a single, unified plot, from which no part could be broken off without damage to the whole structure. In *Volpone*, Jonson carefully observed the unities of time and place but ignored the unity of action. The play profits both by the rules it obeys and the rule it breaks.

First, unity of *time*. The whole action of *Volpone* takes place on a single day, starting with Volpone's morning worship of his gold and ending with his judgement in the evening. This allows the action to be tightly concentrated, and more importantly to gain speed, impetus and momentum as it proceeds. For example, the first act begins with Volpone's solitary self-revelation (just as the third and fifth acts begin in momentary quiet and soliloquy). It allows us important insights into his motives and priorities before we meet Mosca, and encounter the central partnership of the play. The play performed by Volpone's mascots not only gives us an early visual symbol of human deformity, but prepares the way for the play's larger spectacle of degraded animalism and folly. Then come the visits of the suitors. In this preparatory act they are kept apart, but their separate appearances follow a steadily rising intensity of effect. The forward impetus within this act is repeated in the play as a whole, in a pattern of gathering speed, mounting complexity, increasing urgency and risk, as Volpone and Mosca fight against mounting odds to keep their victims apart in the safe insulation of the opening. The concentration offered by the unity of time allows the play to gain an intricate and satisfying structure and an exhilarating sense of acceleration and precarious control.

It was Jonson's practice to begin a new scene every time a new character appears, even when, as often, the action is continuous. In this edition, Jonson's breaks of scene have all been kept, but where the action is unbroken the scene heading has been placed in brackets. If these breaks are examined, it should appear quite clearly how small units of action are subtly linked and blended to their maximum effect in a swift and often continuous flow of action.

Unity of *place* presented Jonson with no problems: everything takes place in Venice. However, it is worth noticing how our sense of Venice – as a society dominated by materialism, corruption and intrigue – is deepened and enriched by the sub-plot. The story of Sir Politic Would-be and Peregrine is Jonson's offence against the unity of *action*, since the sub-plot is almost completely detachable from the main plot and is indeed frequently cut in order to shorten a very long play. The sub-plot has its accusers and its supporters. Some people argue, for example, that it gives the play an example of folly to set against the main plot's vice, or that it provides some needful relaxation from the main plot's pace and intensity, or that it provides a comic parallel and parody for the story of Volpone. Not the least of its effects, however, is to present us with a comic perspective on Venice: absurd, eccentric and ridiculous, certainly, but touched throughout with a nervous alien's sense of strangeness and wonder. Sir Politic's bizarre observations give Venice a kind of distorted civic realism – one which can believably include the more local and intimate corruptions which the main plot follows through.

If unity of action is one 'classical' precept which Jonson ignores, the other is his sacrifice of comedy's happy ending in place of something far more sombre, complex and unorthodox. If we look now at Volpone himself, we shall see why he needed such an ending.

Energy: Volpone and the elements of tragedy

I said earlier that Volpone derives sensual pleasure not only from lust for Celia but from contempt for his victims. Contemptuous manipulation of the foolish and the greedy is for him a rich emotional delight. In this respect he differs from Mosca, who until their final break is otherwise so fine a partner for him. Both of them are conceited egotists, delighting as much in the excellence of their own performances as they do in the profits they reap. Mosca's soliloquy at the beginning of Act III is a piece of fantastic self-glorification as extravagant as any of Volpone's. All the same, Mosca is at root a colder and more practical being, whose brilliant skills are chiefly aimed at loot. Volpone's activities are not directed by material need: he is rich already. Mosca is poor, a parasite who needs the food he steals so cleverly. It is significant that their break in Act V comes when Volpone begins to torture his victims for the satisfaction of torment alone, with no further hope of profit. At this point Mosca goes his own way, becoming for a brief time a hugely successful version of the legacy-hunters themselves. His downfall comes because at the last, in their final climax of bluff and acting, he underestimates Volpone.

Volpone's sensual love of degrading his fellow-beings is an ugly characteristic, and should be a warning to us not to sentimentalize him. His defects of character (and he above all is character, not caricature) are many and serious. His overweening egotism is unsparing in the hurt it causes. He is quite ruthless. He delights in fraud and exults in successful deception; his religion is a satiric version of true religion, holding gleaming heaps of metal sacred; he is a frustrated rapist; he takes pleasure in ruining the innocent. He desecrates noble achievement, and strengthens the bestial tendencies of those he deals with. Morally, his final downfall should strike us as just and satisfying.

The experience of many readers and audiences is just the opposite. It seems in practice that Volpone wins and keeps a stature which is near-heroic, and that his ultimate fate is close to tragedy. How does such an obnoxious figure manage to gain our admiration as he does?

There seem to be several reasons. One is his strange function as a moral agent in the play. Despite his own blatant immorality, Volpone is largely an accurate moral judge. The opinions he forms of his victims are, we feel, morally correct opinions. He accurately pinpoints human deformity and debasement, and his activities expose and punish them. There is, of course, nothing virtuous in his intentions, any more than there is in Mosca's. In nailing moral corruption as he does, he is merely furthering an elaborate and self-indulgent game, designed to inflate further his massive self-esteem. The fact remains that, apart from a few pale or self-righteous utterances from Bonario and Celia, he is the most trustworthy moral voice in the play. For us in the audience, the immoralist becomes our moral spokesman.

A reminder of ourselves in the audience will light up the second of Volpone's great enticements. The play *Volpone* is a theatrical event, which we experience from the audience. We are therefore specially drawn in amused connivance towards Volpone's own theatricality. We see him several times as an audience himself – quite openly when he watches the freaks' play and secretly when he eavesdrops on Mosca's game with the will in Act V. For much of the time when he is playing an old, sick man, he is part actor (counterfeiting disease) and part audience (enjoying the scenes stage-managed for him by Mosca). His wooing of Celia has for him the unknown audience of Bonario, but he also enjoys imagining an audience for his love-making. In his youth he 'acted young Antinous', and acting is still at the very heart of his life. His disguises and performances, first as Scoto the mountebank and later as the *commandadore*, drive him from the safety of his house to risky public ventures in the streets. The love of acting – of skilled professional deceit, glorying in making what is not so seem so – drives him to more and more elaborations of his game. For Volpone's acting, we are his audience 'in the know'. We watch him perform for a stage-audience of the ignorant, and play his histrionic tricks for their confusion. His brilliance as an actor and director removes him partly from the world of theatrical illusion and brings him nearer to ourselves. It is almost as if Volpone, like the audience, has *chosen* to enjoy the play.

Above all there is his energy (the more unmistakably impressive because it contrasts so sharply with the feebleness he usually imitates). In the theatre, as so often in life, energy and zest define themselves as virtues for us, regardless of the uses they are put to. The spectacle of energy puts our moral sense to sleep more certainly than anything else. Faced with such energy as Volpone's, we cannot and should not forgive its perversions, but we can and do forget them. Volpone has a vivid, exhilarating intelligence in a world of corrupt fools; he has strong sexual passions in a world of feeble and perverted jealousies; he has a gift for malign joy in a world of base and sordid satisfactions; he has energy which places him on a different plane of existence from his fellows. Our formal recognition of his own corruption and malignity is displaced by an appalled delight.

To the question 'Is justice done to Volpone?' the answer must be first that it is, and therefore the logic of comedy is satisfied – even down to the poetic exactness of the court's savage sentence. Yet this very savagery – for the court's sentence on Volpone is a *death* sentence, as his response makes plain – calls from us a protest at *in*justice, together with a sense of tragic loss at the extinction of a being whose vitality and intensity of living have so captured us. All those qualities we admire in Volpone are gathered together in his superb farewell line 'This is called mortifying of a fox'. Volpone the perverted yet dependable moralist is in some ways pronouncing a moral judgement on himself. Volpone the great and compulsive actor is doing something very complex: he is speaking almost as a member of the audience, giving the judgement of an ironic, objective, unpained spectator, yet he is also Volpone the rogue, speaking as himself, and it is a proof of his achieved heroism that the line is convincingly his own. He is spectator and actor at once, confronting his death sentence with sardonic courage. As the figure of abundant and enticing energy and ruthless intelligence, he is resolutely carrying those qualities through to the end. In that conclusion, the terms of moral comedy are broken, and tragedy steps in. The play observes the formal disciplines – of law, morality and comedy alike – but it also undermines them with a bolder and more sombre truth.

TO THE MOST NOBLE
AND MOST ÆQVALL
SISTERS
THE TWO FAMOVS VNIVERSITIES,

FOR THEIR LOVE
AND
ACCEPTANCE

SHEW'N TO HIS POEME
IN THE PRESENTATION:

BEN: IONSON

THE GRATEFVLL ACKNOWLEDGER
DEDICATES
BOTH IT, AND HIMSELFE.

There followes an *Epistle*, if
you dare venture on
the length.

¶

The dedication from the Quarto

Volpone
or
The Fox

1–3 Never ... favourers to it: *However fine a man's intelligence it cannot prosper without opportunities and the help of friends.*

1 most equal sisters: *the two universities (between which Jonson carefully refuses to discriminate).*

 wit: *intellectual ability.*

1–2 so presently excellent: *so quick to reveal its quality.*

4 and that: *and if it is also true that.*

5–6 to provide ... accidents: *to cultivate such incidental aids as opportunities and friendly assistance.*

9 studious: *careful.*

10 your act: *i.e. the regard which the universities had shown for his play.*

 satisfying: *enough.*

11 professors: *practitioners.*

12 hear so ill: *hear themselves so abused.*

12–13 there will ... subject: *the beneficiary of their approval (Jonson himself) will be expected to defend his own work.*

14 forehead: *conviction.*

14–15 too-much licence ... poetasters: *excessive indulgence given to bad poets.*

15 mistress: *i.e. poetry itself.*

17 But ... petulancy: *But merely because of the bad poets' insolence.*

21 asquint: *with bias.*

25 inform: *mould.*

28 recover: *restore.*

29 that comes forth: *who professes to be.*

30–1 a master in manners: *an authority on moral behaviour.*

31–2 effect ... mankind: *cause mankind's affairs to be properly conducted.*

32 I take him: *as I see it.*

33 railing: *abusive.*

The Epistle

Never (most equal sisters) had any man a wit so presently excellent as that it could raise itself, but there must come both matter, occasion, commenders, and favourers to it. If this be true, and that the fortune of all writers doth daily prove it, it behoves the careful to provide well toward these accidents; and, having acquired them, to preserve that part of reputation most tenderly, wherein the benefit of a friend is also defended. Hence is it, that I now render myself grateful, and am studious to justify the bounty of your act, to which, though your mere authority were satisfying, yet (it being an age wherein poetry and the professors of it hear so ill on all sides) there will a reason be looked for in the subject. It is certain, nor can it with any forehead be opposed, that the too-much licence of poetasters in this time hath much deformed their mistress; that every day their manifold and manifest ignorance doth stick unnatural reproaches upon her. But for their petulancy it were an act of the greatest injustice either to let the learned suffer, or so divine a skill (which indeed should not be attempted with unclean hands) to fall under the least contempt. For, if men will impartially, and not asquint, look toward the offices and function of a poet, they will easily conclude to themselves the impossibility of any man's being the good poet, without first being a good man. He that is said to be able to inform young men to all good disciplines, inflame grown men to all great virtues, keep old men in their best and supreme state, or, as they decline to childhood, recover them to their first strength; that comes forth the interpreter and arbiter of nature, a teacher of things divine no less than human, a master in manners; and can alone (or with a few) effect the business of mankind: this, I take him, is no subject for pride and ignorance to exercise their railing rhetoric upon. But it

5

10

15

20

25

30

36   inverted: *the very opposite of their traditional qualities.*

41   I dare not . . . this: *Jonson's concern is to set his own work apart from the general low level of public drama, and to claim for it both the literary discipline and the moral stature of classical poetry.*

42   abortive features: *bad plays (i.e. works that have 'miscarried').*

48–9 have loathed . . . bawdry: *There is plenty of obscenity in Jonson's plays, but he implies that in his work it serves a respectable moral purpose.*

50   food of the scene: *material for the stage.*

52   lust: *delight.*

52–4 and not my youngest . . . teeth: *and they will say that all my plays, including the most recent, have proved on their appearance to have sharp and provocative content.*

54   supercilious politics: *scornful and critical commentators on public affairs.*

54–5 what nation . . . provoked?: *Jonson had, in fact, been accused of ridiculing the Scots, the King, the Court, the law and the army in his earlier plays.*

58   allowed: *approved by the censor.*

58–9 I speak . . . entirely mine: *several plays of which Jonson was co-author with other dramatists had got him into trouble.*

59   broad: *indecent.*

61   mimic: *burlesque actor.*

62   taxed: *criticized.*

62–4 so pointingly . . . disease: *Jonson says that even in mounting well-deserved attacks he has not been so specific in his personal references that his victims have forfeited either the merit of confession or the chance to deny guilt.*

65   entitle me: *give me a right to claim (Jonson is being ironic).*

67   carried: *carried out.*

67–8 obnoxious to construction: *liable to misinterpretation.*

68   marry: *indeed.*

69   Application: *the discovery (true or imagined) of references in men's writings to real people or events.*

will here be hastily answered, that the writers of these
days are other things; that not only their manners but   35
their natures are inverted; and nothing remaining with
them of the dignity of poet but the abused name, which
every scribe usurps; that now, especially in dramatic or
(as they term it) stage poetry, nothing but ribaldry, pro-
fanation, blasphemy, all licence of offence to God and   40
man, is practised. I dare not deny a great part of this (and
am sorry I dare not), because in some men's abortive features (and would they had never boasted the light) it is
over-true; but that all are embarked in this bold adventure
for hell is a most uncharitable thought, and, uttered, a   45
more malicious slander. For my particular, I can (and
from a most clear conscience) affirm that I have ever trem-
bled to think toward the least profaneness; have loathed
the use of such foul and unwashed bawdry as is now made
the food of the scene. And, howsoever I cannot escape   50
from some the imputation of sharpness, but that they will
say I have taken a pride or lust to be bitter, and not my
youngest infant but hath come into the world with all his
teeth, I would ask of these supercilious politics, what
nation, society, or general order, or state I have provoked?   55
What public person? Whether I have not (in all these)
preserved their dignity, as mine own person, safe? My
works are read, allowed (I speak of those that are entirely
mine) – look into them. What broad reproofs have I used?
Where have I been particular? Where personal? except to   60
a mimic, cheater, bawd, or buffoon – creatures (for their
insolencies) worthy to be taxed? Yet to which of these so
pointingly as he might not either ingenuously have con-
fessed or wisely dissembled his disease? But it is not
rumour can make men guilty, much less entitle me to   65
other men's crimes. I know that nothing can be so in-
nocently writ or carried, but may be made obnoxious to
construction; marry, whilst I bear mine innocence about
me, I fear it not. Application is now grown a trade with

70 there are: *there are those.*

73 fames: *reputations.*

74–5 who cunningly ... meanings: *who use the innocent writings of others as a cover for the publication of their own malicious slanders.*

76 by faults: *by exposing faults.*

76 raked up: *raked over and hidden.*

77 honesty: *decency (Jonson is attacking those who make scurrilous gossip by reviving scandals which have long been quietly forgotten).*

79 whose living ... styles: *whose living faces they disfigure with the marks of their insolent pens.*

83 providing: *anticipating.*

85 fools ... barbarism retrieved: *revival of early unsophisticated theatre, with its crude jesters and comic devils.*
antique: *obsolete, antiquated.*

88 'Sibi ... odit': *quoted from Horace Satires, II,i,23, which Jonson paraphrases as 'In satires, each man (though untouched) complains/As he were hurt; and hates such biting strains.*

89–90 And men ... sports: *And, if the writer persists in such compositions, men may justly blame him for arousing such indignation merely for his own entertainment.*

90–1 lust in liberty: *delight in licence.*

92 misc'line interludes: *miscellaneous entertainments.*

96 prolepses: *anachronisms.*
brothelry: *obscenity.*

100 divers honest and learned: *various honest and learned men.*

101 name: *title (i.e. that of 'poet').*

103 vernaculous: *scurrilous.*

many; and there are, that profess to have a key for the   70
deciphering of everything. But let wise and noble persons
take heed how they be too credulous, or give leave to these
invading interpreters to be over-familiar with their fames,
who cunningly and often utter their own virulent malice
under other men's simplest meanings. As for those that   75
will (by faults which charity hath raked up or common
honesty concealed) make themselves a name with the multitude, or (to draw their rude and beastly claps) care not
whose living faces they entrench with their petulant styles,
may they do it without a rival, for me – I choose rather to   80
live graved in obscurity than share with them in so preposterous a fame. Nor can I blame the wishes of those
severe and wiser patriots, who, providing the hurts these
licentious spirits may do in a state, desire rather to see
fools and devils and those antique relics of barbarism re-   85
trieved, with all other ridiculous and exploded follies, than
behold the wounds of private men, of princes, and nations.
For, as Horace makes Trebatius speak, among these,
   – *Sibi quisque timet, quamquam est intactus, et odit*
And men may justly impute such rages, if continued, to
the writer, as his sports. The increase of which lust in   90
liberty, together with the present trade of the stage, in all
their misc'line interludes, what learned or liberal soul
doth not already abhor? – where nothing but the filth of
the time is uttered, and that with such impropriety of
phrase, such plenty of solecisms, such dearth of sense, so   95
bold prolepses, so racked metaphors, with brothelry able
to violate the ear of a pagan, and blasphemy to turn the
blood of a Christian to water. I cannot but be serious in a
cause of this nature, wherein my fame and the reputations
of divers honest and learned are the question; when a   100
name so full of authority, antiquity, and all great mark, is
(through their insolence) become the lowest scorn of the
age; and those men subject to the petulancy of every vernaculous orator, that were wont to be the care of kings and

7

105   rapt me: *carried me forcibly.*

107   stand off from them: *keep myself detached and aloof from the bad poets.*

109–110   have seen ... approved: *Volpone was performed at both universities during the period (of approximately one to two years) between the writing of the play and its publication, when the Dedication and Epistle were added.*

109   to my crown: *to my honour.*

111   reduce: *restore.*

111–112   not only .... scene: *not only the forms but the true spirit of classical comedy.*

112   easiness: *apparent effortlessness.*

113   end: *purpose.*

114   reason of living: *basis for living (in terms of manners and moral conduct).*

115   catastrophe: *dénouement.*

115–116   catastrophe ... censure: *Jonson makes this concession because the tone of the play's ending is not 'happy' in the strict sense demanded by the form of comedy. See pages xxiii–xxiv and xxxiv–xxxv.*

116   as turning back to my promise: *not matching my claim to be restoring the ancient classical forms.*

118   of industry: *deliberately.*

119   nearer his scale: *to fit the critic's standards of judgement.*

121   put the snaffle in their mouths: *gag the Puritans.*

122   interludes: *for the Puritans 'interlude' was a derogatory word for any kind of play.*

124   goings out: *endings.*

127   mulcted: *'fined', or (more generally) 'punished'.*

129   gentle affections: *noble emotions.*

132   the understanding: *men of sense and perception.*

134–5   maturing ... fruits: *completion of some better plays.*

135   if my muses be true to me: *i.e. if my poetic inspiration continues.*

138   adulterated: *debased.*
      primitive habit: *original dress.*

happiest monarchs. This it is, that hath not only rapt me   105
to present indignation, but made me studious heretofore,
and by all my actions to stand off from them; which may
most appear in this my latest work (which you, most
learned arbitresses, have seen, judged, and to my crown,
approved) wherein I have laboured, for their instruction   110
and amendment, to reduce not only the ancient forms, but
manners of the scene – the easiness, the propriety, the innocence, and last the doctrine, which is the principal end
of poesy: to inform men in the best reason of living. And
though my catastrophe may, in the strict rigour of comic   115
law, meet with censure, as turning back to my promise, I
desire the learned and charitable critic to have so much
faith in me to think it was done of industry. For with what
ease I could have varied it nearer his scale (but that I fear
to boast my own faculty) I could here insert. But my   120
special aim being to put the snaffle in their mouths that
cry out, we never punish vice in our interludes, &c., I took
the more liberty – though not without some lines of example drawn even in the ancients themselves, the goings out
of whose comedies are not always joyful, but oft-times the   125
bawds, the servants, the rivals, yea, and the masters are
mulcted; and fitly, it being the office of a comic poet to
imitate justice and instruct to life, as well as purity of language, or stir up gentle affections. To which I shall take
the occasion elsewhere to speak. For the present (most re-   130
verenced sisters) as I have cared to be thankful for your
affections past, and here made the understanding acquainted with some ground of your favours, let me not
despair their continuance, to the maturing of some worth-
ier fruits; wherein, if my muses be true to me, I shall raise   135
the despised head of poetry again, and stripping her out of
those rotten and base rags wherewith the times have
adulterated her form, restore her to her primitive habit,
feature and majesty, and render her worthy to be
embraced and kissed of all the great and master-spirits of   140

141 affected: *loved*.

142 inward: *familiar*.

143 her: *i.e. poetry*.

146 'genus irritabile': *sensitive and angry race of people (i.e. true poets)*.

146–7 spout ink in their faces that: *attack in their writings those who . . .*

148 Cinnamus: *Cinnamus was a surgeon-barber, referred to by the Roman poet Martial (Epigram VI, lxiv, 24–6) who had particular skill in removing brands. Jonson says the written attacks mounted by genuine poets against scurrilous writers will be too deeply imprinted for anyone to erase.*

our world. As for the vile and slothful, who never affected
an act worthy of celebration, or are so inward with their
own vicious natures as they worthily fear her, and think it
a high point of policy to keep her in contempt with their
declamatory and windy invectives: she shall out of just   145
rage incite her servants (who are *genus irritabile*) to spout
ink in their faces that shall eat farther than their marrow,
into their fames; and not Cinnamus the barber with his art
shall be able to take out the brands, but they shall live and
be read till the wretches die, as things worst deserving of 150
themselves in chief, and then of all mankind.

From my house in the Blackfriars this 11. of February. 1607

The names of the Venetian characters are based on seventeenth-century Italian. They are usually explained with the aid of Florio's Italian-English dictionary.

VOLPONE	*Italian for 'fox'. Florio explained the word as 'an old fox, an old reynard; an old, crafty, sly, subtle companion; sneaking, lurking, wily deceiver'.*
'magnifico'	*nobleman of Venice.*
MOSCA	*Italian for 'fly'.*
'parasite'	*someone who lives at other people's expense and makes no contribution of his own.*
VOLTORE	*vulture (Florio described it as 'a ravenous bird'. Vultures feed on carrion.)*
'advocate'	*lawyer.*
CORBACCIO	*raven ('filthy great raven', according to Florio).*
CORVINO	*crow. Crows also feed on carrion.*
BONARIO	*Florio explained the word as 'honest, good, uncorrupt'.*
SIR POLITIC	*'politic' man – sophisticated and worldly-wise. Abbreviated to 'Pol', the name indicates a parrot.*
PEREGRINE	*falcon; also a traveller.*
NANO	*the name means 'dwarf'.*
CASTRONE	*the name means 'castrated man' or 'eunuch'.*
ANDROGYNO	*i.e. 'androgynous', combining the sexual characteristics of both men and women.*

CHARACTERS

in the play

VOLPONE, *a magnifico*
MOSCA, *his parasite*
VOLTORE, *an advocate*
CORBACCIO, *an old gentleman*
CORVINO, *a merchant*
BONARIO, *son of Corbaccio*
CELIA, *wife of Corvino*
SIR POLITIC WOULD-BE, *a knight*
PEREGRINE, *a gentleman traveller*
LADY WOULD-BE, *wife of Sir Politic*
NANO, *a dwarf*
CASTRONE, *a eunuch*
ANDROGYNO, *a hermaphrodite*
AVOCATORI, *four magistrates*
NOTARIO, *a notary*
MERCATORI, *three merchants*
COMMANDADORI, *officers*
SERVANTS
WAITING-WOMEN
A CROWD

The Scene:
VENICE

13

2   state: *estate.*

5   which ope themselves: *which develop.*

7   sold: *betrayed.*

3   palates of the season: *tastes of the time.*

5   bid to credit from our poet: *asked by our poet to believe.*
6   scope: *aim*

10   railing: *violent abuse.*
12   He was a year about them: *At a time when most playwrights wrote prolifically (though not of course able to match quantity with consistent quality) Jonson's restricted output of about one play a year exposed him to sarcasm from his fellow writers.*
13–14 To these . . . feature: *the creation of this play alone, which did not exist two months ago, is enough to discredit them.*
17–18 coadjutor . . . tutor: *the various kinds of dramatic collaboration. Probably a coadjutor was an equal partner; a novice was an apprentice; a journeyman was a hack writer; and a tutor was someone who corrected drafts of plays.*
20–28 no eggs . . . fable: *Jonson summarizes the crude characteristics of badly-written, slapstick plays which he despises.*

The Argument

V OLPONE, childless, rich, feigns sick, despairs,
O ffers his state to hopes of several heirs,
L ies languishing; his parasite receives
P resents of all, assures, deludes; then weaves
O ther cross-plots, which ope themselves, are told.   5
N ew tricks for safety are sought; they thrive; when, bold,
E ach tempts th'other again, and all are sold.

Prologue

Now, luck God sent us, and a little wit
    Will serve to make our play hit;
According to the palates of the season,
    Here is rhyme, not empty of reason:
This we were bid to credit from our poet,   5
    Whose true scope, if you would know it,
In all his poems still hath been this measure,
    To mix profit with your pleasure;
And not as some (whose throats their envy failing)
    Cry hoarsely, 'All he writes, is railing';   10
And, when his plays come forth, think they can flout them,
    With saying, 'He was a year about them.'
To these there needs no lie but this his creature,
    Which was, two months since, no feature;
And, though he dares give them five lives to mend it,   15
    'Tis known, five weeks fully penned it –
From his own hand, without a coadjutor,
    Novice, journeyman, or tutor,
Yet, thus much I can give you, as a token
    Of his play's worth: no eggs are broken;   20

21 quaking custards: *the link between custard and faint-heart-edness survives in the jingle 'Cowardy, cowardy custard'. Jonson is probably referring to the huge custard which was put on the table at Lord Mayor's feasts for the jester to jump into – an event which he considered to be old-fashioned entertainment. He is also taking a chance to mock his enemy, the dramatist John Marston, who had written a satire containing the line 'Let custards quake, my rage must freely run'. As a whole, the line is a contemptuous reference to slapstick drama.*

22 your rout: *the rabble.*

23 Nor . . . reciting: *nor does he drag in a foolish character to repeat tags, proverbs and old jokes.*

26 make . . . faction: *give the lunatics of Bedlam some compe-tition. (Bedlam was the London lunatic asylum, St Mary of Bethlehem.)*

28 jests . . . fable: *comedy appropriate for his plot.*

29 quick: *lively.*

31 laws: *the laws of Renaissance literary criticism. They claimed to be, but were not, derived from Aristotle's* Poetics. *According to them (i) the action of a play was restricted to one day, and specific events shown on stage should match the time they would take in real life; (ii) the place of action was limited to one city or district; (iii) in comedy, characters should be fixed types rather than individuals. Another law stressed that 'unity of action' required a single unified plot. Jonson omits any mention of this, since the sub-plot of Sir Politic Would-be breaks it. However, his reference to 'needful' rules in line 32 is designed to cover him against such inconvenient charges.*

33 gall and copperas: *ingredients of ink. Both suggest bitterness, gall because of its link with the gall-bladder and copperas because it was acid.*

34 salt: *salt was not used in ink-making. It was, however, used for cleaning and the reference here suggests the cleansing power of comedy.*

Nor quaking custards with fierce teeth affrighted,
   Wherewith your rout are so delighted;
Nor hales he in a gull, old ends reciting,
   To stop gaps in his loose writing;
With such a deal of monstrous and forced action,   25
   As might make Bedlam a faction;
Nor made he his play for jests stol'n from each table,
   But makes jests to fit his fable.
And so presents quick comedy, refined
   As best critics have designed;   30
The laws of time, place, persons he observeth,
   From no needful rule he swerveth.
All gall and copperas from his ink he draineth,
   Only a little salt remaineth,
Wherewith he'll rub your cheeks, till, red with laughter,   35
   They shall look fresh a week after.

1–26 *This opening speech is full of blasphemous expressions which apply religious terminology to the worship of gold. It sets the mood for the energetic but perverted materialism which runs through the play as a whole.*

3   the world's soul: *'anima mundi', the divine power supposed to be the source of all life.*

5   the celestial Ram: *The sun enters the sign of the Ram, Aries, at the vernal equinox on 21 March. The earth is fertile ('teeming') and longing for the sun to restore new life after the winter.*

8–9 or . . . Chaos: *Volpone compares gold with light, the first creation of God at the beginning of the world. See Genesis 1, 2–4.*

10   centre: *centre of the earth.*

      Sol: *personification of the sun.*

12   relic: *relics were normally the sacred remnants of a dead saint or martyr, and accordingly venerated. Volpone substitutes gold.*

15   that age: *the Golden Age, celebrated in Greek and Roman poetry as a time of unequalled happiness for humankind.*

19   when . . . ascribe: *classical poets habitually described Venus Aphrodite as 'golden'.*

20   twenty thousand Cupids: *Cupid was the son of Venus. Volpone suggests that a goddess worthy to be associated with gold should have been endowed with the fertility to produce many children. Again gold is associated with fertility.*

24   The price of souls: *this is the most blasphemous phrase in the speech, making a direct parallel between the 'purchasing power' of gold and the price paid by Christ in order to redeem humankind.*

24   to boot: *as part of the bargain.*

Act One

Scene one

VOLPONE'S *House*
Enter VOLPONE, MOSCA

VOLPONE
    Good morning to the day; and, next, my gold!
    Open the shrine, that I may see my saint.
                           (MOSCA *reveals the treasure*)
    Hail the world's soul, and mine! More glad than is
    The teeming earth to see the longed-for sun
    Peep through the horns of the celestial Ram,   5
    Am I, to view thy splendour, darkening his;
    That, lying here, amongst my other hoards,
    Show'st like a flame by night; or like the day
    Struck out of Chaos, when all darkness fled
    Unto the centre. O, thou son of Sol   10
    (But brighter than thy father) let me kiss,
    With adoration, thee, and every relic
    Of sacred treasure in this blessed room.
    Well did wise poets by thy glorious name
    Title that age which they would have the best,   15
    Thou being the best of things – and far transcending
    All style of joy, in children, parents, friends,
    Or any other waking dream on earth.
    Thy looks, when they to Venus did ascribe,
    They should have given her twenty thousand Cupids;   20
    Such are thy beauties, and our loves! Dear saint,
    Riches, the dumb god that giv'st all men tongues;
    That canst do naught, and yet mak'st men do all things;
    The price of souls; even hell, with thee to boot,
    Is made worth heaven! Thou art virtue, fame,   25
    Honour, and all things else! Who can get thee,
    He shall be noble, valiant, honest, wise –

28–9 Riches ... nature: *In medieval thought there was a commonplace distinction between gifts of fortune (wealth and rank)
and those of nature (qualities of mind and body).*

31 purchase: *acquisition. The first clear indication that Volpone
is not, as his victims are, interested in wealth for its own sake
alone.*

33 common: *commonplace.*

venture: *risky business enterprise.*

35 shambles: *slaughterhouse.*

36 or men: *note the unnerving effect of this carefully placed phrase,
with its suggestion that not only raw materials were ground down
in the mills of industry, but the bodies and bones of the men who
worked in them.*

37 I blow ... glass: *Venice was (and is) famous for its
glassware.*

subtle: *fine, delicate.*

39 turn no moneys: *circulate no money.*

40 usure: *usury, i.e. lending out money for interest. Usury was a
controversial practice at this period because on the one hand it was
an essential part of the growing capitalist economy, but on the
other hand it conflicted with the traditional doctrines of the church.*

41 Soft prodigals: *spendthrifts who can easily be exploited.*

41–2 swallow ... heir: *cheat a young man out of the riches he has
just inherited.*

42 glibly: *smoothly.*

42–3 Dutch ... butter: *the Dutch were famous for their love of
butter.*

43 purge: *take a laxative. Their untroubled 'digestion' of the unfortunate heir suggests that the usurers' malpractice went
unpunished.*

45–7 coffin them ... rotten: *ironically this anticipates what is
to be Volpone's ultimate punishment.*

47 forth-coming: *coming out. They will not leave prison alive.*

56 mallows: *medicinal herbs.*

58 Romagnìa: *sweet wine from Greece.*

Candian: *wine from Candy, in Crete.*

MOSCA

    And what he will, sir. Riches are in fortune

    A greater good than wisdom is in nature.

VOLPONE

    True, my beloved Mosca. Yet, I glory   30

    More in the cunning purchase of my wealth

    Than in the glad possession; since I gain

    No common way: I use no trade, no venture;

    I wound no earth with ploughshares; fat no beasts

    To feed the shambles; have no mills for iron,   35

    Oil, corn, or men, to grind 'em into powder;

    I blow no subtle glass; expose no ships

    To threat'nings of the furrow-facèd sea;

    I turn no moneys in the public bank;

    Nor usure private –

MOSCA   No sir, nor devour   40

    Soft prodigals. You shall ha' some will swallow

    A melting heir as glibly as your Dutch

    Will pills of butter, and ne'er purge for't;

    Tear forth the fathers of poor families

    Out of their beds, and coffin them, alive,   45

    In some kind, clasping prison, where their bones

    May be forth-coming when the flesh is rotten.

    But your sweet nature doth abhor these courses;

    You loathe, the widow's or the orphan's tears

    Should wash your pavements, or their piteous cries   50

    Ring in your roofs, and beat the air for vengeance –

VOLPONE

    Right, Mosca, I do loathe it.

MOSCA   And besides, sir,

    You are not like the thresher, that doth stand

    With a huge flail, watching a heap of corn,

    And, hungry, dares not taste the smallest grain,   55

    But feeds on mallows and such bitter herbs;

    Nor like the merchant, who hath filled his vaults

    With Romagnìa and rich Candian wines,

59 lees of Lombard's vinegar: *dregs of cheap wine from Lombardy.*

62–3 You know ... observer: *Mosca's extravagant flattery of Volpone's correct use of riches has all been directed towards this delicate request for a tip. He gets one, however, which shows us that, whatever Volpone's faults may be, he is not a miser. It also shows that Volpone is not immune to flattery. ('Observer' means deferential follower.)*

71 cocker up my genius: *indulge my appetites.*

74 substance: *possessions.*

75 observe: *treat me with fulsome respect.*

82 engross me, whole: *absorb me, completely.*

83 counter-work ... other: *undermine each other's plans.*

84 Contend ... love: *Compete with each other in the value of their gifts, as if these reflected the proportions of their love for me.*

85 suffer: *allow.*

87 kindness: *the word is used with mocking irony.*

88 bearing them in hand: *leading them on.*

89 cherry: *reference to the game of bob-cherry, in which the player tries to bite a cherry dangling on a string.*

Yet drinks the lees of Lombard's vinegar;
You will not lie in straw, whilst moths and worms   60
Feed on your sumptuous hangings and soft beds.
You know the use of riches, and dare give, now,
From that bright heap, to me, your poor observer,
Or to your dwarf, or your hermaphrodite,
Your eunuch, or what other household trifle.   65
Your pleasure allows maintenance –

VOLPONE   Hold thee, Mosca,
                                        (*Gives him money*)
Take, of my hand; thou strik'st on truth in all,
And they are envious, term thee parasite.
Call forth my dwarf, my eunuch, and my fool,
And let 'em make me sport. (*Exit* MOSCA) What should I
    do   70
But cocker up my genius and live free
To all delights my fortune calls me to?
I have no wife, no parent, child, ally,
To give my substance to; but whom I make
Must be my heir – and this makes men observe me.   75
This draws new clients, daily, to my house,
Women and men, of every sex and age,
That bring me presents, send me plate, coin, jewels,
With hope that when I die (which they expect
Each greedy minute) it shall then return   80
Tenfold upon them; whilst some, covetous
Above the rest, seek to engross me, whole,
And counter-work the one unto the other,
Contend in gifts, as they would seem in love.
All which I suffer, playing with their hopes,   85
And am content to coin 'em into profit,
And look upon their kindness, and take more,
And look on that; still bearing them in hand,
Letting the cherry knock against their lips,
And draw it by their mouths, and back again. How
    now!   90

23

> *The cynical interlude now played by Volpone's household is loosely adapted from part of* The Cock, *a dialogue by the Greek satirist Lucian. The play, based on Pythagoras' doctrine that souls migrate from one living body to another ('transmigration of souls'), relates the journey of a soul which once lived in Pythagoras himself. Its journeyings carry it from great figures of classical antiquity to a collection of birds and animals. The interlude is an ironic prelude to the coming drama.*

2 university show: *an example of neo-classical academic drama.*

3 rehearse: *recite.*

4 the false pace . . . verse: *the interlude is written in irregular verse, with four stresses to the line. It was frequently used in Morality plays, of which this is a distorted version.*

6 Pythagoras: *Pythagoras was a great mathematician and philosopher of the sixth century BC.*

7 juggler: *(i) buffoon; (ii) magician.*

8 fast and loose: *shifting, inconstant (based on a game played with a stick and a belt and used to cheat people at fairs).*

9 Aethalides: *son of Mercury and herald of the Argonauts. Mercury granted him faultless and undying memory, which accounts for Pythagoras' unique recall of his earlier existences.*

13 the cuckold of Sparta: *Menelaus, husband of the faithless Helen of Troy.*

14 charta: *the paper on which his speech is written.*

17 sophist of Greece: *i.e. Pythagoras.*

19 Hight: *called.*
    Aspasia: *Aspasia was a distinguished figure in classical Athenian society. She was the lifelong companion of the great statesman Pericles, and a friend of Socrates. Like other famous figures in this interlude, she is treated with undeserved scorn.*
    meretrix: *prostitute.*

21 Crates the Cynic: *Greek philosopher of the fourth century BC, and member of the sect called 'cynics'.*
    itself: *i.e. the soul.*

22 Since: *since that time.*

(*Scene two*)

Enter MOSCA, *with* NANO, ANDROGYNO, *and* CASTRONE, *ready to enter-tain* VOLPONE

NANO

Now, room for fresh gamesters, who do will you to know,
    They do bring you neither play nor university show;
And therefore do intreat you that whatsoever they
    rehearse
      May not fare a whit the worse for the false pace of the
      verse.
If you wonder at this, you will wonder more ere we pass,   5
    For know (*Pointing to* ANDROGYNO), here is enclosed
    the soul of Pythagoras,
That juggler divine, as hereafter shall follow;
    Which soul (fast and loose, sir) came first from
    Apollo,
And was breathed into Aethalides, Mercurius his son,
    Where it had the gift to remember all that ever was
    done.   10
From thence it fled forth, and made quick
    transmigration
    To goldy-locked Euphorbus, who was killed in good
    fashion
At the siege of old Troy, by the cuckold of Sparta.
    Hermotimus was next (I find it in my charta)
To whom it did pass, where no sooner it was missing.   15
    But with one Pyrrhus, of Delos, it learned to go
    a-fishing;
And thence did it enter the sophist of Greece.
    From Pythagore, she went into a beautiful piece
Hight Aspasia, the meretrix; and the next toss of her
    Was, again, of a whore – she became a philosopher,   20
Crates the Cynic (as itself does relate it).
    Since, kings, knights, and beggars, knaves, lords and
    fools gat it,

23   brock: *badger.*

24   cobbler's cock: *in Lucian's dialogue* The Cock, *a cockerel claiming to possess this soul has a conversation with a poor cobbler.*

26   his great oath, 'By Quater!':   *Pythagoras developed a complicated symbolism of numbers, based on the mystical powers of the number four ('Quater').*

27   musics: *Pythagoras believed in the laws of celestial harmony which produced the 'music of the spheres'.*

       trigon: *a trigon is a triangle of dots, with four dots on each side; it formed part of Pythagoras' symbolism of numbers.*

       golden thigh: *It was said that Pythagoras' thigh was made of gold.*

28   how elements shift: *i.e. how the traditional four elements – earth, air, fire and water – change their relationships.*

29   translation: *transformation.*

30   reformation: *i.e. the Protestant Reformation.*

31–2   a fool . . . heresy: *Jonson was a Catholic when he wrote* Volpone. *He refers ironically here to those who believe that the 'new learning' of the Reformation is the only truth.*

33   forbid meats: *reference to Pythagoras' curious ban on the eating of various foods.*

34   Carthusian: *Carthusian monks observed a strict self-denial in their diet.*

35   dogmatical silence: *followers of Pythagoras were also instructed to observe a five-year silence.*

36   obstreperous: *the word originally meant 'bawling'. The soul's progress allows Jonson a dig at the noisy eloquence of lawyers, and prepares the ground for Voltore's facile tongue.*

40   beans: *beans were one of the foods that Pythagoras forbade.*

43   precise . . . brother: *Puritan. The words refer to their estimate of themselves, not to Jonson's opinion of them, which was low.*

44   Of those: *One of those who.*

Besides ox, and ass, camel, mule, goat, and brock,
    In all which it hath spoke, as in the cobbler's cock.
But I come not here, to discourse of that matter,   25
    Or his one, two, or three, or his great oath, 'By
    Quater!'
His musics, his trigon, his golden thigh,
    Or his telling how elements shift; but I
Would ask, how of late thou hast suffered translation,
    And shifted thy coat in these days of reformation?   30

ANDROGYNO
    Like one of the reformèd, a fool, as you see,
        Counting all old doctrine heresy.

NANO
    But not on thine own forbid meats hast thou ventured?

ANDROGYNO
    On fish, when first a Carthusian I entered.

NANO
    Why, then thy dogmatical silence hath left thee?   35

ANDROGYNO
    Of that an obstreperous lawyer bereft me.

NANO
    O wonderful change! when Sir Lawyer forsook thee,
        For Pythagore's sake, what body then took thee?

ANDROGYNO
    A good dull mule.

NANO   And how! by that means
        Thou wert brought to allow of the eating of beans?   40

ANDROGYNO
    Yes.

NANO   But, from the mule, into whom did'st thou pass?

ANDROGYNO
        Into a very strange beast, by some writers called an
        ass;
    By others, a precise, pure, illuminate brother,
        Of those devour flesh, and sometimes one another;

27

46   nativity-pie: *so called by the Puritans in order to avoid the Popish implications of '-mas' in the word Christmas.*

47   nation: *class of persons.*

52   take up thy station: *live in permanently.*

55–8 Alas . . . distressèd: *So the general movement of the soul in this sketch from is extreme beauty (Apollo) to deformity (Androgyno); from wisdom to folly; and from idealized humankind to the animals. The soul's final satisfaction with this downward progress is a sign of the decadence which the play as a whole shows to be deeply rooted in Venetian society. There too, there is much deformity, much folly, much bestiality.*

59   as: *as if.*

62   that: *i.e. foolishness.*

And will drop you forth a libel, or a sanctified lie,   45
   Betwixt every spoonful of a nativity-pie.

NANO

  Now quit thee, for heaven, of that profane nation;
   And gently report thy next transmigration.

ANDROGYNO

  To the same that I am.

NANO   A creature of dèlight?
   And, what is more than a fool, an hermaphrodite?   50
  Now pray thee, sweet soul, in all thy variation,
   Which body would'st thou choose, to take up thy
    station?

ANDROGYNO

  Troth, this I am in, even here would I tarry.

NANO

  'Cause here the delight of each sex thou canst vary?

ANDROGYNO

  Alas, those pleasures be stale and forsaken;   55
   No, 'tis your fool, wherewith I am so taken;
  The only one creature that I can call blessèd,
   For all other forms I have proved most distressèd.

NANO

  Spoke true, as thou wert in Pythagoras still.
   This learned opinion we celebrate will,   60
  Fellow eunuch, as behoves us, with all our wit and art,
  To dignify that whereof ourselves are so great and
    special a part.

VOLPONE

  Now very, very pretty! Mosca, this
  Was thy invention?

MOSCA   If it please my patron,
  Not else.

VOLPONE   It doth, good Mosca.

MOSCA   Then it was, sir.   65

Song: *This was probably sung by* NANO *and* CASTRONE, *both parts being played by boys with trained singing voices. The song contains many commonplace conceptions about the Fool and his status, including his freedom to speak candid and uncomfortable truths without being punished for it.*

70 Selves: *they themselves.*

74 bauble: *carved stick carried by a professional Fool, with a play on its alternative bawdy meaning of 'penis'.*

76 free from slaughter: *without punishment.*

79 trencher: *platter.*

82 Hee, hee, hee?: *both 'he, he, he', and a giggle as the song tails off.*

85–6 gown . . . night caps: *the dress of an invalid. It would be appropriate if his 'furs' included a fox fur.*

86 is changing: *is being changed.*

88 Without: *outside.*

89 visitation: *(i) polite social calls; (ii) sick visits.*

89–90 vulture . . . gor-crow: *the names are very precise symbols, with distinct personal references. (The 'kite' is presumably Lady Would-be.) All are birds of prey which partly feed on carrion. The visitors' hunger for gold will be 'fed', they hope, by Volpone's dead body.*

90 gor-crow: *carrion crow.*

30

Song

Fools, they are the only nation
Worth men's envy or admiration;
Free from care or sorrow-taking,
Selves and others merry making. 70
All they speak, or do, is sterling:
Your fool, he is your great man's darling,
And your ladies' sport and pleasure;
Tongue and bauble are his treasure.
E'en his face begetteth laughter, 75
And he speaks truth, free from slaughter;
He's the grace of every feast,
And sometimes the chiefest guest;
Hath his trencher and his stool,
When wit waits upon the fool. 80
   O, who would not be
   Hee, hee, hee?

One knocks without

VOLPONE

Who's that? Away!

(Exeunt NANO, CASTRONE*)*

Look Mosca!

MOSCA   Fool, begone!

Exit ANDROGYNO

'Tis Signior Voltore, the advocate;
I know him by his knock.

VOLPONE   Fetch me my gown, 85
My furs, and night caps; say my couch is changing;
And let him entertain himself awhile
Without i' th' gallery. *(Exit* MOSCA*)* Now, now, my clients
Begin their visitation! vulture, kite,
Raven, and gor-crow, all my birds of prey, 90

95–7 a fox ... crow: *This is usually explained as a reference to Aesop's fable in which a fox tricked a crow into dropping its cheese by praising its singing voice and so causing it to open its beak in song. However, it may refer to another belief about foxes. They were said to 'sham dead', attracting the attention of carrion-eating birds which hoped to feed on the corpses. When one came near enough, the fox would spring to life and seize it, so the bird and not the fox was eaten. Such a fox-trick closely resembles Volpone's.*

96 sleights: *cunning tricks.*

97 gaping: *open-mouthed, ready to bite.*

102 fetch you: *lure you into bequeathing all to him.*

106 foot-cloths: *richly ornamented cloths which hung over horses' backs and reached the ground on each side.*

108 mule: *mules were ridden by judges, serjeants-at-law and advocates.*

    lettered: *learned.*

111–2 rich / Implies it: *Volpone has hinted at the difference between being called learned and actually being learned. Mosca takes the hint and says that wealth hides the difference. True values in Venice are corrupted by materialism. It is because Volpone and Mosca perceive this so clearly and exploit it so scornfully that their activities take on a kind of perverted rightness. We cannot be wholly appalled by them because their trickery is somewhere rooted in accurate moral judgement.*

112 reverend purple: *doctor of divinity wore a purple hood.*

113 ambitious: *(i) aspiring; (ii) soaring into the air.*

That think me turning carcass, now they come –
I am not for 'em yet. How now? the news?

Re-enter MOSCA

MOSCA

    A piece of plate, sir.

VOLPONE   Of what bigness?

MOSCA   Huge,

    Massy, and antique, with your name inscribed,
    And arms engraven.

VOLPONE   Good! and not a fox   95
    Stretched on the earth, with fine delusive sleights,
    Mocking a gaping crow? ha, Mosca?

MOSCA   Sharp, sir.

VOLPONE

    Give me my furs. Why dost thou laugh so, man?

MOSCA

    I cannot choose, sir, when I apprehend
    What thoughts he has, without, now, as he walks: 100
    That this might be the last gift he should give;
    That this would fetch you; if you died today
    And gave him all, what he should be tomorrow;
    What large return would come of all his ventures;
    How he should worshipped be, and reverenced;   105
    Ride, with his furs, and foot-cloths; waited on
    By herds of fools and clients; have clear way
    Made for his mule, as lettered as himself;
    Be called the great and learned advocate;
    And then concludes, there's naught impossible.   110

VOLPONE

    Yes, to be learned, Mosca.

MOSCA   O, no – rich
    Implies it. Hood an ass with reverend purple,
    So you can hide his two ambitious ears,
    And he shall pass for a cathedral doctor.

VOLPONE

    My caps, my caps, good Mosca. Fetch him in.   115

117 dispatch: *hurry.*

121 And hundred . . . succession: *Mosca flatters Volpone to absurd lengths by imagining for him an immortality of successful
deceit. It is a kind of game between them. The falsity of such excessive flattery cannot go unnoticed, as Mosca knows. Volpone is
aware of it, but it pleases him nevertheless. Mosca's blatant ex-
travagance and Volpone's susceptibility are an early sign of potential weakness in their partnership.*

123 Still: *always.*
harpies: *fabulous monsters which had a woman's face and body
and a bird's wings and claws. They were grasping and filthy.
Their greed, together with the mingling of human and bird in their
appearance, makes them an appropriate image for the legacy-
hunters.*

125 phthisic: *consumption.*

127 posture: *imposture.*

1 what you were: *i.e. Volpone's favourite amongst the suitors.*

4 notes: *tokens.*
5 good meaning to: *benevolent intentions towards.*
6 grateful: *pleasing.*

MOSCA
    Stay, sir, your ointment for your eyes.

VOLPONE   That's true;
    Dispatch, dispatch – I long to have possession
    Of my new present.

MOSCA   That, and thousands more,
    I hope to see you lord of.

VOLPONE   Thanks, kind Mosca.

MOSCA
    And that, when I am lost in blended dust,   120
    And hundred such as I am, in succession –

VOLPONE
    Nay, that were too much, Mosca.

MOSCA   You shall live,
    Still, to delude these harpies.

VOLPONE   Loving Mosca!
    'Tis well. My pillow now, and let him enter.

                              (*Exit* MOSCA)

    Now, my feigned cough, my phthisic, and my gout,   125
    My apoplexy, palsy, and catarrhs,
    Help, with your forced functions, this my posture,
    Wherein, this three year, I have milked their hopes.
    He comes, I hear him – uh! uh! uh! uh! O –

(*Scene three*)

Enter MOSCA, *with* VOLTORE *bearing a piece of plate*

MOSCA
    You still are what you were, sir. Only you –
    Of all the rest – are he, commands his love;
    And you do wisely to preserve it thus,
    With early visitation, and kind notes
    Of your good meaning to him, which, I know,   5
    Cannot but come most grateful. Patron, sir.
    Here's Signior Voltore is come –

7   What say you?:   *Volpone pretends to be deaf. His comic imi-*
    tation of this disability will sharply contrast with the genuine poor
    hearing of Corbaccio.

10   of St Mark: *from the shops near the basilica of St Mark.*

15   I long ... here, sir: *As Volpone pretends to stretch out feebly*
    for a friendly hand-clasp, Mosca delights in mentioning frankly
    what it is that Volpone is really reaching for!

20   as well: *as easily.*

21-2   Your love/Hath taste in this: *Your love shows itself in this*
    gift.

VOLPONE   What say you?

MOSCA
  Sir, Signior Voltore is come this morning
  To visit you.
VOLPONE   I thank him.
MOSCA   And hath brought
  A piece of antique plate, bought of St Mark,   10
  With which he here presents you.
VOLPONE   He is welcome.
  Pray him to come more often.
MOSCA   Yes.
VOLPONE   What says he?
MOSCA
  He thanks you, and desires you see him often.
VOLPONE
  Mosca!
MOSCA   My patron?
VOLPONE   Bring him near, where is he?
  I long to feel his hand.
MOSCA   The plate is here, sir.   15
VOLTORE
  How fare you, sir?
VOLPONE   I thank you, Signior Voltore.
  Where is the plate? Mine eyes are bad.
VOLTORE   I'm sorry
  To see you still thus weak.
MOSCA (*Aside*)   That he is not weaker.
VOLPONE
  You are too munificent.
VOLTORE   No, sir, would to heaven
  I could as well give health to you as that plate.   20
VOLPONE
  You give, sir, what you can. I thank you. Your love
  Hath taste in this, and shall not be unanswered.
  I pray you see me often.
VOLTORE   Yes, I shall, sir.

33 inscribed: *written into his will.*

35 write ... family: *write my name in your 'household book' as
one of your servants.*

35–6 All my hopes ... worship: *Mosca pretends to transfer his
services and dependence from Volpone to whichever suitor he is bent
on flattering. They trust him the more because they think they own
him, a materialistic delusion he encourages.*

40 offices: *services.*
your keys: *i.e. the keys to Volpone's treasure, which Mosca
encourages Voltore to think of as if it were already his.*

44 Husband: *look after.*

VOLPONE

Be not far from me.

MOSCA (*Aside to* VOLTORE) Do you observe that, sir?

VOLPONE

Hearken unto me still. It will concern you.   25

MOSCA

You are a happy man, sir; know your good.

VOLPONE

I cannot now last long –

MOSCA (*Aside to* VOLTORE) You are his heir, sir.

VOLTORE

Am I?

VOLPONE I feel me going – uh! uh! uh! uh! –

I am sailing to my port – uh! uh! uh! uh! –

And I am glad I am so near my haven.   30

MOSCA

Alas, kind gentleman; well, we must all go –

VOLTORE

But, Mosca –

MOSCA   Age will conquer.

VOLTORE   Pray thee hear me.

Am I inscribed his heir for certain?

MOSCA   Are you?

I do beseech you, sir, you will vouchsafe

To write me i' your family. All my hopes   35

Depend upon your worship. I am lost,

Except the rising sun do shine on me.

VOLTORE

It shall both shine and warm thee, Mosca.

MOSCA   Sir,

I am a man that have not done your love

All the worst offices; here I wear your keys,   40

See all your coffers and your caskets locked,

Keep the poor inventory of your jewels,

Your plate, and moneys; am your steward, sir,

Husband your goods here.

49–50 Thy modesty . . . know it: *i.e. you underrate your own part in gaining the inheritance for me.*

50   know: *acknowledge.*

we: *the royal plural, a mark of Voltore's pride in his anticipated wealth and stature.*

51–66:   *This speech, full of supposed admiration for lawyers, is actually heavy with irony and under the cloak of praise is a bitter attack on the legal profession.*

51   course: *procedure (in twisting the law to suit his clients' convenience).*

took: *delighted.*

53   large: *(i) numerous; (ii) expansive and fluent in public speaking.*

54   mere contraries: *absolute opposites, impossible to reconcile with each other (i.e. the lawyer could with equal confidence defend first one view and then its complete reverse).*

58   forkèd: *equivocal; ambiguous.*

58–9 take provoking . . . put it up: *accept bribes or fees from both parties to a legal dispute, and pocket them. (To 'provoke' is to ask a court or lawyer to take up one's case.)*

60   humility: *There is vicious irony in Mosca's reference to the spiritual virtue of humility, since his evidence for it has been a series of 'humble' refusals to make any stand for truth or professional integrity.*

62   suffering: *again ironic: patient; reluctant to complain.*

63   perplexed: *perplexing, bewildering.*

66   chequeen: *Venetian gold coin.*

70–1 lard . . . honey: *These are not easy substances to swim in! Wealth is equated with a suffocating excess of fat and sweetness and the images are calculated to arouse disgust.*

72   fatness: *excessive richness.*

73   but: *only.*

VOLTORE   But am I sole heir?

MOSCA

Without a partner, sir, confirmed this morning;   45
The wax is warm yet, and the ink scarce dry
Upon the parchment.

VOLTORE   Happy, happy, me!
By what good chance, sweet Mosca?

MOSCA   Your desert, sir;
I know no second cause.

VOLTORE   Thy modesty
Is loath to know it; well, we shall requite it.   50

MOSCA

He ever liked your course, sir – that first took him.
I oft have heard him say how he admired
Men of your large profession, that could speak
To every cause, and things mere contraries,
Till they were hoarse again, yet all be law;   55
That, with most quick agility, could turn,
And re-turn; make knots, and undo them;
Give forkèd counsel; take provoking gold
On either hand, and put it up – these men,
He knew, would thrive, with their humility.   60
And, for his part, he thought he should be blest
To have his heir of such a suffering spirit,
So wise, so grave, of so perplexed a tongue,
And loud withal, that would not wag, nor scarce
Lie still, without a fee; when every word   65
Your worship but lets fall, is a chequeen!

                                        (*Another knocks*)

Who's that? one knocks; I would not have you seen, sir.
And yet – pretend you came and went in haste;
I'll fashion an excuse. And, gentle sir,
When you do come to swim in golden lard,   70
Up to the arms in honey, that your chin
Is borne up stiff with fatness of the flood,
Think on your vassal; but remember me:

76 Anon!: *Coming in a minute!* (*Shouted offstage to whoever has knocked.*)

78 Put business in your face: *look businesslike.*

2 multiply: *The pile of loot will 'multiply' as each caller adds to it. The idolatrous regard for gold is reinforced by a blasphemous reminder of God's instruction to Adam and Eve: 'Be fruitful, and multiply' (Genesis, 1, 22).*

4 this: *i.e. Volpone.*

7 What? mends he?: *Mosca's contrast in lines 3–5 between Corbaccio's impotence and Volpone's pretence of it is now borne out when we see a genuine instance of the deafness which Volpone had earlier feigned.*

I ha' not been your worst of clients.

VOLTORE   Mosca –

MOSCA

When will you have your inventory brought, sir?   75
Or see a copy of the will? (*Knocking again*) Anon!
I'll bring 'em to you, sir. Away, be gone;
Put business in your face.

Exit VOLTORE

VOLPONE   Excellent, Mosca!
Come hither, let me kiss thee.

MOSCA   Keep you still, sir.
Here is Corbaccio.

VOLPONE   Set the plate away.   80
The vulture's gone, and the old raven's come.

(*Scene four*)

MOSCA

Betake you to your silence, and your sleep.
(*To the plate*) Stand there, and multiply. Now shall we
    see
A wretch who is indeed more impotent
Than this can feign to be; yet hopes to hop
Over his grave. (*Enter* CORBACCIO) Signior Corbaccio!   5
You're very welcome, sir.

CORBACCIO   How does your patron?

MOSCA

Troth, as he did, sir, no amends.

CORBACCIO   What? mends he?

MOSCA

No, sir – he is rather worse.

CORBACCIO   That's well. Where is he?

MOSCA

Upon his couch, sir, newly fall'n asleep.

11   but slumbers: *only dozes.*

13   opiate: *sedative.*

18   Ay, his last sleep: *Volpone suggests that the drug is poisoned.*

19   say you?: *What's that you say?*

20–35: *The satirical attack on lawyers in Scene III lines 51–66 is now matched by a similar assault on doctors.*

21   your doctors: *'your' is a colloquial idiom which suggests both familiarity with the person you are talking to and a rather contemptuous knowledge of the subject you are discussing.*

27   flay: *literally, 'skin alive'. Here 'strip all his money from him'.*

28   conceive: *understand.*

29   do it by experiment: *test new treatments on their patients, which kill them.*

CORBACCIO
    Does he sleep well?

MOSCA   No wink, sir, all this night,   10
    Nor yesterday, but slumbers.

CORBACCIO   Good! He should take
    Some counsel of physicians; I have brought him
    An opiate here, from mine own doctor –

MOSCA
    He will not hear of drugs.

CORBACCIO   Why? I myself
    Stood by while 't was made, saw all th'ingredients,   15
    And know it cannot but most gently work.
    My life for his, 'tis but to make him sleep.

VOLPONE (*Aside*)
    Ay, his last sleep, if he would take it.

MOSCA   Sir,
    He has no faith in physic.

CORBACCIO   Say you, say you?

MOSCA
    He has no faith in physic: he does think   20
    Most of your doctors are the greater danger,
    And worse disease t'escape. I often have
    Heard him protest that your physician
    Should never be his heir.

CORBACCIO   Not I his heir?

MOSCA
    Not your physician, sir.

CORBACCIO   O, no, no, no,   25
    I do not mean it.

MOSCA   No, sir, nor their fees
    He cannot brook; he says, they flay a man
    Before they kill him.

CORBACCIO   Right, I do conceive you.

MOSCA
    And then, they do it by experiment;
    For which the law not only doth absolve 'em,   30

32 hire: *pay for.*

35 kill him, too: *i.e. the judge, when he seeks medical treatment.*

39 was wont: *used to be.*

41 O, good: *Corbaccio, himself visibly decrepit and infirm, takes imbecile pleasure in Mosca's account of Volpone's supposed decline. Both the language and the visual stage effect make avarice appear vicious, foolish and grotesque.*

46 Not from his brain?: *Not out of his mind?*

48 rheum: *watery discharge.*

46

But gives them great reward; and he is loath
To hire his death so.
CORBACCIO   It is true, they kill
With as much licence as a judge.
MOSCA   Nay, more;
For he but kills, sir, where the law condemns,
And these can kill him, too.
CORBACCIO   Ay, or me –   35
Or any man. How does his apoplex?
Is that strong on him still?
MOSCA   Most violent.
His speech is broken, and his eyes are set.
His face drawn longer than 't was wont –
CORBACCIO   How? How?
Stronger than he was wont?
MOSCA   No, sir; his face   40
Drawn longer, than 't was wont.
CORBACCIO   O, good.
MOSCA   His mouth
Is ever gaping, and his eyelids hang.
CORBACCIO   Good.
MOSCA
A freezing numbness stiffens all his joints,
And makes the colour of his flesh like lead.
CORBACCIO   'Tis good.
MOSCA
His pulse beats slow, and dull.
CORBACCIO   Good symptoms still.   45
MOSCA
And, from his brain –
CORBACCIO   Ha? How? Not from his brain?
MOSCA
Yes, sir, and from his brain –
CORBACCIO   I conceive you, good.
MOSCA
Flows a cold sweat, with a continual rheum,

49 resolvèd: *drooping.*

53 left to snort: *ceased snorting.*

62 about his testament: *in the process of making his will.*

67 By your own scale: *Mosca says that Corbaccio judges Voltore by his own standards, and correctly guesses Voltore's motive because he shares it.*

Forth the resolvèd corners of his eyes.

CORBACCIO

Is't possible? Yet I am better, ha!   50
How does he, with the swimming of his head?

MOSCA

O, sir, 'tis past the scotomy; he now
Hath lost his feeling, and hath left to snort;
You hardly can perceive him, that he breathes.

CORBACCIO

Excellent, excellent, sure I shall outlast him;   55
This makes me young again, a score of years.

MOSCA

I was a-coming for you, sir.

CORBACCIO   Has he made his will?
What has he given me?

MOSCA   No, sir.

CORBACCIO   Nothing? ha?

MOSCA

He has not made his will, sir.

CORBACCIO   Oh, oh, oh.
What then did Voltore, the lawyer, here?   60

MOSCA

He smelt a carcass, sir, when he but heard
My master was about his testament –
As I did urge him to it, for your good –

CORBACCIO

He came unto him, did he? I thought so.

MOSCA

Yes, and presented him this piece of plate.   65

CORBACCIO

To be his heir?

MOSCA   I do not know, sir.

CORBACCIO   True,
I know it too.

MOSCA (*Aside*) By your own scale, sir.

CORBACCIO   Well,

68   prevent: *forestall*.

70   weigh down: *outweigh*.

71   sacred medicine: *once again gold is credited with divine powers,
      this time linked to the gift of healing.*

72   to: *compared to.*
      elixir: *alchemists sought a substance called the 'elixir', which was
      reputed to prolong life indefinitely and to transmute other metals into
      gold.*

73   'aurum palpabile', if not 'potabile': *aurum potabile was
      'drinkable gold', a solution of gold in oil believed to act as a res-
      torative medicine for the heart and circulation. Aurum palpabile
      is 'touchable gold', which Corbaccio suggests may still have a
      medicinal effect even if Volpone cannot drink it.*

74   It shall . . . bowl?: *Mosca develops Corbaccio's remark by sug-
      gesting that he will present Corbaccio's chequeens to Volpone in
      his feeding-bowl, as if they were a medicinal food.*

77   recover: *restore.*

80   therefore forbear: *Mosca makes a slight tactical error. To
      stimulate Corbaccio into offering gifts he suggests that the bag of
      chequeens will be good for Volpone's health. Since this is not what
      Corbaccio wants, he decides to retrieve his gift. Mosca is able to
      put things right, but the mistake is a sign of the tightrope which
      the deceivers are always walking.*
      Venture: *speculative gift.*

81   At no hand: *by no means.*

I shall prevent him yet. See, Mosca, look,
Here, I have brought a bag of bright chequeens,
Will quite weigh down his plate.

MOSCA   Yea, marry, sir!   70
This is true physic, this your sacred medicine,
No talk of opiates, to this great elixir.

CORBACCIO
'Tis *aurum palpabile*, if not *potabile*.

MOSCA
It shall be ministered to him, in his bowl?

CORBACCIO
Ay, do, do, do.

MOSCA   Most blessed cordial!   75
This will recover him.

CORBACCIO   Yes, do, do, do.

MOSCA
I think it were not best, sir.

CORBACCIO   What?

MOSCA   To recover him.

CORBACCIO
O, no, no, no; by no means.

MOSCA   Why, sir, this
Will work some strange effect if he but feel it.

CORBACCIO
'Tis true, therefore forbear, I'll take my venture;   80
Give me't again.

MOSCA   At no hand, pardon me;
You shall not do yourself that wrong, sir. I
Will so advise you, you shall have it all.

CORBACCIO
How?

MOSCA All, sir, 'tis your right, your own; no man
Can claim a part; 'tis yours, without a rival,   85
Decreed by destiny.

CORBACCIO   How? how, good Mosca?

51

87 This fit he shall recover: *He will recover from this attack.*

89 gained: *regained.*

96–7 that colour . . . taking: *that pretence will make it much more enticing.*

97 but: *merely. (Even Corbaccio has momentary compunction about disinheriting his son. Mosca needs to offer quick assurance that only a pretence is intended.)*

99 enforce: *emphasize.*

100 Your cares, your watchings: *your concern and attendance at his bedside.*

103 proper issue: *own offspring.*

MOSCA

I'll tell you, sir. This fit he shall recover –

CORBACCIO

I do conceive you.

MOSCA   And, on first advantage

Of his gained sense, will I re-importune him

Unto the making of his testament,   90

And show him this.

CORBACCIO   Good, good.

MOSCA   'Tis better yet,

If you will hear, sir.

CORBACCIO   Yes, with all my heart.

MOSCA

Now, would I counsel you, make home with speed;

There, frame a will, whereto you shall inscribe

My master your sole heir.

CORBACCIO   And disinherit   95

My son?

MOSCA   O, sir, the better – for that colour

Shall make it much more taking.

CORBACCIO   O, but colour?

MOSCA

This will, sir, you shall send it unto me.

Now, when I come to enforce (as I will do)

Your cares, your watchings, and your many prayers,   100

Your more than many gifts, your this day's present,

And, last, produce your will; where (without thought

Or least regard unto your proper issue,

A son so brave and highly meriting)

The stream of your diverted love hath thrown you   105

Upon my master, and made him your heir.

He cannot be so stupid, or stone dead,

But, out of conscience, and mere gratitude –

CORBACCIO

He must pronounce me his?

MOSCA   'Tis true.

109–10 This plot ... before: *Corbaccio now begins to claim that each of Mosca's ideas was first of all his own.*

110 I do believe it: *Mosca is being ironic.*

114 Being so lusty: *The more preposterous his compliments are, the greater delight Mosca takes in getting his victims to believe them. Both Mosca and Volpone find it hard to miss any opportunity to push their deceits a little further and increase the pleasures of risk. It is an exhilarating game, but dangerous.*

115 See, how he should be: *Look how he is.*

116 organ: *i.e. voice.*

119 Still my invention: *He is still saying what I had previously thought.*

CORBACCIO   This plot
  Did I think on before.
MOSCA   I do believe it.   110
CORBACCIO
  Do you not believe it?
MOSCA   Yes, sir.
CORBACCIO   Mine own project.
MOSCA
  Which when he hath done, sir –
CORBACCIO   Published me his heir?
MOSCA
  And you so certain to survive him –
CORBACCIO   Ay.
MOSCA
  Being so lusty a man –
CORBACCIO   'Tis true.
MOSCA   Yes, sir –
CORBACCIO
  I thought on that too. See, how he should be   115
  The very organ to express my thoughts!
MOSCA
  You have not only done yourself a good –
CORBACCIO
  But multiplied it on my son?
MOSCA   'Tis right, sir.
CORBACCIO
  Still my invention.
MOSCA   'Las, sir, heaven knows,
  It hath been all my study, all my care,   120
  (I e'en grow grey withal) how to work things –
CORBACCIO
  I do conceive, sweet Mosca.
MOSCA   You are he
  For whom I labour here.
CORBACCIO   Ay, do, do, do.

124   straight: *straightaway.*
       Rook go with you: *May you be fooled (or 'rooked').*

125   You do lie: *Mosca takes advantage of Corbaccio's deafness to speak an open truth.*

128   gull . . . blessing: *If Corbaccio becomes Mosca's foster-father, Bonario will be his brother. Hence 'I do not doubt that I shall cheat my brother of his blessing'. The reference is to Genesis 27, where Jacob cheated his brother Esau out of the blessing of their father, Isaac.*

133   Let out my sides: *Let me breathe! Volpone pretends to be suffocating from choked mirth, and hence to need his clothing loosened.*
134   flux: *discharge, flow.*
       this hope: *the hope of the inheritance.*

137   let me kiss thee: *compare Act I Scene III line 79. As the legacy-hunters depart, Volpone's delight in Mosca's performances breaks out in genuine demonstrative affection.*
138   so rare a humour: *such a clever and inventive mood.*
140   give 'em words: *deceive them with words.*
141   oil: *flattery.*

I'll straight about it.

MOSCA (*Quietly*)   Rook go with you, raven.

CORBACCIO

  I know thee honest.

MOSCA   You do lie, sir.

CORBACCIO   And –   125

MOSCA

  Your knowledge is no better than your ears, sir.

CORBACCIO

  I do not doubt to be a father to thee.

MOSCA

  Nor I, to gull my brother of his blessing.

CORBACCIO

  I may ha' my youth restored to me, why not?

MOSCA

  Your worship is a precious ass –

CORBACCIO   What say'st thou?   130

MOSCA

  I do desire your worship to make haste, sir.

CORBACCIO

  'Tis done, 'tis done, I go

                          Exit CORBACCIO

VOLPONE   O I shall burst;

  Let out my sides, let out my sides –

MOSCA   Contain

  Your flux of laughter, sir – you know this hope

  Is such a bait, it covers any hook.   135

VOLPONE

  O, but thy working, and thy placing it!

  I cannot hold; good rascal, let me kiss thee –

  I never knew thee in so rare a humour.

MOSCA

  Alas, sir, I but do as I am taught;

  Follow your grave instructions; give 'em words;   140

  Pour oil into their ears; and send them hence.

142–3 What a . . . itself: *traditional moral saying. Volpone, who has no use for morality, enjoys the chance to utter it in solemn-voiced mockery.*

144–59 So many cares . . . air!: *The first half of this speech copies a long tradition of lamentations about the miseries of life and old age. This prepares for a satirical attack in the second half of the speech on those like Corbaccio whose hopes and behaviour are grossly out of keeping with their physical decrepitude and senility. Corbaccio's avarice and his clinging to delusions of life and health are shown to be not just stupid but grotesque.*

148 going: *ability to walk.*

155 belying: *falsifying.*

156 Aeson: *father of Jason, whose youth was restored by the magic practices of Jason's wife, Medea.*

157 battens: *grows fat.*

158 cheated on: *deceived.*

159 all turns air!: *treats the grim realities of old age as if they did not exist.*

160 Close: *hide yourself.*

161 spruce: *trim and smart. (The word prepares us for a younger man, with some pretensions to fashion – a sharp contrast with Corbaccio.)*

VOLPONE

    'Tis true, 'tis true. What a rare punishment
    Is avarice to itself!

MOSCA   Ay, with our help, sir.

VOLPONE

    So many cares, so many maladies,
    So many fears attending on old age,   145
    Yea, death so often called on, as no wish
    Can be more frequent with 'em. Their limbs faint,
    Their senses dull, their seeing, hearing, going,
    All dead before them; yea, their very teeth,
    Their instruments of eating, failing them –   150
    Yet this is reckoned life! Nay, here was one,
    Is now gone home, that wishes to live longer!
    Feels not his gout, nor palsy, feigns himself
    Younger, by scores of years, flatters his age
    With confident belying it, hopes he may   155
    With charms, like Aeson, have his youth restored;
    And with these thoughts so battens, as if fate
    Would be as easily cheated on as he,
    And all turns air!

                                    (*Another knocks*)

            Who's that, there, now? a third?

MOSCA

    Close, to your couch again; I hear his voice.   160
    It is Corvino, our spruce merchant.

VOLPONE (*Lying down*)   Dead.

MOSCA

    Another bout, sir, with your eyes. (*Applying more ointment*)

                    Who's there?

5 How shall I do, then?: *How shall I manage to present my gift?* (*Volpone and Mosca, carried away by the impulse to feign Volpone's imminent death, have momentarily overlooked the problems they cause for their victims! Mosca is once again adroit in mending their small error.*)

8 still: *always.*

9 orient: *term for the most brilliant and precious pearls, which in ancient times came from the East.*

10 the like: *one to equal it.*

14 it . . . carat: *it weighs twenty-four carats. A carat is a measure of weight used for precious stones.*

(*Scene five*)

Enter CORVINO

MOSCA

Signior Corvino! come most wished for! O,
How happy were you, if you knew it, now!

CORVINO

Why? what? wherein?

MOSCA   The tardy hour is come, sir.

CORVINO

He is not dead?

MOSCA   Not dead, sir, but as good;
He knows no man.

CORVINO   How shall I do, then?

MOSCA   Why, sir?   5

CORVINO

I have brought him, here, a pearl.

MOSCA   Perhaps he has
So much remembrance left, as to know you, sir;
He still calls on you; nothing but your name
Is in his mouth. Is your pearl orient, sir?

CORVINO

Venice was never owner of the like.   10

VOLPONE (*Faintly*)

Signior Corvino.

MOSCA   Hark.

VOLPONE   Signior Corvino.

MOSCA

He calls you, step and give it him. He's here, sir.
And he has brought you a rich pearl.

CORVINO   How do you, sir?
Tell him, it doubles the twelfth carat.

MOSCA   Sir,
He cannot understand, his hearing's gone;   15
And yet it comforts him to see you –

CORVINO   Say

20 See, how he grasps it!: *Just as Voltore's plate was offered to a feebly reaching hand, and Corbaccio's chequeens presented in an invalid's feeding bowl, so Corvino's pearl is clasped in palsied fingers! The firm grasp of Volpone's own cheating avarice is each time movingly disguised as a half-conscious and enfeebled clutching.*

23 visor: *mask.*

35 still: *always.*

37 stage direction: *The direction 'They embrace' is Jonson's own. It is another example of the demonstrative shows of affection which are stirred up in this perverted world by successful plotting and material loot.*

39 No more than a blind harper: *harpists were proverbially blind.*

42–3 Not those . . . Bastards: *In this mention of Volpone's children, Mosca is once again embroidering his tale in order to emphasize Volpone's comatose state. However, the mention of children is imprudent, since children may inherit estates. Corvino is alarmed by this possibility, so Mosca has to make yet another quick adjustment. Bastards had no legal claim on their father's wealth, so it is safe to invent them!*

I have a diamond for him, too.

MOSCA   Best show't, sir,
Put it into his hand; 'tis only there
He apprehends – he has his feeling yet.
See, how he grasps it!

CORVINO   'Las, good gentleman!   20
How pitiful the sight is!

MOSCA   Tut, forget, sir.
The weeping of an heir should still be laughter
Under a visor.

CORVINO   Why, am I his heir?

MOSCA
Sir, I am sworn, I may not show the will
Till he be dead. But here has been Corbaccio,   25
Here has been Voltore, here were others too,
I cannot number 'em, they were so many,
All gaping here for legacies; but I,
Taking the vantage of his naming you,
'Signior Corvino, Signior Corvino', took   30
Paper, and pen, and ink, and there I asked him,
Whom he would have his heir? 'Corvino'. Who
Should be executor? 'Corvino'. And
To any question he was silent to,
I still interpreted the nods he made   35
Through weakness, for consent; and sent home
    th'others,
Nothing bequeathed them but to cry, and curse.

They embrace

CORVINO
O, my dear Mosca. Does he not perceive us?

MOSCA
No more than a blind harper. He knows no man,
No face of friend, nor name of any servant,   40
Who 'twas that fed him last, or gave him drink;
Not those he hath begotten or brought up
Can he remember.

44–5 Some dozen ... drunk: *Mosca is inspired to yet bolder details of Volpone's supposed depravity, not least because he knows Volpone will relish it. Even if Volpone happens to be offended, he is in no position to protest. In short, Mosca's imagination is emboldened by power. It can release high comedy, as here; it can precipitate disaster, as it does later.*

45 black-moors: *general term for African negroes and other dark-skinned races.*

46 fable: *gossip.*

47 The dwarf ...his: *There is no reason to question Volpone's earlier declaration (Act I Scene I line 73) that he has no children. This is another of Mosca's inventions. All the same, such malformed and pitiful offspring would be* symbolically *appropriate for such a warped, licentious being as Volpone.*

48 true father of his family: *real father of his servants, not just the head of his household.*

51 credit your own sense: *believe what your senses tell you.*

54 your incontinence ... it: *i.e. your lechery has deserved the pox.*

55 Throughly, and throughly: *through and through.*

56 once: *once and for all.*

59 Nay, help, sir: *Come and help me to jeer at him.*

63 culverin: *naval cannon.*

66 draught: *cesspool.*

CORVINO   Has he children?
MOSCA   Bastards,
   Some dozen, or more, that he begot on beggars,
   Gipsies and Jews, and black-moors, when he was drunk.   45
   Knew you not that, sir? 'Tis the common fable.
   The dwarf, the fool, the eunuch are all his;
   He's the true father of his family,
   In all save me – but he has given 'em nothing.
CORVINO
   That's well, that's well. Art sure he does not hear us?   50
MOSCA
   Sure, sir? Why, look you, credit your own sense.
                        (*Shouts in* VOLPONE'S *ear*)
   The pox approach and add to your diseases,
   If it would send you hence the sooner, sir.
   For your incontinence, it hath deserved it
   Throughly, and throughly, and the plague to boot.   55
   – (*To* CORVINO) You may come near, sir. – Would you
     once close
   Those filthy eyes of yours, that flow with slime
   Like two frog-pits; and those same hanging cheeks,
   Covered with hide instead of skin – Nay, help, sir –
   That look like frozen dish-clouts, set on end.   60
CORVINO
   Or, like an old smoked wall, on which the rain
   Ran down in streaks.
MOSCA   Excellent, sir, speak out;
   You may be louder yet; a culverin
   Dischargèd in his ear would hardly bore it.
CORVINO
   His nose is like a common sewer, still running.   65
MOSCA
   'Tis good! And what his mouth?
CORVINO   A very draught.
MOSCA
   O, stop it up –

68 rarely: *skilfully*. (*Again Mosca coaxes the situation towards excess, this time by proposing murder.*)

69 should keep: *might look after*.

75 to take my pearl: *i.e. from the invalid's stiff grasp!*

76 needless care: *unnecessary concern* (*i.e. why trouble to take your jewels away, since all the wealth here will shortly be yours?*)

78 creature: (*i*) *creation*; (*ii*) *dependant*.

82 gallant: *beautiful. Corvino's prompt and wordless exit the moment his wife is mentioned introduces to the play at one stroke both Celia's beauty and Corvino's jealousy.*

85 outgone: *excelled*.

CORVINO   By no means.

MOSCA   Pray you, let me.
　Faith, I would stifle him rarely with a pillow,
　As well as any woman that should keep him.

CORVINO
　Do as you will, but I'll be gone.

MOSCA   Be so;   70
　It is your presence makes him last so long.

CORVINO
　I pray you, use no violence.

MOSCA   No, sir? why?
　Why should you be thus scrupulous, pray you, sir?

CORVINO
　Nay, at your discretion.

MOSCA   Well, good sir, be gone.

CORVINO
　I will not trouble him now, to take my pearl?   75

MOSCA
　Puh! nor your diamond. What a needless care
　Is this afflicts you! Is not all here yours?
　Am not I here? whom you have made? your creature?
　That owe my being to you?

CORVINO   Grateful Mosca!
　Thou art my friend, my fellow, my companion,   80
　My partner, and shalt share in all my fortunes.

MOSCA
　Excepting one.

CORVINO   What's that?

MOSCA   Your gallant wife, sir.

(*Exit* CORVINO)

　Now is he gone; we had no other means
　To shoot him hence but this.

VOLPONE   My divine Mosca!
　Thou hast today outgone thyself.

(*Another knocks*)
                    Who's there?   85

90   purchase: *acquisition.*

91   better . . . yet: *even better than robbing churches.*

92   eating . . . man: *consuming one man's wealth each month by fraud. Although the reference is to preying on wealth, the suggestion of preying on a man's actual body, and hence of cannibalism, is clear.*

95   This is the style . . . me: *This is the form of announcement she has instructed me to use.*

96   tonight: *last night.*

98   Some three hours hence: *it is a sign of the play's compressed time-scale that Lady Would-be actually returns in Act III.*

98   squire: *personal attendant.*

100–102 I wonder . . . encounters!:   *English travellers reported that Italians guarded their wives jealously (as Corvino does). England itself, on the other hand, had a reputation amongst foreigners for allowing women exceptional freedom.*

104   affect: *(i) affectedly puts on; (ii) is fond of.*
       strange: *(i) foreign; (ii) peculiar.*

105   hath not . . .dishonest: *is not even handsome enough to be seduced.*

108–109 a wench . . . year: *young and beautiful woman. There may be a reference to the Old Testament, where animals 'of the first year, without blemish' were chosen as suitable for sacrifice.*

I will be troubled with no more. Prepare
Me music, dances, banquets, all delights;
The Turk is not more sensual in his pleasures
Than will Volpone. (*Exit* MOSCA) Let me see, a pearl!
A diamond! plate! chequeens! Good morning's
   purchase;   90
Why, this is better than rob churches yet;
Or fat, by eating once a month a man.
(*Enter* MOSCA)
   Who is't?
MOSCA   The beauteous Lady Would-be, sir.
  Wife to the English knight, Sir Politic Would-be,
  (This is the style, sir, is directed me)   95
  Hath sent to know how you have slept tonight,
  And if you would be visited.
VOLPONE   Not now.
  Some three hours hence –
MOSCA   I told the squire so much.
VOLPONE
  When I am high with mirth and wine, then, then.
  'Fore heaven, I wonder at the desperate valour   100
  Of the bold English, that they dare let loose
  Their wives to all encounters!
MOSCA   Sir, this knight
  Had not his name for nothing; he is politic,
  And knows, howe'er his wife affect strange airs,
  She hath not yet the face to be dishonest.   105
  But had she Signior Corvino's wife's face –
VOLPONE
  Has she so rare a face?
MOSCA   O, sir, the wonder,
  The blazing star of Italy! a wench
  O' the first year! a beauty ripe as harvest!
  Whose skin is whiter than a swan, all over!   110
  Than silver, snow, or lilies! a soft lip,
  Would tempt you to eternity of kissing!

113 And flesh . . . blood!: *(i) flesh so demurely responsive that she instantly blushes when touched; (ii) body which melts into sexual passion when she's embraced.*

114 Bright as your gold!: *Even female beauty and sexual attractiveness are finally measured against gold as the ultimate criterion of value. While confirming the material dominance of gold over other objects of desire, the comparison serves to give gold itself a sensuous and ravishing quality.*

119 abroad: *out of the house.*

121–2 watched . . . they are: *guarded as closely as the first crops of fruit.*

124 his whole household: *i.e. Corvino's.*

124–6 each . . . examined: *each domestic spy is briefed to watch not only Celia but his fellow-servants, and every time Corvino enters or leaves the house they are all interrogated about their duties to observe her and each other. (Mosca cannot be unaware of the effect this tantalizing story will have on Volpone, both for the sensual lure it offers and the risky challenge it presents.)*

129 shape still the same: *consistent appearance; i.e. his role as a dying man must be consistently maintained, so he must adopt another disguise.*

And flesh that melteth in the touch to blood!
Bright as your gold! and lovely as your gold!

VOLPONE
Why had not I known this before?

MOSCA   Alas, sir,   115
Myself but yesterday discovered it.

VOLPONE
How might I see her?

MOSCA   O, not possible;
She's kept as warily as is your gold –
Never does come abroad, never takes air
But at a window. All her looks are sweet   120
As the first grapes or cherries – and are watched
As near as they are.

VOLPONE   I must see her –

MOSCA   Sir,
There is a guard, of ten spies thick, upon her –
All his whole household – each of which is set
Upon his fellow, and have all their charge,   125
When he goes out, when he comes in, examined.

VOLPONE
I will go see her, though but at her window.

MOSCA
In some disguise then.

VOLPONE   That is true. I must
Maintain mine own shape still the same; we'll think.

                                                        Exeunt

After the confined and claustrophobic world of Volpone's sick-room, this Act takes us out into the larger world of Venice. Its portrait of external social reality is typically distorted, however, because we are shown it through the eyes of a foolish foreign observer. Peregrine's role is partly to highlight the absurdities in Sir Politic's colourful vision of Venice.

1 soil: *birthplace.*

4 protest: *declare.*
 salt: *wanton.*

5–7 shifting . . . bred: *Sir Politic denies the usual accusations levelled against travellers. One was that travel exposed good Protestants to Roman Catholic influences, and another that it weakened national loyalty.*

8 plots: *plans.*
 brought me out: *prompted me to travel.*

9 antique: *antiquated (Sir Politic is so keen to appear up-to-date and sophisticated that he rejects all unfashionable reasons for travelling, even sensible ones.)*

10 with Ulysses: *as it was in the case of Ulysses. (The good example of Ulysses was widely quoted by defenders of travel.)*

11 peculiar: *(i) particular; (ii) curious.*
 humour: *(i) state of mind; (ii) whim.*

12 Laid . . . Venice: *directed towards this latitude of Venice.*

13 quote: *take notes.*

14 licence: *official permission. English subjects required a licence from the Privy Council in order to travel abroad.*

15 dare . . . converse: *I run less risk if I am seen talking to you.*

17 my lord ambassador: *the English ambassador at this time was Sir Henry Wotton, who offered much hospitality to English travellers.*

18 vents our climate: *is spread around in our country.*

21 seconded: *followed up.*

Act Two

Scene one

The Square, near CORVINO'S *House*
Enter SIR POLITIC WOULD-BE, PEREGRINE

SIR POLITIC

    Sir, to a wise man, all the world's his soil.
    It is not Italy, nor France, nor Europe,
    That must bound me, if my fates call me forth.
    Yet, I protest, it is no salt desire
    Of seeing countries, shifting a religion,   5
    Nor any disaffection to the state
    Where I was bred (and unto which I owe
    My dearest plots) hath brought me out; much less
    That idle, antique, stale, grey-headed project
    Of knowing men's minds and manners, with Ulysses;   10
    But a peculiar humour of my wife's,
    Laid for this height of Venice, to observe,
    To quote, to learn the language, and so forth –
    I hope you travel, sir, with licence?

PEREGRINE   Yes.

SIR POLITIC

    I dare the safelier converse – How long, sir,   15
    Since you left England?

PEREGRINE   Seven weeks.

SIR POLITIC   So lately!
    You ha' not been with my lord ambassador?

PEREGRINE

    Not yet, sir.

SIR POLITIC   Pray you, what news, sir vents our
    climate?
    I heard, last night, a most strange thing reported
    By some of my lord's followers, and I long   20
    To hear how 'twill be seconded.

22–3 raven . . . King's: *doubly ominous event. Ravens were birds of ill omen, and it was considered sinister for any birds to nest on ships.*

22 should build: *is said to have built.*

24 gull: *make a fool of.*
   trow?: *do you think?*

25 that speaks him: *that gives away his character.*

27 Lies: *lodges.*
   intelligence: *information.*

28 tires: *head-dresses.*

29 courtesans: *Venetian prostitutes were widely esteemed for their beauty and intelligence.*

30 the spider and the bee: *since Peregrine has provokingly linked Lady Would-be with the whores, Sir Politic defends her with a proverb, suggesting that the good and the bad sip the same nectar.*

32 I cry you mercy: *I beg your pardon.*

34 lion's whelping in the Tower: *a lioness in the Tower of London menagerie gave birth to a cub in 1604 and again in 1605. Sir Politic's enthusiastic, superstitious reaction to this news marks him out as a naive, provincial gossip, despite his efforts to be sophisticated.*

36 The fires at Berwick: *a curious apparition of battle which occurred at Halidon Hill, near Berwick, in the winter of 1604–5. It could have been a display of aurora borealis, which at this time would have been an alarming and wholly mysterious event.*

37 new star: *a supernova appeared in September 1604, and remained visible for seventeen months.*
   concurring: *coinciding.*

40 porpoises: *a large porpoise was reputedly captured at West Ham in January 1606. This, the sturgeon and the whale were a series of apparitions which caused a popular stir in London during that year. Peregrine is mocking Sir Politic's obvious taste for such wonders.*

PEREGRINE   What was't, sir?

SIR POLITIC

Marry, sir, of a raven, that should build
In a ship royal of the King's.

PEREGRINE (*Aside*)   –This fellow,
Does he gull me, trow? or is gulled? – Your name, sir?

SIR POLITIC

My name is Politic Would-be.

PEREGRINE (*Aside*)   –O, that speaks him –   25
A knight, sir?

SIR POLITIC   A poor knight, sir.

PEREGRINE   Your lady
Lies here in Venice, for intelligence
Of tires, and fashions, and behaviour,
Among the courtesans? The fine Lady Would-be?

SIR POLITIC

Yes, sir, the spider and the bee oft-times   30
Suck from one flower.

PEREGRINE   Good Sir Politic!
I cry you mercy; I have heard much of you.
'Tis true, sir, of your raven.

SIR POLITIC   On your knowledge?

PEREGRINE

Yes, and your lion's whelping in the Tower.

SIR POLITIC

Another whelp!

PEREGRINE   Another, sir.

SIR POLITIC   Now, heaven!   35
What prodigies be these? The fires at Berwick!
And the new star! These things concurring, strange!
And full of omen! Saw you those meteors?

PEREGRINE

I did, sir.

SIR POLITIC Fearful! Pray you sir, confirm me,
Were there three porpoises seen above the bridge,   40
As they give out?

49 Stode: *now called Stade; port near Hanover, on the Elbe estuary, used by ships of the English merchant adventurers.*

50–2 'Twas ... projects?: *despite the peace made in 1604 between England and Spain, Sir Politic believes that Catholic plots are still afoot against the English.*

50 the Archdukes: *the joint title of the Infanta Isabella, daughter of Philip II of Spain, and her husband Albert of Austria. They ruled the Protestant Netherlands for Spain.*

51 Spinola: *commander of the Spanish forces in the Netherlands, and a capable soldier who was credited in English gossip with remarkable feats of military cunning. Sir Politic apparently believes that Spinola has recruited a whale to the Spanish ranks.*
    credit: *reputation.*

53 Stone the fool: *popular jester, about whom little is known.*

55 Mas': *contraction of 'Master'.*

58–9 He that ... fellow: *anyone who put a character like Sir Politic in a play.*

60 Stone dead!: *Sir Politic accidentally produces a hideous pun!*

61 apprehend: *feel.*

62 He was no kinsman to you?: *Peregrine's innocent query about Sir Politic's excessive feeling hides the insinuation that Stone, being a fool, is certainly 'kin' to Sir Politic.*
    That I know of: *i.e. not that I know of.*

63 unknown: *underestimated.*

PEREGRINE   Six, and a sturgeon, sir.

SIR POLITIC
  I am astonished!

PEREGRINE   Nay, sir, be not so;
  I'll tell you a greater prodigy than these –

SIR POLITIC
  What should these things portend?

PEREGRINE   The very day
  (Let me be sure) that I put forth from London,   45
  There was a whale discovered in the river,
  As high as Woolwich, that had waited there,
  Few know how many months, for the subversion
  Of the Stode fleet.

SIR POLITIC   Is't possible? Believe it,
  'Twas either sent from Spain, or the Archdukes!   50
  Spinola's whale, upon my life, my credit!
  Will they not leave these projects? Worthy sir,
  Some other news.

PEREGRINE   Faith, Stone the fool is dead,
  And they do lack a tavern fool extremely

SIR POLITIC
  Is Mas' Stone dead?

PEREGRINE   He's dead, sir. Why, I hope   55
  You thought him not immortal? (*Aside*) – O, this knight
  (Were he well known) would be a precious thing
  To fit our English stage. He that should write
  But such a fellow, should be thought to feign
  Extremely, if not maliciously.

SIR POLITIC   Stone dead!   60

PEREGRINE
  Dead. Lord! how deeply, sir, you apprehend it!
  He was no kinsman to you?

SIR POLITIC   That I know of.
  Well! that same fellow was an unknown fool.

PEREGINE
  And yet you knew him, it seems?

70 cabbages: *cabbages were imported from the Low Countries.*

72–4 oranges . . . cockles: *when Stone passed on information to the ambassador, he used more elevated gastronomic transport than the humble cabbage. All these eatables were scarce, prized and expensive delicacies.*

76 ordinary: *public eating house serving meals at fixed prices.*

77 advertisement: *instructions, information.*

78 concealed statesman: *disguised political agent.*

81–2 the meat was . . . character: *the meat was cut out in the form of a code. It was a fashionable custom to cut up meat in intricate shapes.*

85 In polity: *as a diplomatic device.*

86 had your languages: *was a good linguist.*

87 to't: *into the bargain.*
  noddle: *head, intelligence.*

87–9 I have heard . . . China: *Peregrine tempts Sir Politic by talking elaborate and confidential rubbish. Sir Politic (lines 90–7) duly falls into the trap, and produces yet more absurd 'secrets of state'.*

SIR POLITIC   I did so. Sir,
  I knew him one of the most dangerous heads   65
  Living within the state, and so I held him.

PEREGRINE
  Indeed, sir?

SIR POLITIC   While he lived, in action.
  He has received weekly intelligence,
  Upon my knowledge, out of the Low Countries,
  For all parts of the world, in cabbages;   70
  And those dispensed again to ambassadors,
  In oranges, musk-melons, apricots,
  Lemons, pome-citrons, and such-like – sometimes
  In Colchester oysters, and your Selsey cockles.

PEREGRINE
  You make me wonder!

SIR POLITIC   Sir, upon my knowledge.   75
  Nay, I have observed him, at your public ordinary,
  Take his advertisement, from a traveller
  (A concealed statesman) in a trencher of meat;
  And, instantly, before the meal was done,
  Convey an answer in a toothpick.

PEREGRINE   Strange!   80
  How could this be, sir?

SIR POLITIC   Why, the meat was cut
  So like his character, and so laid, as he
  Must easily read the cipher.

PEREGRINE   I have heard
  He could not read, sir.

SIR POLITIC   So 'twas given out,
  In polity, by those that did employ him;   85
  But he could read, and had your languages,
  And to't, as sound a noddle –

PEREGRINE   I have heard, sir,
  That your baboons were spies; and that they were
  A kind of subtle nation near to China.

90 'Mamuluchi': *originally a group of slaves who had risen to become the ruling class in Egypt. The connection of ideas in Sir Politic's curious mind is obscure and probably non-existent. The Mamuluchi have no links with baboons, or China, or French plotters.*

93 discovery: *disclosure.*

94 advices: *news.*

95 one of their own coat: *one of their party.*

96 relations: *reports.*

97 stand fair: *are ready.*

100–105 I do love . . . state: *Sir Politic sees himself as a keen but detached observer, carefully watching the tides and currents of politics move to and fro without actually getting wet himself. This imaginary stance is a clear indication that any actual involvement with politics would frighten him extremely; something that Peregrine is able to use against him later.*

106 tie: *debt. (Peregrine is blessing his luck, though not for the reason that Sir Politic supposes.)*

113 vulgar grammar: *common grammar book (which would probably include wise sayings and advice).*

114 cried: *called out (i.e. 'taught').*

115 brave bloods: *well-born and spirited young men.*

117 bark: *outward appearance.*

118 of ingenuous race: *of honourable descent.*

SIR POLITIC
    Ay, ay, your *Mamuluchi*. Faith, they had   90
    Their hand in a French plot or two; but they
    Were so extremely given to women, as
    They made discovery of all; yet I
    Had my advices here, on Wednesday last,
    From one of their own coat, they were returned,   95
    Made their relations, as the fashion is,
    And now stand fair for fresh employment.

PEREGRINE (*Aside*)   'Heart!
    This Sir Pol will be ignorant of nothing.
    It seems, sir, you know all?

SIR POLITIC   Not all, sir. But
    I have some general notions; I do love   100
    To note and to observe, though I live out,
    Free from the active torrent, yet I'd mark
    The currents and the passages of things,
    For mine own private use; and know the ebbs
    And flows of state.

PEREGRINE   Believe it, sir, I hold   105
    Myself in no small tie unto my fortunes
    For casting me thus luckily upon you;
    Whose knowledge, if your bounty equal it,
    May do me great assistance, in instruction
    For my behaviour, and my bearing, which   110
    Is yet so rude and raw.

SIR POLITIC   Why, came you forth
    Empty of rules for travel?

PEREGRINE   Faith, I had
    Some common ones from out that vulgar grammar
    Which he that cried Italian to me taught me.

SIR POLITIC
    Why, this it is that spoils all our brave bloods;   115
    Trusting our hopeful gentry unto pedants –
    Fellows of outside, and mere bark. You seem
    To be a gentleman, of ingenuous race –

119 I not profess it: *it is not my profession. (Sir Politic protects his social status by explaining that he does not offer his expertise as a paid tutor, but as an amateur gentleman who will freely offer the benefit of his experience.)*

121 high kind: *important role.*
touching: *concerning.*

Stage direction: 'mountebank': *wandering quack who sold his goods with the aid of story-telling, elaborate speech, tricks, and often with the assistance of a clown. They did indeed 'mount a bank' (climb on a bench or elevated platform) – hence the name. Volpone's performance as a mountebank uses many of the tricks which such quacks employed in real life, and his efforts are highly convincing.*

3 dear tongues: *esteemed languages.*

5 quacksalvers: *quack-doctors.*
6 venting: *selling.*

12 cabinet counsellors: *confidential advisers.*
13 only languaged: *most skilled in languages.*
14 lewd: *ignorant.*
15 terms, and shreds: *jargon, and common tags.*
15–16 no less beliers ... medicines: *they make equally false claims about the favours they enjoy from great men and about the supposed merits of their worthless medicines.*

I not profess it, but my fate hath been
To be where I have been consulted with,   120
In this high kind, touching some great men's sons,
Persons of blood and honour –

PEREGRINE (*Seeing people approach*) Who be these, sir?

(*Scene two*)

Enter MOSCA *and* NANO, *disguised as a mountebank's attendants,*
with materials for a stage, which they proceed to erect.

MOSCA

Under that window, there't must be. The same.

SIR POLITIC

Fellows, to mount a bank! Did your instructor
In the dear tongues never discourse to you
Of the Italian mountebanks?

PEREGRINE   Yes, sir.

SIR POLITIC   Why,
Here shall you see one.

PEREGRINE   They are quacksalvers,   5
Fellows that live by venting oils and drugs?

SIR POLITIC

Was that the character he gave you of them?

PEREGRINE

As I remember.

SIR POLITIC   Pity his ignorance.
They are the only knowing men of Europe!
Great general scholars, excellent physicians,   10
Most admired statesmen, professed favourites
And cabinet counsellors to the greatest princes!
The only languaged men of all the world!

PEREGRINE

And I have heard they are most lewd impostors;
Made all of terms, and shreds; no less beliers   15
Of great men's favours than their own vile medicines;

17   utter, upon: *offer for sale, with the aid of.*

19   crowns: *silver coins, worth about five shillings (25 new pence in precise equivalence, but the actual value in Jonson's time was of course vastly higher).*

22   Scoto of Mantua: *the leader of a troupe of Italian actors in the sixteenth century, famous in England for his conjuring skills.*

24   phant'sied: *inaccurately described. (Sir Politic is predictably gullible about mountebanks and keenly anticipates the performance that is sure to alter Peregrine's low opinion of them.)*

26   in this nook: *in this obscure corner (outside Corvino's house).*

27   In face of the Piazza!: *facing onto the main square.*

28   zany: *mountebank's assistant.*

30   May write . . . bank: *i.e. whose credit is worth ten thousand crowns.*

31   I do use to observe: *I habitually watch.*

32   The state . . . getting up!: *the ceremony he observes in mounting the platform.*

36   Portico to the 'Procuratìa': *the colonnade of the Procuratie Vecchie (the residence of the Procurators on the north side of St Mark's).*

Which they will utter, upon monstrous oaths –
Selling that drug for twopence, ere they part,
Which they have valued at twelve crowns before.

SIR POLITIC

    Sir, calumnies are answered best with silence.   20
    Yourself shall judge. Who is it mounts, my friends?

MOSCA

    Scoto of Mantua, sir.

SIR POLITIC   Is't he? Nay, then
    I'll proudly promise, sir you shall behold
    Another man than has been phant'sied to you.
    I wonder, yet, that he should mount his bank   25
    Here in this nook, that has been wont t'appear
    In face of the Piazza! Here he comes.

Enter VOLPONE, *as a mountebank; a crowd gathers*

VOLPONE (*To* NANO)

    Mount, zany.

CROWD   Follow, follow, follow, follow, follow.

SIR POLITIC

    See how the people follow him! He's a man
    May write ten thousand crowns in bank here. Note,   30
    Mark but his gesture! I do use to observe
    The state he keeps in getting up!

                    VOLPONE *mounts the stage*

PEREGRINE   'Tis worth it, sir.

VOLPONE

    Most noble gentlemen, and my worthy patrons, it may
    seem strange that I, your Scoto Mantuano, who was
    ever wont to fix my bank in face of the public Piazza,   35
    near the shelter of the Portico to the *Procuratìa*, should
    now (after eight months' absence from this illustrious
    city of Venice) humbly retire myself into an obscure
    nook of the Piazza.

SIR POLITIC

    Did not I now object the same?

42   cold on my feet: *in such desperate need that I have to sell my goods cheaply.*

45   Buttone: *nothing is known of this person, who may be a mere invention.*

47   'sforzato':   *galley-slave (from the Italian 'sforzare', to force).*

47–8 Cardinal Bembo's cook: *Cardinal Bembo was a versatile and richly-gifted Renaissance humanist, one of the greatest Venetians of his time, and made distinguished contributions to literature and philosophy. It is typical of Volpone's distorted world that it degrades distinction. In this case, the pause before 'cook' insinuates that the word conceals a sexual relationship.*

48   attached: *taken a hold on me.*

50   ground 'ciarlitani':   *poor mountebanks who speak from ground level rather than from a platform.*

52   feats of activity: *acrobatics.*

53   Boccaccio: *author of the* Decameron, *a rich supply of material for Renaissance story-tellers.*
      Tabarine: *literally 'short cloak', a name for the zany or clown in a company of Italian comedians.*

61   turdy-facy-nasty-paty-lousy-fartical: *compound adjectives of this sort, made up of linked abusive words, were a speciality of the Greek dramatist Aristophanes: 'facy' means 'impudent' The word 'paty' (from 'pate' or 'head') when linked with the offensive anal suggestions of the other words, adds up to an accusation that the 'rogues' are villainous 'from top to bottom'.*

62   groatsworth: *a groat was worth fourpence.*

63   several 'scartoccios':   *separate scraps of paper.*

64   and play: *and make a good living from it.*

66   earthy oppilations: *obstructions (i.e. material concerns).*
      want: *lack.*

69   purge . . . world: *i.e. kill them.*

PEREGRINE   Peace, sir.   40

VOLPONE

Let me tell you: I am not (as your Lombard proverb
saith) cold on my feet, or content to part with my com-
modities at a cheaper rate than I accustomed – look not
for it. Nor, that the calumnious reports of that impudent
detractor and shame to our profession (Alessandro But-   45
tone, I mean) who gave out, in public, I was con-
demned a *sforzato* to the galleys for poisoning the Cardinal
Bembo's cook, hath at all attached, much less dejected
me. No, no, worthy gentlemen; to tell you true, I cannot
endure to see the rabble of these ground *ciarlitani*, that   50
spread their cloaks on the pavement as if they meant to
do feats of activity, and then come in lamely with their
mouldy tales out of Boccaccio, like stale Tabarine the
fabulist – some of them discoursing their travels, and of
their tedious captivity in the Turks' galleys, when in-   55
deed (were the truth known) they were the Christians'
galleys, where very temperately they ate bread and
drunk water, as a wholesome penance (enjoined them
by their confessors) for base pilferies.

SIR POLITIC

Note but his bearing, and contempt of these.   60

VOLPONE

These turdy-facy-nasty-paty-lousy-fartical rogues, with
one poor groatsworth of unprepared antimony, finely
wrapped up in several *scartoccios*, are able, very well, to
kill their twenty a week, and play; yet these meagre
starved spirits, who have half stopped the organs of   65
their minds with earthy oppilations, want not their
favourers among your shrivelled, salad-eating artisans,
who are overjoyed that they may have their ha'p'orth of
physic; though it purge 'em into another world, 't makes
no matter.   70

SIR POLITIC

Excellent! Ha' you heard better language, sir?

74 'canaglia': *base common people.*

80 Terra Firma: *Venetian possessions on the Italian mainland.*
83 splendidous: *variant of 'splendid'.*
84 magazines: *storehouses.*
85 'moscadelli': *muscatel wines.*
87 cocted: *boiled.*

O, health!: *the play, which deals so heavily with the fact and imagery of disease, is strengthened in its imaginative effect by this mockery of health and medicine.*

93 end: *purpose. Peregrine is echoing and mocking Sir Politic's use of 'end' in line 77. Sir Politic naively believed the mountebank's 'end', or purpose, to be non-commercial. Peregrine breaks into a different point in the performance to show up the delayed and cunning salesmanship which is now appearing.*

94 humid flux: *discharge of mucus.*

mutability of air: *change in the air.*

96–8: take you ... work: *Volpone is pointing out that gold and health are unrelated, and that wealth cannot cure sickness. This obvious truth is used as a tactic to persuade his audience into parting with their money for worthless medicines. It is typical of the play's method that even commonsense truth about riches is turned into a device for avaricious trickery.*

98 'unguento': *ointment.*

99 that hath only power: *that has the sole power.*

VOLPONE

Well, let 'em go. And gentlemen, honourable gentlemen, know that for this time our bank, being thus removed from the clamours of the *canaglia*, shall be the
scene of pleasure and delight. For I have nothing to sell,   75
little or nothing to sell.

SIR POLITIC

I told you, sir, his end.

PEREGRINE   You did so, sir.

VOLPONE

I protest, I, and my six servants, are not able to make of
this precious liquor so fast as it is fetched away from my
lodging, by gentlemen of your city, strangers of the Ter-   80
ra Firma, worshipful merchants, ay, and senators too,
who ever since my arrival have detained me to their
uses, by their splendidous liberalities. And worthily.
For what avails your rich man to have his magazines
stuffed with *moscadelli*, or of the purest grape, when his   85
physicians prescribe him – on pain of death – to drink
nothing but water, cocted with aniseeds? O, health!
health! the blessing of the rich! the riches of the poor!
who can buy thee at too dear a rate, since there is no
enjoying this world without thee? Be not then so sparing   90
of your purses, honourable gentlemen, as to abridge the
natural course of life –

PEREGRINE

You see his end?

SIR POLITIC   Ay, is't not good?

VOLPONE

For, when a humid flux, or catarrh, by the mutability of
air, falls from your head into an arm, or shoulder, or   95
any other part, take you a ducat, or your chequeen of
gold, and apply to the place affected: see what good
effect it can work. No, no, 'tis this blessed *unguento*, this
rare extraction, that hath only power to disperse all

100 malignant humours: *medical theory held that a man was made up of four 'humours' or fluids. They were* blood *(hot and moist);* phlegm *(cold and moist);* bile *(hot and dry); and* black bile *(cold and dry). Each contributed its effect not only on health but on the temperament and state of mind, and the supremacy of any one humour could decide the bias of a man's personality as well as his health. 'Blood' produced a sanguine temperament, 'phlegm' a phlegmatic one, 'bile' a choleric or angry one, and 'black bile' a melancholy one. Illness was caused by a failure of balance in the humours.*

102 dry: *'dry' is the correct term for which Volpone has substituted 'windy'.*

103 crude: *poor in its digestive powers.*

106 fricace: *massage.*
'vertigine': *dizziness.*

108 'mal caduco': *falling sickness, or epilepsy.*

109 'tremor-cordia': *palpitations.*

110 retired nerves: *shrunken sinews.*
ill vapours: *disorders. (The spleen was an important organ in medical theory, since it affected the blood.)*

111 strangury: *painful urination.*
'hernia ventosa': *rupture causing flatulence.*

112 'iliaca passio': *intestinal colic.*

113 torsion of the small guts: *griping pains in the small intestine.*
'melancolia hypocondriaca': *the 'hypochondria' were the liver, gall-bladder and spleen, thought to be the root of melancholy.*

115 receipt; 'bill': *prescription.*

119 theoric . . . art: *theory and practice of medicine. Aesculapius was the Greek god of healing.*

120 Zan Fritada: *well-known zany, or mountebank's assistant.*

123 But alchemy: *except for alchemy (since alchemists sought a medicine which would give eternal youth and health).*

124 Broughton: *Hugh Broughton was a rabbinical scholar and earnest Puritan, the author of obscure theological works. Peregrine is commenting ironically on the incomprehensible 'expertise' of Volpone's speech.*

malignant humours that proceed either of hot, cold,   100
moist, or windy causes –

PEREGRINE

I would he had put in dry too.

SIR POLITIC   Pray you, observe.

VOLPONE

To fortify the most indigest and crude stomach, ay,
were it of one that through extreme weakness vomited
blood, applying only a warm napkin to the place, after   105
the unction and fricace; for the *vertigine* in the head, put-
ting but a drop into your nostrils, likewise behind the
ears, a most sovereign and approved remedy; the *mal
caduco*, cramps, convulsions, paralyses, epilepsies, *tremor-cordia*, retired nerves, ill vapours of the spleen, stop-   110
pings of the liver, the stone, the strangury, *hernia ventosa*,
iliaca passio; stops a *disenteria* immediately; easeth the
torsion of the small guts; and cures *melancolia hypocondriaca*, being taken and applied, according to my printed
receipt. (*Pointing to his bill and his glass*) For this is the   115
physician, this the medicine; this counsels, this cures;
this gives the direction, this works the effect; and, in
sum, both together may be termed an abstract of the
theoric and practic in the Aesculapian art. 'Twill cost
you eight crowns. And, Zan Fritada, pray thee sing a   120
verse, extempore, in honour of it.

SIR POLITIC

How do you like him, sir?

PEREGRINE   Most strangely, I!

SIR POLITIC

Is not his language rare?

PEREGRINE   But alchemy,

I never heard the like – or Broughton's books.

NANO *sings*

125   Hippocrates ... Galen: *Greek physicians, born respectively in about 460 BC and about AD 130. Hippocrates invented the theory of humours and Galen gave it systematic expression.*

129   murderers ... paper: *i.e. written so much.*

130   hurtless: *harmless.*

132   sassafras: *stimulant obtained from the bark of the sassafras tree.*

133–135 Ne ... Ne: *neither ... nor.*

133   guacum: *the wood and resin of the guaiacum, a West Indian tree, were both used medicinally.*

134   Raymond Lully: *Raymond Lull, or Lully (1235–1315) was a philosopher, linguist and mystic. Certain writings on alchemy were attributed to him in the Renaissance, though probably falsely. His reputation as an alchemist caused him to be credited with discovering the elixir of life. This is another of several instances in* Volpone *of a great historical figure being belittled and derided.*

135   Gonswart: *unidentified figure.*

136   Paracelsus: *the boastful pseudonym of Theophrastus Bombastus von Hohenheim (1493–1541), an eccentric but gifted German-Swiss physician. He transported his drugs and medicines in a long sword with a hollow pommel.*

138   if: *if only.*

139   'oglio del Scoto': *i.e. oil of Scoto.*

144   on my part: *on my behalf.*

144–5 Signiory of the 'Sanità': *body which had power to issue licences to physicians and mountebanks in Venice.*

152   divers: *various (other mountebanks).*

153   experimented receipts: *tested medications.*

154   apes: *imitators.*

Song

Had old Hippocrates, or Galen,	125
(That to their books put med'cines all in)	
But known this secret, they had never	
(Of which they will be guilty ever)	
Been murderers of so much paper,	
Or wasted many a hurtless taper;	130
No Indian drug had ere been famèd,	
Tobacco, sassafras not namèd;	
Ne yet of guacum one small stick, sir,	
Nor Raymond Lully's great elixir;	
Ne had been known the Danish Gonswart,	135
Or Paracelsus, with his long sword.	

PEREGRINE

All this, yet, will not do; eight crowns is high.

VOLPONE

No more. Gentlemen, if I had but time to discourse to
you the miraculous effects of this my oil, surnamed *oglio
del Scoto*; with the countless catalogue of those I have   140
cured of th'aforesaid and many more diseases; the pa-
tents and privileges of all the princes and common-
wealths of Christendom; or but the depositions of those
that appeared on my part before the Signiory of the
Sanità and most learned college of physicians; where I   145
was authorized, upon notice taken of the admirable virtues of my medicaments, and mine own excellency in
matter of rare and unknown secrets, not only to disperse
them publicly in this famous city, but in all the territor-
ies that happily joy under the government of the most   150
pious and magnificent states of Italy. But may some
other gallant fellow say, 'O, there be divers that make
profession to have as good and as experimented receipts
as yours.' Indeed, very many have assayed, like apes, in
imitation of that which is really and essentially in me, to   155

93

157 alembics: *vessels used in distilling*.
158–9 several simples: *separate herbal ingredients*.

160 conglutination: *glueing together*.
161 decoction: *boiling to extract the soluble parts*.
162 in 'fumo': *in smoke*.

167 book: *make a record of*.

172 the four elements: *the four substances – fire, air, earth and water – of which all created matter was believed to consist*.

175 'balloo': *'balloon' – ball game played in Venice*.

179 And that withal: *and so is that. (Peregrine once again counters Sir Pol's idealization of mountebanks by drawing attention to their sales technique and mercenary purposes. See note to line 93)*.

187 Cardinals Montalto, Fernese: *historical figures of importance. Montalto became Pope Sixtus V*.

make of this oil; bestowed great cost in furnaces, stills, alembics, continual fires and preparation of the ingredients (as indeed there goes to it six hundred several simples, besides some quantity of human fat, for the conglutination, which we buy of the anatomists), but, 160 when these practitioners come to the last decoction, blow, blow, puff, puff, and all flies in *fumo*. Ha, ha, ha! Poor wretches! I rather pity their folly and indiscretion than their loss of time and money; for those may be recovered by industry, but to be a fool born is a disease 165 incurable. For my self, I always from my youth have endeavoured to get the rarest secrets, and book them; either in exchange, or for money; I spared nor cost nor labour where anything was worthy to be learned. And gentlemen, honourable gentlemen, I will undertake, by 170 virtue of chemical art, out of the honourable hat that covers your head, to extract the four elements – that is to say, the fire, air, water, and earth – and return you your felt without burn or stain. For, whilst others have been at the *balloo*, I have been at my book; and am now 175 past the craggy paths of study, and come to the flowery plains of honour and reputation.

SIR POLITIC
I do assure you, sir, that is his aim.

VOLPONE
But, to our price –

PEREGRINE   And that withal, Sir Pol.

VOLPONE
You all know, honourable gentlemen, I never valued 180 this *ampulla*, or vial, at less than eight crowns; but for this time I am content to be deprived of it for six; six crowns is the price; and less, in courtesy, I know you cannot offer me; take it or leave it, howsoever, both it, and I, am at your service. I ask you not as the value of 185 the thing, for then I should demand of you a thousand crowns, so the Cardinals Montalto, Fernese, the great

188   Duke of Tuscany: *title conferred on Cosimo de' Medici in 1569.*

      gossip: *godfather; also 'familiar acquaintance'. This claim is not so outrageous as it may appear, since the Italian nobility did commonly stand as godparents for the children of their favourites.*

192   offices: *affairs.*

      framed: *directed.*

197   painful circumstance: *elaborate and painstaking ceremony.*

198   'gazets':   *Venetian coins worth approximately one penny.*

199   i'th' whole: *altogether.*

201   coil: *fuss.*

204   Tart: *keen.*

205   Moist of hand?:   *sign of youth, health and sexual vigour.*

206   come nearer to't: *come to the point.*

209   achès: *pronounced as two syllables ('aitches').*

210   for the nones: *for just this purpose.*

211   in a humour: *in the mood.*

217   ducat: *a ducat was worth about 4s 8d in equivalent English money at this time. It is not possible to give precise equivalents in modern coinage. What matters is that the coins and prices quoted vary between the huge and the trivial. Note that Jonson habitually refers to both Italian and English coins. In terms of their values at that time, his equivalences between the two currencies are fairly exact.*

      'moccenigo':   *Venetian coin worth about nine gazets (or nine pence, in equivalent English coinage).*

Duke of Tuscany, my gossip, with divers other princes
have given me; but I despise money. Only to show my
affection to you, honourable gentlemen, and your illus-   190
trious state here, I have neglected the messages of these
princes, mine own offices, framed my journey hither,
only to present you with the fruits of my travels. (*To*
NANO *and* MOSCA) Tune your voices once more to the
touch of your instruments, and give the honourable   195
assembly some delightful recreation.

PEREGRINE

What monstrous and most painful circumstance
Is here, to get some three or four *gazets*!
Some threepence i'th' whole, for that 'twill come to.

Song

You that would last long, list to my song: 200
Make no more coil, but buy of this oil.
Would you be ever fair? and young?
Stout of teeth? and strong of tongue?
Tart of palate? quick of ear?
Moist of hand? and light of foot?   205
Or, I will come nearer to't –
Would you live free from all diseases?
Do the act your mistress pleases;
Yet fright all achès from your bones?
Here's a med'cine for the nones.   210

VOLPONE

Well, I am in a humour, at this time, to make a present
of the small quantity my coffer contains: to the rich, in
courtesy, and to the poor, for God's sake. Wherefore,
now mark; I asked you six crowns; and six crowns at
other times you have paid me; you shall not give me six   215
crowns, nor five, nor four, nor three, nor two, nor one;
nor half a ducat; no, nor a *moccenigo*; six – pence it will

219   banner of my front: *banner hung out by the mountebank, listing the diseases he professed to cure.*
        bate a 'bagatine':   *reduce the price by a farthing.*

222   toss your handkerchiefs: *customers would throw their handkerchiefs to the mountebank with the money tied into them, and the mountebank would return them with his wares knotted inside.*

223   be advertised: *take notice.*

227   double pistolet: *valuable Spanish gold coin.*

228   spark: *man-about-town.*

229   prevented: *forestalled.*

236–7   if I should . . . worth: *if I should try to value it.*

239   pilgrimage . . . life: *Volpone is mocking the common religious image of life as a pilgrim's journey towards heaven. He is ostensibly mocking a hackneyed image, but in reality is also scoffing at the religious idea it expresses.*

247   derived to Helen: *passed down to Helen of Troy.*

250   moiety: *half; part.*

cost you, or six hundred pound – expect no lower price,
for by the banner of my front, I will not bate a *bagatine*;
that I will have, only, a pledge of your loves, to carry 220
something from amongst you, to show I am not con-
temned by you. Therefore now, toss your handkerchiefs,
cheerfully, cheerfully; and be advertised, that the first
heroic spirit that deigns to grace me with a handkerchief, I will give it a little remembrance of something 225
beside, shall please it better than if I had presented it
with a double pistolet.

PEREGRINE

Will you be that heroic spark, Sir Pol?
O, see! the window has prevented you.

     CELIA *at the window throws down her handkerchief*

VOLPONE

Lady, I kiss your bounty; and for this timely grace you 230
have done your poor Scoto of Mantua, I will return you,
over and above my oil, a secret of that high and inestim-
able nature shall make you for ever enamoured on that
minute wherein your eye first descended on so mean
(yet not altogether to be despised) an object. Here is a 235
powder, concealed in this paper, of which, if I should
speak to the worth, nine thousand volumes were but as
one page, that page as a line, that line as a word – so
short is this pilgrimage of man (which some call life) to
the expressing of it. Would I reflect on the price, why! 240
the whole world were but as an empire, that empire as a
province, that province as a bank, that bank as a private
purse, to the purchase of it. I will only tell you: it is the
powder that made Venus a goddess (given her by Apollo), that kept her perpetually young, cleared her wrink- 245
les, firmed her gums, filled her skin, coloured her hair;
from her, derived to Helen, and at the sack of Troy un-
fortunately lost; till now, in this our age, it was as happily recovered by a studious antiquary out of some ruins
of Asia, who sent a moiety of it to the court of France 250

251 sophisticated: *adulterated.*

253 extracted to a quintessence: *distilled and refined to its purest form.*

255 seats: *firmly fixes (in the gums).*

256 virginal jacks: *a virginal is a small keyboard instrument. To the back of each note is fixed a piece of wood or 'jack', with a quill attached to the top of it. When the note is played, the 'jack' rises and the quill plucks the string, thus producing the sound.*

 1 Blood . . . shame!:   *Corvino appears and effectively completes the speech he has interrupted, comparing the disguised Volpone with the devil.*

3–9 Signior . . . town: *Corvino sums up the situation in terms of the 'commedia dell'arte', or professionals' comedy, in which travelling actors improvized dialogue on the framework of outline plots and stock comic roles. Flaminio was a frequent name for the high-ranking lover in such performances, Franciscina for an impudent and lively serving-maid, and Pantalone di Besogniosi for an ageing merchant – sometimes a merchant married to a young and unfaithful wife. In publicly casting himself in this last humiliating role, Corvino betrays his jealous insecurity and anticipates the self-inflicted public shaming he will undergo later in the play. It is part of Corvino's character to create his degradation in the very process of seeking to avoid it.*

 6 properties: *stage props.*

10 home: *go home.*

11 It may be . . . you: *Peregrine does not of course believe this. He is teasing Sir Pol, whose political pretentions are apt to turn on the slightest pretext to political anxieties.*

12 best: *best policy.*

100

(but much sophisticated), wherewith the ladies there
now colour their hair. The rest, at this present, remains
with me, extracted to a quintessence, so that, wherever
it but touches, in youth it perpetually preserves, in age
restores the complexion; seats your teeth, did they   255
dance like virginal jacks, firm as a wall; makes them
white as ivory, that were black as –

(*Scene three*)

Enter CORVINO

CORVINO

    Blood o' the devil, and my shame! come down here;
    Come down! No house but mine to make your scene?
                  (*He beats away the mountebank, & c.*)
    Signior Flaminio, will you down, sir? down?
    What, is my wife your Franciscina, sir?
    No windows on the whole piazza here   5
    To make your properties, but mine? but mine?
    Heart! ere tomorrow I shall be new christened,
    And called the *Pantalone di Besogniosi*
    About the town.

                               Exit

PEREGRINE   What should this mean, Sir Pol?

SIR POLITIC

    Some trick of state, believe it. I will home.   10

PEREGRINE

    It may be some design on you.

SIR POLITIC   I know not.

    I'll stand upon my guard.

PEREGRINE   It is your best, sir.

SIR POLITIC

    This three weeks, all my advices, all my letters,
    They have been intercepted.

PEREGRINE   Indeed, sir?

1 without: *externally.*

3 bolting: *shooting an arrow.*

6 ambitious: *rising.*

7 Whose vent is stopped: *the imagery is a little confused. A fire needs a vent in order to burn fiercely, whereas Volpone is saying that his fire of passion is all the fiercer because it has no vent or outlet. The meaning may be, however, that Volpone is experiencing the discomfort of confined emotional heat, instead of the pleasurable fires of fulfilled passion, which would find their outlet in the presence and body of Celia.*

9 liver: *supposedly the seat of passion.*

16–17 to effect . . . torment: *to do my best to relieve your suffering.*

Best have a care.

SIR POLITIC   Nay, so I will.

Exit   *Exit*

PEREGRINE   This knight,   15

I may not lose him, for my mirth, till night.

Exit

Scene four

Enter VOLPONE, MOSCA

VOLPONE

O, I am wounded.

MOSCA   Where, sir?

VOLPONE   Not without;

Those blows were nothing – I could bear them ever.

But angry Cupid, bolting from her eyes,

Hath shot himself into me like a flame,

Where now he flings about his burning heat,   5

As in a furnace an ambitious fire

Whose vent is stopped. The fight is all within me.

I cannot live, except thou help me, Mosca;

My liver melts, and I, without the hope

Of some soft air from her refreshing breath,   10

Am but a heap of cinders.

MOSCA   'Las, good sir!

Would you had never seen her.

VOLPONE   Nay, would thou

Hadst never told me of her.

MOSCA   Sir, 'tis true;

I do confess, I was unfortunate,

And you unhappy: but I'm bound in conscience,   15

No less than duty, to effect my best

To your release of torment, and I will, sir.

18 Dear Mosca ... more than dear: *another indication of the intimate, affectionate relationship between the two, which at this stage of the play has only occasional hints of the tension and conflicting interests which will finally sever them.*

21 My better angel: *My good angel. The idea that every man has a good and bad angel receives its finest dramatic expression in Marlowe's* Dr Faustus.

22 devotion: *disposal. 'Devotion' links with 'angel' as a play on religious language, misapplied and abused as usual. Volpone's restored wit suggests his recovery of self-control and hope after the impassioned disorder of his mood at the start of this scene. His venture into the streets and inflaming encounter with Celia is following a sequence of risk, despair, hope and revival which is repeated several times in the play, and finally achieves a near-tragic intensity.*

23 coin me, too: *convert me into coinage too. Volpone's idea of the body as potential currency is a powerful instance of the all-consuming materialism which the play depicts.*

28 horn him: *make him a cuckold. The drama of this period is full of jokes about the horns which a cuckold was said to wear on his forehead.*

30 colour: *probably red, like a fox.*

31 make me known: *give me away.*

I did it well: *characteristically, Volpone is torn between pride in his performance as an actor and fear that the deception may not have been complete. His insecurities prey on him, and yet he thrives on them.*

32 mine: *my own 'art' (of disguise and acting).*

33 happiness: *skill.*

34 your epilogue: *i.e. being beaten by Corvino.*

37 I have not time ... now: *but Mosca has just been flattering Volpone! Volpone will take the words to mean that Mosca is just stating the simple truth about his great performance. Privately, Mosca is making an ironic jibe at Volpone's obvious taste for flattery, and shrugging off his own contribution to it.*

VOLPONE
    Dear Mosca, shall I hope?

MOSCA   Sir, more than dear,
    I will not bid you to despair of aught,
    Within a human compass.

VOLPONE   O, there spoke   20
    My better angel. Mosca, take my keys,
    Gold, plate, and jewels, all's at thy devotion;
    Employ them how thou wilt; nay, coin me, too,
    So thou, in this, but crown my longings. – Mosca?

MOSCA
    Use but your patience.

VOLPONE   So I have.

MOSCA   I doubt not   25
    To bring success to your desires.

VOLPONE   Nay, then,
    I not repent me of my late disguise.

MOSCA
    If you can horn him, sir, you need not.

VOLPONE   True.
    Besides, I never meant him for my heir.
    Is not the colour o' my beard and eyebrows   30
    To make me known?

MOSCA   No jot.

VOLPONE   I did it well.

MOSCA
    So well, would I could follow you in mine
    With half the happiness; and yet, I would
    Escape your epilogue.

VOLPONE   But were they gulled
    With a belief that I was Scoto?

MOSCA   Sir,   35
    Scoto himself could hardly have distinguished!
    I have not time to flatter you now. We'll part;
    And, as I prosper, so applaud my art.

                                              Exeunt

                                                        105

2 tooth-drawing: *mountebanks habitually acted as dentists.*

4 strained action . . . faces: *forced theatrical performance and limited range of facial expressions.*

5 itching: *eager.*

7 satyrs: *creatures from mythology, part man and part beast, noted for lustfulness.*

8 favours: *small gifts and approving gestures given by a lady to her admirers.*

9 hot: *lustful.*

12 saffron jewel: *i.e. cheap trinket glazed with saffron to make it look like gold.*

12 toad-stone: *in mediaeval times, stones supposed to be found in the head of a toad were believed to have magical powers.*

13 cope-stitch: *the stitch used for the straight edges of ornate cloaks.*

14 hearse-cloth: *black funeral pall.*

tilt-feather: *part of the plume worn by knights when jousting.*

17 fricace, for the mother: *massage for hysteria. But Corvino is making a bitter sexual innuendo. This expression like others in the scene ('mount', 'tilt', 'cope') derive from his obsessive imaginings of Celia engaged in sexual intercourse with a lover.*

18 mount: *literally 'mount the bank' to the mountebank's platform (from which elevation she will be visible 'down to th'foot'); but 'mount' has a direct sexual implication.*

21 cittern: *guitar-like instrument, often played by mountebanks' women and by prostitutes.*

22 dealer with the virtuous man: *go into trade with the mountebank ('virtuous man' is of course ironic).*

23 Make one: *join the discreditable company.*

I'll but protest . . . cuckold: *ironic anticipation of what Corvino will eventually do.*

24 save your dowry: *an adulteress forfeited her dowry.*

Dutchman: *i.e. phlegmatic. Italians, he suggests, behave less patiently, so she must have mistaken his nationality.*

Scene five

CORVINO'S *House*
Enter CORVINO, CELIA

CORVINO
    Death of mine honour, with the city's fool?
    A juggling, tooth-drawing, prating mountebank?
    And at a public window? where, whilst he,
    With his strained action and his dole of faces,
    To his drug lecture draws your itching ears,   5
    A crew of old, unmarried, noted lechers
    Stood leering up, like satyrs; and you smile,
    Most graciously! and fan your favours forth,
    To give your hot spectators satisfaction!
    What, was your mountebank their call? their whistle?   10
    Or were you enamoured on his copper rings?
    His saffron jewel, with the toad-stone in't?
    Or his embroidered suit, with the cope-stitch,
    Made of a hearse-cloth? or his old tilt-feather?
    Or his starched beard? Well! you shall have him, yes.   15
    He shall come home, and minister unto you
    The fricace, for the mother. Or, let me see,
    I think you'd rather mount? Would you not mount?
    Why, if you'll mount, you may; yes truly, you may;
    And so you may be seen, down to th'foot.   20
    Get you a cittern, Lady Vanity,
    And be a dealer with the virtuous man;
    Make one – I'll but protest myself a cuckold,
    And save your dowry. I am a Dutchman, I!
    For, if you thought me an Italian,   25
    You would be damned ere you did this, you whore!
    Thou'dst tremble to imagine that the murder
    Of father, mother, brother, all thy race,
    Should follow as the subject of my justice.
CELIA
    Good sir, have patience!

34 goatish: *lustful.*

41 in the receipt: *in receiving it.*

43 point: *appoint.*

44 serve the turn: *answer the need; but the phrase carries another sexual innuendo.*

49 To: *compared to.*
50 light: *window.*

55–6 conjuror ... laid: *a magician who summoned up devils was able to control them provided he remained within his magic circle, but could not safely step outside it until he had sent them back to hell.*
57 lock: *chastity belt.*
58 backwards: *at the back of the house.*

CORVINO   What couldst thou propose   30
  Less to thyself, than, in this heat of wrath,
  And stung with my dishonour, I should strike
                      (*Threatening her with his sword*)
  This steel into thee, with as many stabs
  As thou wert gazed upon with goatish eyes?

CELIA
  Alas, sir, be appeased! I could not think   35
  My being at the window should more now
  Move your impatience than at other times.

CORVINO
  No? not to seek and entertain a parley
  With a known knave? before a multitude?
  You were an actor, with your handkerchief!   40
  Which he, most sweetly, kissed in the receipt,
  And might, no doubt, return it with a letter,
  And point the place where you might meet; your
     sister's,
  Your mother's, or your aunt's might serve the turn.

CELIA
  Why, dear sir, when do I make these excuses?   45
  Or ever stir abroad but to the church?
  And that so seldom –

CORVINO   Well, it shall be less;
  And thy restraint before was liberty
  To what I now decree, and therefore, mark me:
  First, I will have this bawdy light dammed up;   50
  And, till't be done, some two or three yards off,
  I'll chalk a line; o'er which if thou but chance
  To set thy desp'rate foot, more hell, more horror,
  More wild remorseless rage shall seize on thee
  Than on a conjurer that had heedless left   55
  His circle's safety ere his devil was laid.
  Then, here's a lock, which I will hang upon thee;
  And, now I think on't, I will keep thee backwards;
  Thy lodging shall be backwards; thy walks backwards;

60 prospect: *view*.

64 subtle: *keen*.

66 passengers: *passers-by*.

70 anatomy: *body used for dissection*.

Thy prospect – all be backwards; and no pleasure   60
That thou shalt know, but backwards. Nay, since you force
My honest nature, know it is your own
Being too open, makes me use you thus.
Since you will not contain your subtle nostrils
In a sweet room, but they must snuff the air   65
Of rank and sweaty passengers –

                               (*Knock within*)
                One knocks.
Away, and be not seen, pain of thy life;
Not look toward the window; if thou dost –
Nay, stay, hear this – let me not prosper, whore,
But I will make thee an anatomy,   70
Dissect thee mine own self, and read a lecture
Upon thee to the city, and in public.
Away! (*Exit* CELIA) Who's there?

Enter SERVANT

SERVANT   'Tis Signior Mosca, sir.

(*Scene six*)

CORVINO

Let him come in. (*Exit* SERVANT)
                      His master's dead. There's yet
Some good, to help the bad. (*Enter* MOSCA)
                              My Mosca, welcome –
I guess your news.

MOSCA   I fear you cannot, sir.

CORVINO

Is't not his death?

MOSCA   Rather the contrary.

CORVINO

Not his recovery?

MOSCA   Yes, sir.

6 crosses: *afflictions. The very word suggests trials imposed by God as a test of patience and devotion, so its use in this context is a sharp Jonsonian irony.*

7 with Scoto's oil: *note how Mosca makes one element in their plottings work for the benefit of another.*

12 virtue: *healing power.*

14 'osterìa': *inn, hostelry.*
tumbling: *performing acrobatics; but also 'tumbling' in sexual activity.*

15 forced: *(i) forced upon him by poverty; (ii) clumsily contrived.*

19 sod: *boiled.*

20 fasting spittle: *the spittle of one who is fasting, and therefore hungry.*

23 recovered: *restored.*

24 fricace: *massage. The very word 'fricace' is calculated to stir Corvino to frenzy, because of his own neurotic use of it. (See Act II Scene V line 17.)*

25 officious: *helpful.*

29–32 Where ... skins: *these exotic remedies give Jonson another chance to satirize doctors. (Compare Act I Scene IV lines 20–35.)*

29 cataplasm: *poultice.*

32–5 at last ... by him: *compare 1 Kings 1,1–4. When King David was old and 'gat no heat', the selfsame remedy was tried for him.*

CORVINO   I am cursed,   5
  I am bewitched, my crosses meet to vex me.
  How? how? how? how?
MOSCA   Why, sir, with Scoto's oil!
  Corbaccio and Voltore brought of it,
  Whilst I was busy in an inner room –
CORVINO
  Death! that damned mountebank! But for the law,   10
  Now I could kill the rascal; 't cannot be
  His oil should have that virtue. Ha' not I
  Known him a common rogue, come fiddling in
  To th'*osteria* with a tumbling whore,
  And, when he has done all his forced tricks, been glad   15
  Of a poor spoonful of dead wine, with flies in't?
  It cannot be. All his ingredients
  Are a sheep's gall, a roasted bitch's marrow,
  Some few sod earwigs, pounded caterpillars,
  A little capon's grease, and fasting spittle –   20
  I know 'em to a dram.
MOSCA   I know not, sir,
  But some on't, there, they poured into his ears,
  Some in his nostrils, and recovered him,
  Applying but the fricace.
CORVINO   Pox o' that fricace.
MOSCA
  And since, to seem the more officious   25
  And flattering of his health, there they have had,
  At extreme fees, the college of physicians
  Consulting on him, how they might restore him;
  Where one would have a cataplasm of spices,
  Another, a flayed ape clapped to his breast,   30
  A third would ha' it a dog, a fourth an oil
  With wild cats' skins; at last, they all resolved
  That to preserve him was no other means
  But some young woman must be straight sought out,
  Lusty, and full of juice, to sleep by him;   35

40–1 cross your ends: *obstruct your purposes.*

41 my whole dependence: *as usual, Mosca treats each suitor as his prospective patron and employer.*

42 it: *i.e. find the required young woman.*

delate: *report.*

44 opinion: *good opinion.*

47 present him: *i.e. present him with a woman.*

48 briefly, conclude somewhat: *quickly decide on something.*

49 Prevent: *forestall.*

51 courtesan: *prostitute. Since this is the obvious answer, Mosca has skilfully anticipated it. The fickleness of age, he suggests, combined with the seductive cunning of a prostitute, may divert the whole inheritance to her and ruin all their plans. It is another example of the brilliant foresight and quick-wittedness, especially on Mosca's part, which can achieve marvels of deception and yet finally overreach itself.*

53 again: *on the other hand.*

flexible: *changeable.*

55 Light on a quean: *happen to choose a prostitute.*

57 creature made unto it: *dependent suited to the job.*

59 God's so: *common oath: God's soul.*

Think . . . think, sir: *the emotional pressure is intense. 'Think', repeated several times, suggests desperate urgency, and is directly followed by the blatant suggestion that a close relative might be chosen.*

61 Lupo: *i.e. wolf. The name maintains the animal imagery and further impugns the medical profession.*

And to this service – most unhappily
And most unwillingly – am I now employed,
Which here I thought to pre-acquaint you with,
For your advice, since it concerns you most,
Because I would not do that thing might cross   40
Your ends, on whom I have my whole dependence, sir.
Yet, if I do it not, they may delate
My slackness to my patron, work me out
Of his opinion; and there, all your hopes,
Ventures, or whatsoever, are all frustrate.   45
I do but tell you, sir. Besides, they are all
Now striving, who shall first present him. Therefore –
I could entreat you, briefly, conclude somewhat;
Prevent 'em if you can.

CORVINO   Death to my hopes!
This is my villainous fortune! Best to hire   50
Some common courtesan?

MOSCA   Ay, I thought on that, sir.
But they are all so subtle, full of art,
And age again doting and flexible,
So as – I cannot tell – we may perchance
Light on a quean, may cheat us all.

CORVINO   'Tis true.   55

MOSCA
No, no; it must be one that has no tricks, sir,
Some simple thing, a creature made unto it;
Some wench you may command. Ha' you no
    kinswoman?
God's so – Think, think, think, think, think, think,
    think, sir.
One o' the doctors offered there his daughter.   60

CORVINO
How?

MOSCA   Yes, Signior Lupo, the physician.

CORVINO
His daughter!

MOSCA   And a virgin, sir. Why! Alas,

115

64 blood: *including the 'blood' of sexual arousal.*

66 that part: *i.e. his sexual organs.*

68 give me leave: *excuse me.*

68–9 If any man . . . luck: *What would anyone else do in my position?*

71 blood and my affections: *passions and feelings.*

73 The cases . . . daughter: *There is no difference between offering a wife and offering a daughter. (The persuasive example of Signior Lupo has worked!)*

74 coming: *coming round to it.*

75 'Slight: *exclamation, short for 'God's light'.*

75–6 who is . . . counsel: *who is not involved in Volpone's affairs except as an adviser.*

77–8 that am So deeply in: *that am so heavily involved (because of his financial investment in gifts to Volpone).*

78 prevent: *forestall.*

79 Covetous wretch!: *Corvino is so blind to his own moral condition that he can unselfconsciously accuse 'Lupo' of covetousness! Such unconscious hypocrisy presents a rich dramatic irony.*

80 The party you wot of: *the person you know about (an indirect way of referring to Volpone's prospective bedfellow).*

83 motioned: *proposed.*

84 make your count: *count your gains.*
    you have . . . throats: *you have outmatched all your rivals.*

85 directly: *immediately.*

86 let him go: *allow him to die.*

87 'Tis but . . . head: *We have only to pull away his pillow and let his head drop sharply.*

90 wit: *intelligence.*

He knows the state of 's body, what it is;
That naught can warm his blood, sir, but a fever;
Nor any incantation raise his spirit –   65
A long forgetfulness hath seized that part.
Besides, sir, who shall know it? some one, or two –
CORVINO
I pray thee give me leave. (*Walks aside*) If any man
But I had had this luck – The thing in 't self,
I know, is nothing – Wherefore should not I   70
As well command my blood and my affections
As this dull doctor? In the point of honour,
The cases are all one of wife and daughter.
MOSCA
(*Aside*) I hear him coming.
CORVINO   She shall do 't; 'tis done.
'Slight, if this doctor, who is not engaged,   75
Unless 't be for his counsel (which is nothing),
Offer his daughter, what should I, that am
So deeply in? I will prevent him – wretch!
Covetous wretch! Mosca, I have determined.
MOSCA
How, sir?
CORVINO   We'll make all sure. The party you
    wot of   80
Shall be mine own wife, Mosca.
MOSCA   Sir, the thing
(But that I would not seem to counsel you)
I should have motioned to you at the first;
And, make your count, you have cut all their throats.
Why, 'tis directly taking a possession!   85
And, in his next fit, we may let him go.
'Tis but to pull the pillow from his head,
And he is throttled – 't had been done before,
But for your scrupulous doubts.
CORVINO   Ay, a plague on 't,
My conscience fools my wit. Well, I'll be brief,   90

95 free motion: *voluntary proposition. Corvino wants all the credit for his degradation! Once again this is Corvino's particular speciality in the play's depiction of perverted values.*

96 possess him with: *make him aware of.*

99–100 I have something ... good: *in fact, Mosca wants a breathing space in which to further his other scheme of persuading Corbaccio to disinherit Bonario. Despite this warning, Corvino arrives embarrassingly early.*

3 try: *test.*

4 lightness: *insignificance.*
   occasion: *cause.*

5 confirmed thee: *assured you.*

7 humour: *state of mind.*

8–10 Do not ... gold: *Corvino claims that he knows jealousy be pointless, since women who are sufficiently determined to fulfil their sexual desires will do so regardless of any guard placed on them, and in any case there are no spies who cannot be bribed.*

118

And so be thou, lest they should be before us;
Go home, prepare him, tell him with what zeal
And willingness I do it; swear it was
On the first hearing – as thou mayst do, truly –
Mine own free motion.

MOSCA   Sir, I warrant you,   95
I'll so possess him with it that the rest
Of his starved clients shall be banished, all,
And only you received. But come not, sir,
Until I send, for I have something else
To ripen for your good – you must not know't.   100

CORVINO

But do not you forget to send, now.

MOSCA   Fear not.

(*Exit* MOSCA)

(*Scene seven*)

CORVINO

Where are you, wife? my Celia? wife?
(*Enter* CELIA *weeping*)
                              What, blubbering?
Come, dry those tears. I think thou thought'st me in
    earnest?
Ha? By this light, I talked so but to try thee.
Methinks the lightness of the occasion
Should ha' confirmed thee. Come I am not jealous.   5

CELIA

No?

CORVINO Faith, I am not, I, nor never was;
It is a poor, unprofitable humour.
Do not I know, if women have a will,
They'll do 'gainst all the watches o' the world?
And that the fiercest spies are tamed with gold?   10
Tut, I am confident in thee, thou shalt see't;

16   solemn feast: *rich banquet.*

And see, I'll give thee cause too, to believe it.
Come, kiss me. Go, and make thee ready straight
In all thy best attire thy choicest jewels,
Put 'em all on, and with 'em, thy best looks;   15
We are invited to a solemn feast
At old Volpone's, where it shall appear
How far I am free from jealousy or fear.

Exeunt

1–33: *This is Mosca's great speech of self-justification, in which he takes the seemingly degraded role of parasite and elevates it to the status of an innate gift, vocation and art. In making his extravagant claims, Mosca distinguishes the true parasite (himself) from mere imitators who scrape a living from flattering servility. The key point of the speech is that a true parasite is not a dependant, but only plays out the role of dependency as a professional skill. The speech has a bearing not only on our understanding of Mosca's vanity but on the real nature of his relationship with Volpone.*

2 parts: *talents.*

4 whimsy: *swirling.*

5 wanton: *playful.*

6 subtle: *(i) sinuous and slender; (ii) cunning (like the serpent in Eden).*

7 limber: *supple.*

9 clotpoles: *thick-heads.*

10 I muse: *I am surprised.*
mystery: *professional craft.*
science: *recognised area of learning.*

11 so liberally professed: *so widely practised by gentlemen.*

14 those: *ordinary parasites.*
bare town-art: *basic skills for scraping a living in urban society. Mosca describes these basic skills in lines 15–22.*

15 To know ... feed 'em: *to know where they can be sure of cadging a meal.*

17 bait that sense: *entrap men through their sense of hearing.*

18 Kitchen-invention: *servant's gossip.*

20 court-dog-tricks: *tricks of servile flattery.*
fleer: *smile obsequiously.*

21 Make their revènue ... faces: *Make their living by bowing and smiling*

22 lick ... moth: *a particularly striking image for extreme flattering subservience.*

28 Present ... occasion: *always at the ready to deal with any mood or situation.*

Act Three

Scene one

A Street
Enter MOSCA

MOSCA
    I fear I shall begin to grow in love
With my dear self and my most prosp'rous parts,
They do so spring and burgeon; I can feel
A whimsy i' my blood. I know not how,
Success hath made me wanton. I could skip   5
Out of my skin, now, like a subtle snake,
I am so limber. O! your parasite
Is a most precious thing, dropped from above,
Not bred 'mongst clods and clotpoles, here on earth.
I muse the mystery was not made a science,   10
It is so liberally professed! Almost
All the wise world is little else in nature
But parasites, or sub-parasites. And yet,
I mean not those that have your bare town-art,
To know who's fit to feed 'em; have no house,   15
No family, no care, and therefore mould
Tales for men's ears, to bait that sense; or get
Kitchen-invention, and some stale receipts
To please the belly, and the groin; nor those,
With their court-dog-tricks, that can fawn and fleer,   20
Make their revènue out of legs and faces,
Echo my lord, and lick away a moth;
But your fine, elegant rascal, that can rise
And stoop (almost together) like an arrow;
Shoot through the air as nimbly as a star;   25
Turn short, as doth a swallow; and be here,
And there, and here, and yonder, all at once;
Present to any humour, all occasion;

29   visor: *mask; therefore 'role' or 'expression'.*

32   nature: *natural ability.*
      sparks: *men-about-town.*
33   zanies: *hangers-on; mere assistants.*

2   bound: *on my way.*

4   know thy way: *mind your own business.*

6   mate: *fellow.*

11   Thy means of feeding?:   *the way you earn your living (by fawning on rich men). Bonario accuses Mosca of earning his living in the base way he has just rejected as a description of himself and attributed to the lesser parasites whom he despises. Bonario's scorn draws our attention to the self-idealization and conceit in Mosca's vision of himself.*

14   unequal: *unjust (and also above me in social status).*

15–16 Your sentence . . . censure: *your judgement may be just, but you are not just in making it, since you do not know me and therefore condemn me without evidence.*

17   St Mark: *the patron saint of Venice.*

124

And change a visor swifter than a thought!
This is the creature, had the art born with him;   30
Toils not to learn it, but doth practise it
Out of most excellent nature; and such sparks
Are the true parasites, others but their zanies.

(Scene two)

Enter BONARIO

MOSCA
Who's this? Bonario? old Corbaccio's son?
The person I was bound to seek. Fair sir,
You are happ'ly met.

BONARIO   That cannot be by thee.

MOSCA
Why, sir?

BONARIO   Nay, pray thee know thy way, and leave me;
I would be loath to interchange discourse   5
With such a mate as thou art.

MOSCA   Courteous sir,
Scorn not my poverty.

BONARIO   Not I, by heaven –
But thou shalt give me leave to hate thy baseness.

MOSCA
Baseness?

BONARIO   Ay, answer me, is not thy sloth
Sufficient argument? thy flattery?   10
Thy means of feeding?

MOSCA   Heaven, be good to me!
These imputations are too common, sir,
And eas'ly stuck on virtue when she's poor;
You are unequal to me, and howe'er
Your sentence may be righteous, yet you are not,   15
That ere you know me, thus proceed in censure.
St Mark bear witness 'gainst you, 'tis inhuman.

Weeps

21 careful: *hard-earned.*

23 fain . . . raiment: *forced to make my own poor living.*

24 observance: *dutiful service.*

25–30 But that . . . chastity: *Mosca's tone of injured innocence in this passage is all the more effective dramatically because these are the very things he has done and is currently doing!*

26 Base offices: *dishonourable duties.*

28 mining men with praises: *undermining men with flattery. (By flattery, Mosca persuades men to take him into their confidence and so expose themselves to trickery and exploitation.)*

29 Trained: *deceived.*

32 Prove: *undergo.*

33 redeem . . . estimation: *restore my good name.*

34 Let me here . . . goodness: *this sanctimonious hope is an empty one for Mosca to express. He does not have any 'hope of goodness'.*

35 personated passion: *simulated grief. Bonario's quick credulity establishes the naive innocence of his character (like Celia's) throughout.*

39 main: *serious.*

45 mere: *complete.*

46 engageth: *concerns.*

BONARIO (*Aside*)

    What? does he weep? the sign is soft and good!
    I do repent me that I was so harsh.

MOSCA

    'Tis true that, swayed by strong necessity,   20
    I am enforced to eat my careful bread
    With too much obsequy; 'tis true, beside,
    That I am fain to spin mine own poor raiment
    Out of my mere observance, being not born
    To a free fortune. But that I have done   25
    Base offices, in rending friends asunder,
    Dividing families, betraying counsels,
    Whispering false lies, or mining men with praises,
    Trained their credulity with perjuries,
    Corrupted chastity, or am in love   30
    With mine own tender ease, but would not rather
    Prove the most rugged and laborious course
    That might redeem my present estimation,
    Let me here perish, in all hope of goodness.

BONARIO (*Aside*)

    This cannot be a personated passion! –   35
    I was to blame, so to mistake thy nature;
    Pray thee forgive me, and speak out thy business.

MOSCA

    Sir, it concerns you; and though I may seem
    At first, to make a main offence in manners,
    And in my gratitude unto my master,   40
    Yet, for the pure love which I bear all right,
    And hatred of the wrong, I must reveal it.
    This very hour, your father is in purpose
    To disinherit you –

BONARIO   How!

MOSCA   And thrust you forth

    As a mere stranger to his blood; 'tis true, sir.   45
    The work no way engageth me, but as

49 for which mere respect: *for which reason alone.*

53 lend it any thought: *even consider it.*

56 piety: *natural feelings as a son.*

65 common issue . . . earth: *of obscure or unknown parentage.*

67 score: *mark.*
    front: *forehead.*

I claim an interest in the general state
Of goodness and true virtue, which I hear
T'abound in you; and, for which mere respect,
Without a second aim, sir, I have done it.   50
BONARIO
    This tale hath lost thee much of the late trust
    Thou hadst with me; it is impossible –
    I know not how to lend it any thought,
    My father should be so unnatural.
MOSCA
    It is a confidence that well becomes   55
    Your piety; and formed, no doubt, it is
    From your own simple innocence – which makes
    Your wrong more monstrous and abhorred. But, sir,
    I now will tell you more. This very minute,
    It is, or will be doing; and if you   60
    Shall be but pleased to go with me, I'll bring you,
    I dare not say where you shall see, but where
    Your ear shall be a witness of the deed;
    Hear yourself written bastard, and professed
    The common issue of the earth.
BONARIO   I'm mazed!   65
MOSCA
    Sir, if I do it not, draw your just sword,
    And score your vengeance on my front and face;
    Mark me your villain. You have too much wrong,
    And I do suffer for you, sir. My heart
    Weeps blood, in anguish –
BONARIO   Lead. I follow thee.   70
                                                   Exeunt

1   stays long: *is away a long time. (Volpone is impatiently waiting for Mosca to return from Corvino.)*

4   whether: *which.*
5   known: *acknowledged.*
     delicates: *amusements.*

8   set . . . school: *teach you both a lesson.*

10 as: *as far as.*

15 feat: *dainty.*

17 Admit: *let us grant.*
18 come after: *be of secondary importance.*
19 that: *i.e. the laughter aroused by the fool's face.*

23 fair return: *good news. Volpone asks Cupid for help because his objective this time is not gold but Celia.*

Scene three

VOLPONE'S *House*
Enter VOLPONE, *followed by* NANO, ANDROGYNO *and* CASTRONE
VOLPONE

Mosca stays long, methinks. Bring forth your sports
And help to make the wretched time more sweet.

NANO

Dwarf, fool, and eunuch, well met here we be.
    A question it were now, whether of us three –
Being, all, the known delicates of a rich man –   5
    In pleasing him, claim the precedency can?

CASTRONE I claim for myself.

ANDROGYNO   And so doth the fool.

NANO

'Tis foolish indeed; let me set you both to school.
First, for your dwarf, he's little, and witty,
    And every thing, as it is little, is pretty;   10
Else, why do men say to a creature of my shape,
    So soon as they see him, 'It's a pretty little ape?'
And, why a pretty ape? but for pleasing imitation
    Of greater men's action, in a ridiculous fashion.
Beside, this feat body of mine doth not crave   15
    Half the meat, drink, and cloth, one of your bulks will
    have.
Admit, your fool's face be the mother of laughter,
    Yet, for his brain, it must always come after;
And though that do feed him, it's a pitiful case
    His body is beholding to such a bad face.   20

            One knocks

VOLPONE

Who's there? my couch; away, look, Nano, see;
Give me my caps, first – go, enquire.

           Exeunt NANO, ANDROGYNO, CASTRONE
              Now, Cupid
Send it be Mosca, and with fair return.

24 Would-be: *some three eventful hours have therefore elapsed since Lady Would-be's first visit in Act I Scene V.*

25 squire: *escort.*
26 dwell: *hang around.*
27 that my fit were past: *so that I can get the torment of her visit over and done with.*
28 this: *i.e. Lady Would-be.*
29 the other: *i.e. Celia.*

2–3: *Lady Would-be enters inspecting herself in a mirror. She wishes her physical charms to be suitably visible to Volpone.*

2 band: *collar, ruff.*

6 favourably: *sarcasm directed at her maids.*
7–8 Look, see, . . . done this!: *Just look what a mess these insolent women have made of their work!*

11 his: *its.*

14 your fellow: *your fellow servant.*

NANO (*At the entrance*)
    It is the beauteous Madam –
VOLPONE   Would-be – is it?
NANO
    The same.
VOLPONE   Now, torment on me; squire her in –   25
    For she will enter, or dwell here for ever.
    Nay, quickly, that my fit were past, (*Exit* NANO) I fear
    A second hell too, that my loathing this
    Will quite expel my appetite to the other.
    Would she were taking, now, her tedious leave.   30
    Lord, how it threats me, what I am to suffer!

(*Scene four*)

Enter NANO *with* LADY WOULD-BE

LADY WOULD-BE
    I thank you, good sir. Pray you signify
    Unto your patron, I am here. This band
    Shows not my neck enough – I trouble you, sir,
    Let me request you, bid one of my women
    Come hither to me – in good faith, I am dressed   5
    Most favourably today. It is no matter,
    'Tis well enough. Look, see, these petulant things!
    How they have done this!
VOLPONE (*Aside*)   I do feel the fever
    Ent'ring in at mine ears. O, for a charm,
    To fright it hence.
Enter 1st WOMAN
LADY WOULD-BE   Come nearer. Is this curl   10
    In his right place? or this? why is this higher
    Than all the rest? you ha' not washed your eyes yet?
    Or do they not stand even i' your head?
    Where's your fellow? call her.
                                Exit 1st WOMAN

15 Anon: *in a moment.*

17 tire: *head-dress.*
forsooth: *'indeed'; a mild and polite oath. The servant maliciously imitates it, whereupon Lady Would-be can think of nothing wittier than to return the repetitious mockery she has herself provoked.*

20 bird-eyed: *expression used of someone reacting nervously to a threat. The women think Lady Would-be is threatening to hit them.*

21 mend it: *put it right.*

22 by that light: *an oath.*
I muse: *I am surprised.*

23–5 preached ... grace: *Lady Would-be uses in these lines a terminology suitable for serious discussion of religious and intellectual matters. It is a sign of her shallowness and pretension that she applies such words to trivialities of personal appearance.*

24 grounds: *fundamentals.*

25 Disputed: *debated the case in favour of and against an intellectual proposition.*

27 fame: *reputation.*

31 At your return: *on your return to England.*

32 curious: *fastidious.*

37 fucus: *make-up.*

NANO (*Aside*)   Now, St Mark

  Deliver us! Anon, she'll beat her women   15

  Because her nose is red.

Enter 1st *and* 2nd WOMEN

LADY OULD-BE   I pray you, view

  This tire, forsooth – are all things apt, or no?

2nd WOMAN

  One hair a little, here, sticks out, forsooth.

LADY WOULD-BE

  Does't so, forsooth? and where was your dear sight

  When it did so, forsooth? what now? bird-eyed?   20

  And you, too? pray you both approach, and mend it.

  Now, by that light, I muse you're not ashamed!

  I, that have preached these things, so oft, unto you,

  Read you the principles, argued all the grounds,

  Disputed every fitness, every grace,   25

  Called you to counsel of so frequent dressings –

NANO (*Aside*)

  More carefully than of your fame or honour.

LADY WOULD-BE

  Made you acquainted, what an ample dowry

  The knowledge of these things would be unto you,

  Able, alone, to get you noble husbands   30

  At your return; and you, thus, to neglect it?

  Besides, you seeing what a curious nation

  Th'Italians are, what will they say of me?

  'The English lady cannot dress herself' –

  Here's a fine imputation to our country!   35

  Well, go your ways, and stay i' the next room.

  This fucus was too coarse too; it's no matter.

  Good sir, you'll give 'em entertainment?

Exeunt NANO *and* WOMEN

VOLPONE (*Aside*)

  The storm comes tòward me.

LADY WOULD-BE   How does my Volp?

135

41   fury: *the Furies of Greek myth were supernatural avengers who pursued the guilty and wicked. Lady Would-be naturally fails to see any reference to herself!*

47   golden mediocrity: *Lady Would-be's distorted version of the classical 'golden mean', which denoted the virtuous moderate position between two extremes. When Lady Would-be has to improvize a dream without notice, her ideas turn naturally towards gold.*

51   the passion of the heart: *expression which covered several kinds of malady, including heartburn.*

52   Seed-pearl: *solution of seed-pearl was considered a tonic for the heart.*

53   Tincture of gold: *essence of gold; another stimulant when dissolved.*
     coral: *coral was supposed to dispel bad dreams.*

54   elecampane: *plant believed to be good for the stomach.*
     myrobalans: *plum-like fruits thought to relieve melancholy and heartburn.*

55   grasshopper: *because Lady Would-be's talk is unstoppably buzzing and jumping about.*

56   Burnt silk: *taken in water as a cure for smallpox.*
     amber: *ambergris, thought good for the stomach.*
     muscadel: *a perfumed wine.*

57   You will not drink, and part?:   *Won't you have a drink before you go? Even such a strong hint as this will not get rid of Lady Would-be. She thinks Volpone fears her departure, not that he longs for it!*

58   I doubt we shall not get: *I fear we shall be unable to get.*

59   saffron: *saffron taken in wine was another recommended cure for bad stomachs.*

61   Bugloss: *herb used as a heart stimulant.*
     She's in: *She's off.*

63   scarlet cloth: *wrapping the patient in a scarlet cloth was recommended in cases of smallpox. This remedy almost concludes Lady Would-be's adventurous medicinal catalogue.*

VOLPONE
> Troubled with noise, I cannot sleep; I dreamt   40
> That a strange fury entered, now, my house,
> And, with the dreadful tempest of her breath,
> Did cleave my roof asunder.

LADY WOULD-BE   Believe me, and I
> Had the most fearful dream, could I remember't –

VOLPONE (*Aside*)
> Out on my fate; I ha' given her the occasion   45
> How to torment me – she will tell me hers.

LADY WOULD-BE
> Methought the golden mediocrity,
> Polite, and delicate –

VOLPONE   O, if you do love me,
> No more; I sweat and suffer at the mention
> Of any dream – feel how I tremble yet.   50

LADY WOULD-BE
> Alas, good soul! the passion of the heart.
> Seed-pearl were good now, boiled with syrup of apples,
> Tincture of gold, and coral, citron-pills,
> Your elecampane root, myrobalans –

VOLPONE (*Aside*)
> Ay me, I have ta'en a grasshopper by the wing.   55

LADY WOULD-BE
> Burnt silk, and amber; you have muscadel
> Good i' the house –

VOLPONE   You will not drink, and part?

LADY WOULD-BE
> No, fear not that. I doubt we shall not get
> Some English saffron – half a dram would serve –
> Your sixteen cloves, a little musk, dried mints,   60
> Bugloss, and barley-meal –

VOLPONE (*Aside*)   She's in again;
> Before I feigned diseases, now I have one.

LADY WOULD-BE
> And these applied, with a right scarlet cloth –

68   forenoons: *mornings*

72   principal: *principally*

72–3 Plato . . . Pythagoras: *Lady Would-be's learning is a matter of name-dropping rather than knowledge. Plato valued music for its potential contribution to an ideal education, and Pythagoras propounded the influential doctrine of the 'music of the spheres'. Neither was concerned with it as a fashionable social accomplishment, which is Lady Would-be's only interest.*

74   concent: *harmony.*

76   The poet: *i.e. Sophocles,* Ajax, *293, where the expression is 'Women should be seen, not heard'.*

79   Which o' your poets: *Lady Would-be seizes the chance to recite the names of various Italian poets. Every implicit criticism which Volpone directs at Lady Would-be turns into another conversational weapon against him.*

79–81 Petrarch . . . Cieco di Hadria: *These are all Italian poets of the middle ages and Renaissance, and they include, in Petrarch, Dante and Ariosto, some of the greatest poets of that period. None, however, is a classical poet, 'as old in time as Plato', an historical fact of which Lady Would-be is ignorant despite her professed familiarity with their works.*

86   'Pastor Fido':   *i.e. 'The Faithful Shepherd', a fashionable tragicomedy by Guarini, and a work which Jonson did not admire. Some of his contemporaries and rivals, including Marston, approved of it and used it, so Jonson's reference to stealing (line 89) is a malicious joke at their expense.*

VOLPONE (*Aside*)
  Another flood of words! a very torrent!

LADY WOULD-BE
  Shall I, sir, make you a poultice?

VOLPONE   No, no, no;   65
  I'm very well, you need prescribe no more.

LADY WOULD-BE
  I have, a little, studied physic; but now
  I'm all for music – save, i' the forenoons,
  An hour or two for painting. I would have
  A lady, indeed, t'have all letters and arts.   70
  Be able to discourse, to write, to paint,
  But principal (as Plato holds) your music
  (And so does wise Pythagoras, I take it)
  Is your true rapture – when there is concent
  In face, in voice, and clothes – and is, indeed,   75
  Our sex's chiefest ornament.

VOLPONE   The poet
  As old in time as Plato, and as knowing,
  Says that your highest female grace is silence.

LADY WOULD-BE
  Which o' your poets? Petrarch? or Tasso? or Dante?
  Guarini? Ariosto? Aretine?   80
  Cieco di Hadria? I have read them all.

VOLPONE (*Aside*)
  Is everything a cause to my destruction?

LADY WOULD-BE
  I think I ha' two or three of 'em about me.

VOLPONE
  The sun, the sea will sooner, both, stand still
  Than her eternal tongue! nothing can scape it.   85

LADY WOULD-BE
  Here's *Pastor Fido* –

VOLPONE (*Aside*)   Profess obstinate silence,
  That's now my safest.

LADY WOULD-BE   All our English writers,

88   happy in th' Italian: *have a good knowledge of Italian.*

90   Montagnié: *the French essayist Montaigne (1533–92), whose works had been translated into English by Florio and much 'borrowed' by English writers.*

91   modern and facile: *Lady Politic means 'fashionable and readable', but the words could also mean (as Jonson intends them to) 'trivial and superficial'.*

93   Petrarch: *Francesco Petrarch (1304–74) was a great Italian poet whose love sonnets exerted a profound influence on other poets.*

93–4   yet he ... with much: *yet Petrarch, in the times when sonnet writing was fashionable, gave poets plenty of material to borrow.*

95   Dante: *author of the* Divine Comedy; *great Italian poet renowned for his difficulty.*

96   desperate: *reckless.*
      Aretine: *Pietro Aretino (1492–1556), Italian poet famous for his slanderous wit.*

97   pictures: *set of obscene engravings created from designs by Giulio Romano. Aretino wrote sixteen 'Sonnets of Lust' to accompany them.*

102   Encounter: *counteract.*

103   humour: *mood, passion.*

104   politic bodies: *governing bodies of states.*

107   Settling ... subsiding: *Lady Would-be uses chemical terminology to recommend Volpone to cheer himself up by finding new interests and diversions. Her comparison is with a council of state which must not let its judgement be clouded by concentrating too long on one subject ('settling and fixing') and becoming dull and listless ('subsiding').*

108–110 For the incorporating ... mental: *For absorbing these external passions into the mind ... (Lady Would-be's learned prescription is of course largely confused and nonsensical).*

110–111 faeces ... organs: *sediment which clogs up the system.*

114   more a-days: *on more days (compare our word 'nowadays')*

115   lusty: *merry.*

I mean such as are happy in th'Italian,
Will deign to steal out of this author, mainly,
Almost as much as from Montagnié –   90
He has so modern and facile a vein,
Fitting the time, and catching the court-ear.
Your Petrarch is more passionate, yet he,
In days of sonneting, trusted 'em with much:
Dante is hard, and few can understand him.   95
But for a desperate wit, there's Aretine!
Only, his pictures are a little obscene –
You mark me not?

VOLPONE   Alas, my mind's perturbed.

LADY WOULD-BE
Why, in such cases, we must cure ourselves,
Make use of our philosophy –

VOLPONE   O'y me!   100

LADY WOULD-BE
And, as we find our passions do rebel,
Encounter 'em with reason; or divert 'em,
By giving scope unto some other humour
Of lesser danger – as in politic bodies,
There's nothing more doth overwhelm the judgment,   105
And clouds the understanding, than too much
Settling, and fixing, and (as't were) subsiding
Upon one object. For the incorporating
Of these same outward things into that part
Which we call mental, leaves some certain faeces   110
That stop the organs, and, as Plato says,
Assassinates our knowledge.

VOLPONE (*Aside*)   Now the spirit
Of patience help me!

LADY WOULD-BE   Come, in faith, I must
Visit you more a-days, and make you well.
Laugh, and be lusty.

VOLPONE (*Aside*)   My good angel save me!   115

118 Would lie you often: *would often lie.*

120 from the purpose: *off the point.* (*Lady Would-be imagines that this mental distraction arises from the fascination of her interminable talk. On stage, the spectacle of Volpone's anguished boredom is a comic revelation of the truth.*)

121 you are like him, just: *you are just like him.*

122 And't: *even if it . . .*

125 'coaetanei': *of the same age.*

5 The bells in time of pestilence: *The ringing of death-knells in times of plague.*

7 cock-pit: *area used for cock-fighting, made noisy by the excitements of betting.*

11 rid her hence: *get her out.*

LADY WOULD-BE
  There was but one sole man, in all the world,
  With whom I ere could sympathise; and he
  Would lie you often, three, four hours together,
  To hear me speak; and be sometime so rapt,
  As he would answer me quite from the purpose,   120
  Like you, and you are like him, just. I'll discourse –
  And't be but only, sir, to bring you asleep –
  How we did spend our time, and loves, together,
  For some six years.
VOLPONE   Oh, oh, oh, oh, oh, oh.
LADY WOULD-BE
  For we were *coætanei*, and brought up –   125
VOLPONE (*Aside*)
  Some power, some fate, some fortune rescue me!

(*Scene five*)

Enter MOSCA
MOSCA
  God save you, madam.
LADY WOULD-BE   Good sir.
VOLPONE   Mosca! welcome,
  Welcome to my redemption!
MOSCA   Why, sir?
VOLPONE   Oh,
  Rid me of this my torture quickly, there;
  My madam with the everlasting voice;
  The bells in time of pestilence ne'er made   5
  Like noise, or were in that perpetual motion;
  The cock-pit comes not near it. All my house,
  But now, steamed like a bath with her thick breath.
  A lawyer could not have been heard; nor scarce
  Another woman, such a hail of words   10
  She has let fall. For hell's sake, rid her hence.

12 presented: *offered a gift.* (*Mosca, not having suffered with Volpone, keeps his eye on the priorities.*)

15 toy: *trifle.* (*Lady Would-be's gift is absurdly trivial compared with those of the other suitors.*)

17 Marry: *light oath, derived from 'By the Virgin Mary'.*

20 courtesan: *prostitute.*

22 I knew 'twould take: *I knew she would fall for that.*

23 lightly: *commonly.*
24 still: *always.*

27 Again . . . paroxysm: *she's come back! I shall have a fit.*

MOSCA

  Has she presented?

VOLPONE   O, I do not care,

  I'll take her absence upon any price,

  With any loss.

MOSCA   Madam –

LADY WOULD-BE   I ha' brought your patron

  A toy, a cap here, of mine own work –

MOSCA   'Tis well.   15

  I had forgot to tell you, I saw your knight

  Where you'd little think it –

LADY WOULD-BE   Where?

MOSCA   Marry,

  Where yet, if you make haste, you may apprehend him,

  Rowing upon the water in a gondola,

  With the most cunning courtesan of Venice.   20

LADY WOULD-BE

  Is't true?

MOSCA   Pursue 'em, and believe your eyes –

  Leave me to make your gift. (*Exit* LADY WOULD-BE) I

    knew 'twould take.

  For lightly, they that use themselves most licence

  Are still most jealous.

VOLPONE   Mosca, hearty thanks

  For thy quick fiction and delivery of me.   25

  Now, to my hopes, what say'st thou?

Re-enter LADY WOULD-BE

LADY WOULD-BE   But do you hear,

    sir? –

VOLPONE

  Again: I fear a paroxysm.

LADY WOULD-BE   Which way

  Rowed they together?

MOSCA   Toward the *Rialto*.

31–2 stay / But: *only wait for.*

33 straight: *straightaway.*

36 like your wanton gamester at primero: *like a reckless gambler playing primero. Primero is a four-card game, something like poker. Volpone uses several terms from the game. To 'go less' is to wager a smaller stake, something Volpone resolves not to do in his sexual gamble for Celia. To 'lie' is to 'lay' or place a bet. To 'draw' is to take another card from the pack. To 'encounter' is to choose a winning card. Volpone imagines himself as a gambler who is prepared to take risks in the love-game, and also as a lover who will 'lie' in his bed, 'draw' Celia to him and 'encounter' her in a sexual embrace.*

4 imagine this a truth: *i.e. believe what Mosca has already told him about his father's intention to disinherit him.*

2 send: *send for you. See Act II Scene VI line 99. Corvino disturbs Mosca's plans by arriving when he is expecting Corbaccio. Volpone and Mosca habitually expect other characters to behave exactly as they themselves arrange or predict, and incur increasing risks when unexpected behaviour occurs. A part of Jonson's dramatic skill is the suspense or comic surprise he is able to create when his characters suddenly fail to behave in the stereotyped way he has led us to expect.*

LADY WOULD-BE
　　I pray you, lend me your dwarf.
MOSCA　　　　　　　　　　　　I pray you, take him.
　　　　　　　　　　　　　　　(*Exit* LADY WOULD-BE)
　　Your hopes, sir, are like happy blossoms, fair,　　　30
　　And promise timely fruit, if you will stay
　　But the maturing; keep you at your couch –
　　Corbaccio will arrive straight, with the will;
　　When he is gone, I'll tell you more.

　　　　　　　　　　　　　　　　　　　Exit

VOLPONE　　　　　　　　　　　My blood,
　　My spirits are returned; I am alive;　　　　　　　35
　　And like your wanton gamester at primero,
　　Whose thought had whispered to him, not go less,
　　Methinks I lie, and draw – for an encounter.

(*Scene six*)

Enter MOSCA, BONARIO
MOSCA
　　Sir, here concealed, you may hear all. But pray you
　　Have patience, sir; (*One knocks*) the same's your father
　　　knocks;
　　I am compelled to leave you.
BONARIO　　　　　　　　　　Do so. Yet
　　Cannot my thought imagine this a truth.

　　　　　　　　　　　　　　　　Hides himself

(*Scene seven*)

Enter CORVINO, CELIA
MOSCA
　　Death on me! you are come too soon, what meant you?
　　Did not I say I would send?

3   they prevent us: *the other legacy-hunters would forestall us.*

4   horns: *the horns of a cuckold.*

5   A courtier . . . place: *A courtier would not be so pressing in his search for patronage at court.*

7   presently: *immediately.*

9   except you told me: *except what you have already told me.*

11   half an hour: *Mosca has to find some excuse now for delaying his plans for Corbaccio and Bonario while he deals with Corvino and Celia.*

16   doubt: *suspect.*

19   starting back: *calling things off.*

21   move: *suggest.*

22   shifts: *stratagems.*

24   Affect not . . . trials: *Do not pretend to make trial of my virtue in this way. (Celia believes that Corvino is conducting a jealous experiment; she cannot believe he is serious.)*

CORVINO   Yes, but I feared
  You might forget it, and then they prevent us.

MOSCA
  Prevent? *(Aside)* – Did e'er man haste so for his horns?
  A courtier would not ply it so, for a place. –   5
  Well, now there's no helping it, stay here;
  I'll presently return.

                                      Moves toward BONARIO

CORVINO   Where are you, Celia?
  You know not wherefore I have brought you hither?

CELIA
  Not well, except you told me.

CORVINO   Now I will;
  Hark hither.

                                      They whisper apart

MOSCA *(To* BONARIO*)*   Sir, your father hath sent word   10
  It will be half an hour ere he come;
  And therefore, if you please to walk the while
  Into that gallery – at the upper end
  There are some books to entertain the time;
  And I'll take care, no man shall come unto you, sir.   15

BONARIO
  Yes, I will stay there. *(Aside)* I do doubt this fellow.

                                                            Exit

MOSCA
  There, he is far enough; he can hear nothing;
  And for his father, I can keep him off.

                                      Moves to VOLPONE

CORVINO
  Nay, now, there is no starting back; and therefore
  Resolve upon it; I have so decreed.   20
  It must be done. Nor would I move't afore,
  Because I would avoid all shifts and tricks
  That might deny me.

CELIA   Sir, let me beseech you,
  Affect not these strange trials; if you doubt

                                                            149

27 please your fears: *put your fears at rest.*

28 I have no such humour: *I am not engaged in such a pretence.*

30 horn-mad: *maddened by fear of being cuckolded.*

32 train: *trap.*

34 engagements: *obligations.*

35-6 My means ... recovery: *My financial resources, and how much more I need to restore my prosperity.*

37 respect my venture: *support my enterprise.*

38 Honour? tut, a breath: *the bitter dramatic irony of Corvino's speech is emphasized by contrast with his language in Act II Scene III. Honour, which then mattered so much to him, is now a mere word. Cuckoldry, which he then abhorred, is a dishonour he is now actively seeking.*

43 sense: *sensual feelings.*

43-4 takes his meat ... fingers: *has to be helped to feed.*

44-5 only knows ... gums: *can do nothing but gape when food which is too hot is placed in his mouth.*

46 spirit: *evil spirit.*

48 jig: *trifle.*

49 Cry it, on the Piazza!: *Shout aloud in public what you have done.*

50 he, that cannot speak it: *i.e. Volpone, supposed incapable of speech.*

50-1 this fellow ... pocket: *i.e. Mosca, supposed to say only what he has been paid to say.*

51 save yourself: *except yourself.*

My chastity, why, lock me up, for ever!   25
Make me the heir of darkness. Let me live
Where I may please your fears, if not your trust.

CORVINO

Believe it, I have no such humour, I.
All that I speak I mean; yet I am not mad –
Not horn-mad, see you? Go to, show yourself   30
Obedient, and a wife.

CELIA   O heaven!

CORVINO   I say it,

Do so.

CELIA   Was this the train?

CORVINO   I've told you reasons;

What the physicians have set down; how much
It may concern me; what my engagements are;
My means; and the necessity of those means   35
For my recovery; wherefore, if you be
Loyal, and mine, be won, respect my venture.

CELIA

Before your honour?

CORVINO   Honour? tut, a breath;

There's no such thing in nature – a mere term
Invented to awe fools. What is my gold   40
The worse, for touching? clothes, for being looked on?
Why, this's no more. An old, decrepit wretch,
That has no sense, no sinew; takes his meat
With others' fingers; only knows to gape
When you do scald his gums; a voice; a shadow;   45
And what can this man hurt you?

CELIA   Lord! what spirit

Is this hath entered him?

CORVINO   And for your fame,

That's such a jig; as if I would go tell it,
Cry it, on the Piazza! who shall know it,
But he, that cannot speak it, and this fellow,   50
Whose lips are i' my pocket – save yourself?

60 Aretine . . . prints: *see note on Act III Scene IV line 97.*
   conned: *studied.*
62 professed critic: *someone who claims to be an expert.*
63 And: *If.*

66 polity: *discreet action.*
   assure mine own: *take care of my own property (i.e. the anticipated inheritance, of which he speaks as if he already owned it).*

If you'll proclaim't, you may. I know no other
Should come to know it.

CELIA   Are heaven and saints then
    nothing?
Will they be blind, or stupid?

CORVINO   How?

CELIA   Good sir,
Be jealous still, emulate them; and think   55
What hate they burn with tòward every sin.

CORVINO
I grant you, if I thought it were a sin,
I would not urge you. Should I offer this
To some young Frenchman, or hot Tuscan blood,
That had read Aretine, conned all his prints,   60
Knew every quirk within lust's labyrinth,
And were professed critic in lechery –
And I would look upon him, and applaud him,
This were a sin. But here, 'tis contrary,
A pious work, mere charity, for physic,   65
And honest polity to assure mine own.

CELIA
O heaven! canst thou suffer such a change?

VOLPONE
Thou art mine honour, Mosca, and my pride,
My joy, my tickling, my delight! go, bring 'em.

MOSCA (*Advancing*)
Please you draw near, sir.

CORVINO   Come on, what –   70
You will not be rebellious? by that light –

                     Drags her towards the bed

MOSCA
Sir, Signior Corvino, here, is come to see you –

VOLPONE
Oh!

MOSCA   And hearing of the consultation had

153

75 prostitute: *Corvino is usually able to cast himself in a favour-*
    able light despite the evidence, and expert in self-deception. He
    understands 'prostitute' to mean 'offer in devoted sacrifice'. Mosca,
    of course, intends it to be understood in its more usual sense: Cor-
    vino is forcing his helpless wife to become a whore.

78 proper: (i) *his own;* (ii) *comely and attractive.*
78–9 the beauty/Only of price: *the beauty without rival or*
    comparison.

82 for that: *as for that (i.e. the offering of Celia).*
83 e'en: *nothing less than (i.e. as futile as to fight against divine*
    will).

86 gently: *with courteous gratitude.*

97 Cry thee a strumpet ... streets: *note the dramatic irony:*
    Corvino will brand his wife a strumpet for refusing to be one. He
    will accuse her in public, when she is innocent, in the very manner
    which he sarcastically denied that he would do (see lines 48–9)
    if she had consented to be guilty.

So lately for your health, is come to offer,
Or rather, sir, to prostitute –

CORVINO   Thanks, sweet Mosca.   75

MOSCA
Freely, unasked, or unentreated –

CORVINO   Well.

MOSCA
As the true, fervent instance of his love,
His own most fair and proper wife, the beauty
Only of price in Venice –

CORVINO   'Tis well urged.

MOSCA
To be your comfortress, and to preserve you.   80

VOLPONE
Alas, I'm past already! pray you, thank him
For his good care, and promptness; but for that,
'Tis a vain labour; e'en to fight 'gainst heaven;
Applying fire to a stone – uh, uh, uh, uh –
Making a dead leaf grow again. I take   85
His wishes gently, though; and you may tell him
What I've done for him. Marry, my state is hopeless!
Will him to pray for me, and t'use his fortune
With reverence, when he comes to't.

MOSCA   Do you hear, sir?
Go to him, with your wife.

CORVINO   Heart of my father!   90
Wilt thou persist thus? come, I pray thee, come.
Thou seest 'tis nothing. Celia! By this hand,
I shall grow violent. Come, do't, I say.

CELIA
Sir, kill me, rather. I will take down poison,
Eat burning coals, do anything –

CORVINO   Be damned!   95
Heart, I will drag thee hence, home, by the hair;
Cry thee a strumpet through the streets; rip up
Thy mouth, unto thine ears; and slit thy nose,

99   rochet: *fish, the red gurnard.*

100–101 I will buy . . . alive: *Corvino's version of the rapist Tarquin's threat to his victim, Lucrece. His violence in this ugly scene is that of the rapist. The parallel emphasizes the grotesque unnaturalness of Corvino's action in forcibly subjecting his own wife to the rapist intentions of another man.*

104   aquafortis: *nitric acid, used in etching.*

105   corsives: *corrosives.*

109   Think who it is entreats you: *further irony: Corvino is so oblivious to the monstrousness of his action in trying to prostitute Celia that he actually uses his role and authority as her husband as an argument to persuade and plead with her.*

111   What . . . ask: *Whatever you think of and demand.*

112   but: *merely.*

114   Will you disgrace me thus?:   *another instance of Corvino's corrupt and inverted ideas of honour.*
      do you thirst my undoing: *do you want to ruin me?*

116   watched her time: *waited for the right opportunity.*

118   locust: *locust because, like a plague of locusts, she is destroying his expectations of wealth.*

119   Crocodile: *Celia is about to weep. Corvino suggests that, like the crocodile in fable, she will weep over her victim, himself, while in the act of destroying him.*

120   Expecting: *anticipating.*

124   affect: *seek.*

Like a raw rochet – Do not tempt me, come.
Yield I am loath – Death, I will buy some slave,   100
Whom I will kill, and bind thee to him, alive;
And at my window, hang you forth – devising
Some monstrous crime, which I, in capital letters,
Will eat into thy flesh, with aquafortis
And burning corsives, on this stubborn breast.   105
Now, by the blood thou hast incensed, I'll do't.

CELIA

Sir, what you please, you may; I am your martyr.

CORVINO

Be not thus obstinate, I ha' not deserved it.
Think who it is entreats you. Pray thee, sweet;
Good faith, thou shalt have jewels, gowns, attires,   110
What thou wilt think, and ask – Do, but go kiss him.
Or touch him, but. For my sake. At my suit.
This once, No? not? I shall remember this.
Will you disgrace me thus? do you thirst my undoing?

MOSCA

Nay, gentle lady, be advised.

CORVINO   No. no.   115

She has watched her time. God's precious, this is
   scurvy;
'Tis very scurvy; and you are –

MOSCA   Nay, good sir.

CORVINO

An arrant locust, by heaven, a locust. Whore,
Crocodile, that hast thy tears prepared,
Expecting how thou'lt bid 'em flow.

MOSCA   Nay, pray you, sir,   120
She will consider.

CELIA   Would my life would serve
To satisfy –

CORVINO   'Sdeath, if she would but speak to him,
And save my reputation, 'twere somewhat;
But spitefully to affect my utter ruin!

126 quit: *acquit, excuse.*

127 coming: *responsive.*

128 undertake for her: *make myself responsible for her (cooperative) behaviour.*

132 esteem: *consider.*

134 fled: *fled from.*

135 put off: *cast aside.*

136 Is that ... life ...?: *Is honour, which has always been one of life's main objectives ... .?*

137 placed beneath ... circumstance: *valued less than the meanest trifle.*

144 cope-man: *dealer.*

145 mazed: *amazed, bemused.*

146 thy beauty's miracle: *the miracle caused by your beauty.*

147 thy great work: *i.e. the marvel which you are.*

148 shapes: *disguises.*

151 left my practice .... love: *abandoned my schemes to win your love.*

152 In varying figures: *in various roles and disguises.*

158

MOSCA

    Ay, now you've put your fortune in her hands.   125
    Why i'faith, it is her modesty, I must quit her;
    If you were absent, she would be more coming;
    I know it, and dare undertake for her.
    What woman can, before her husband? Pray you,
    Let us depart, and leave her here.

CORVINO   Sweet Celia,   130
    Thou mayst redeem all yet; I'll say no more.
    If not, esteem yourself as lost. (CELIA *starts to leave*) Nay,
       stay there.

                          Exeunt CORVINO, MOSCA

CELIA

    O God, and his good angels! whither, whither
    Is shame fled human breasts? that with such ease
    Men dare put off your honours, and their own?   135
    Is that, which ever was a cause of life,
    Now placed beneath the basest circumstance?
    And modestly an exile made, for money?

VOLPONE

    Ay, in Corvino, and such earth-fed minds,
                  (*He leaps off from his couch*)
    That never tasted the true heaven of love.   140
    Assure thee, Celia, he that would sell thee,
    Only for hope of gain, and that uncertain,
    He would have sold his part of paradise
    For ready money, had he met a cope-man.
    Why art thou mazed to see me thus revived?   145
    Rather applaud thy beauty's miracle;
    'Tis thy great work, that hath, not now alone,
    But sundry times raised me, in several shapes,
    And but this morning like a mountebank,
    To see thee at thy window. Ay, before   150
    I would have left my practice for thy love,
    In varying figures I would have contended

153   blue Proteus: *Proteus was a sea god (described by the poet Virgil as sea-coloured, and therefore blue) who had the power to change his shape at will.*

      hornèd flood: *river. Jonson is referring to the river god Achelous, who fought Hercules for the love of Dejanira. During the contest Achelous changed his shape, first to a serpent and then to a bull, one horn of which was broken off by Hercules. Thus both Proteus and Achelous were shape-shifters, whose skill Volpone vows he would rival in order to win Celia.*

155   imagination: *supposition.*

158   jovial: *i.e. like Jove, the most famous of all those who changed their shapes when in love.*

      plight: *condition.*

160   recitation: *performance.*

161   the great Valois: *the Duke of Anjou, later King Henry III of France and the last monarch of the House of Valois. He was luxuriously entertained in Venice in 1574 while returning to France from Poland to take the throne following his brother's death.*

162   young Antinous: *beautiful youth, favourite of the Roman Emperor Hadrian. The idea of Volpone playing the part is comically incongruous.*

164   footing: *dance.*

165–183   Song: *The song is adapted from the fifth ode of Catullus, 'Vivamus mea Lesbia', which was justly admired and much translated. Volpone's persuasive use of it, however, is a perversion of the original which is a true love lyric and a far cry from Volpone's opportunistic, lustful wooing.*

166   prove: *test.*

175   Fame and rumour are but toys: *Reputation and gossip are mere trivialities. (Ironically, this is exactly what Corvino said to Celia when urging her to cooperate in this scene.)*

178   his: *i.e. Corvino's.*

With the blue Proteus, or the hornèd flood.
Now, art thou welcome.

CELIA   Sir!

VOLPONE   Nay, fly me not.
Nor, let thy false imagination   155
That I was bed-rid, make thee think I am so;
Thou shalt not find it. I am now as fresh,
As hot, as high, and in as jovial plight,
As when – in that so celebrated scene
At recitation of our comedy   160
For entertainment of the great Valois –
I acted young Antinous; and attracted
The eyes and ears of all the ladies present,
T'admire each graceful gesture, note, and footing.

Song   165

Come, my Celia, let us prove,
While we can, the sports of love;
Time will not be ours for ever,
He, at length, our good will sever;
Spend not then his gifts in vain.   170
Suns that set may rise again;
But if, once, we lose this light,
'Tis with us perpetual night.
Why should we defer our joys?
Fame and rumour are but toys.   175
Cannot we delude the eyes
Of a few poor household spies?
Or his easier ears beguile,
Thus removèd, by our wile?
'Tis no sin, love's fruits to steal,   180
But the sweet thefts to reveal;
To be taken, to be seen,
These have crimes accounted been.

161

184   sèrene: *dew or mist, thought to be poisonous.*

189–190 not in expectation/As I feed others: *not with mere hopes and promises, the bait with which I lure the other legacy-hunters. The reference to wealth as food is characteristic of the play.*

191   orient: *see the note to Act I Scene V line 9.*

192   brave: *magnificently arrayed.*

     Egyptian queen caroused: *Cleopatra luxuriously consumed. Having boasted to Antony of the vast sum she would spend on one banquet, Cleopatra fulfilled the boast by dissolving a priceless pearl in vinegar and drinking it.*

193   carbuncle: *red precious stone, i.e. a ruby.*

194   put out: *(i) put to shame; (ii) blind by its brightness.*

     both . . . St Mark: *the reference is uncertain. It may refer to two particular and valued jewels in the Venetian treasury.*

195   would have bought: *i.e. which would have excelled in value.*

     Lollia Paulina: *wife of the Emperor Caligula; her vast inherited treasure had been gained by extortion.*

198   and lose 'em: *and don't bother if you lose them (i.e. there is plenty more where they came from).*

200   but: *merely.*

201   we will . . . meal: *we will spend that much on a single meal. (Note again the association of food with wealth.)*

204   phoenix: *in ancient myth only one phoenix lived at any one time. After a life of several hundred years it died and was burnt, another being born from its ashes.*

205   Though nature lost her kind: *even if it became extinct as a result.*

206   affected: *influenced.*

208   wealthy: *valuable.*

210   taken with: *caught by.*

213   Jùly-flowers: *i.e. gillyflowers (clove-scented pinks).*

215   milk of unicorns: *the unicorn, a one-horned legendary beast, still commanded widespread belief, but was thought so rare that the idea of obtaining its milk is an exotic novelty even by Volpone's standards.*

CELIA

 Some sèrene blast me, or dire lightning strike
 This my offending race.

VOLPONE   Why droops my Celia?   185
 Thou hast in place of a base husband found
 A worthy lover; use thy fortune well,
 With secrecy, and pleasure. See, behold,
 What thou art queen of; not in expectation,
 As I feed others, but possessed, and crowned.   190
 See, here, a rope of pearl, and each more orient
 Than that the brave Egyptian queen caroused;
 Dissolve, and drink 'em. See, a carbuncle,
 May put out both the eyes of our St Mark;
 A diamond, would have bought Lollia Paulina,   195
 When she came in like star-light, hid with jewels
 That were the spoils of provinces; take these,
 And wear, and lose 'em; yet remains an ear-ring
 To purchase them again, and this whole state.
 A gem but worth a private patrimony   200
 Is nothing – we will eat such at a meal.
 The heads of parrots, tongues of nightingales,
 The brains of peacocks, and of ostriches
 Shall be our food; and, could we get the phoenix,
 Though nature lost her kind, she were our dish.   205

CELIA

 Good sir, these things might move a mind affected
 With such delights; but I, whose innocence
 Is all I can think wealthy, or worth th'enjoying,
 And which once lost, I have naught to lose beyond it,
 Cannot be taken with these sensual baits.   210
 If you have conscience –

VOLPONE   'Tis the beggar's virtue;
 If thou hast wisdom, hear me, Celia.
 Thy baths shall be the juice of Jùly-flowers,
 Spirit of roses, and of violets,
 The milk of unicorns, and panthers' breath   215

217   preparèd gold: *see the note on Act I Scene IV line 73. Volpone seems here to be presenting the medicine 'drinkable gold' as an extra luxury at a feast.*

        amber: *ambergris, used in both medicine and cooking.*

220   antic: *fantastic dance.*

221   changèd shapes: *Volpone continues his preoccupation with acting, disguises, and shape-changing. These are not just his means of acquiring profit through deception, but intense pleasures in their own right.*

222   Europa . . . Jove: *Jove (or Jupiter) fell in love with Europa, took on the appearance of a bull, and carried her away to Crete.*

223   Mars . . . Erycine: *Mars is the god of war, Venus the goddess of love. Venus Erycine is one of her numerous names, derived from Mount Eryx in Sicily, where there was a temple to her.*

229   Sophy: *the Shah of Persia.*

230   the Grand Signior: *the Sultan of Turkey.*

232   quick: *lively.*

234–5 Where we may . . . lips: *refers to the idea that in kissing the soul could be sucked forth from the body or transplanted from one to another.*

234   so: *Volpone indicates a kiss, either by actually kissing Celia or by kissing his hand to her.*

        transfuse: *pour out from one vessel to another.*

236–9 That the curious . . . pined: *note that Volpone envisages an audience for his lovemaking, and an envious one whom he can tease with the spectacle of his achievement.*

237   tell: *count.*

239   pined: *tormented.*

240–60:   *The dots in this speech represent the pauses and hesitations which punctuate Celia's fearful and halting delivery of the lines.*

242   any part . . . about you: *anything about you that still proclaims you a man.*

243   If you have touch . . .:   *If you have the least trace . . .*

Gathered in bags, and mixed with Cretan wines.
Our drink shall be preparèd gold and amber;
Which we will take, until my roof whirl round
With the vertigo; and dwarf shall dance,
My eunuch sing, my fool make up the antic.   220
Whilst we, changèd shapes, act Ovid's tales,
Thou like Europa now, and I like Jove,
Then I like Mars, and thou like Erycine,
So of the rest, till we have quite run through
And wearied all the fables of the gods.   225
Then will I have thee in more modern forms,
Attirèd like some sprightly dame of France,
Brave Tuscan lady, or proud Spanish beauty;
Sometimes unto the Persian Sophy's wife;
Or the Grand Signior's mistress; and, for change,   230
To one of our most artful courtesans,
Or some quick Negro, or cold Russian;
And I will meet thee in as many shapes;
Where we may, so, transfuse our wand'ring souls,
Out at our lips, and score up sums of pleasures,   235

                                                            (*Sings*)

             That the curious shall not know
             How to tell them as they flow;
             And the envious, when they find
             What their number is, be pined.

CELIA (*Haltingly*)
If you have ears that will be pierced ... or eyes   240
That can be opened ... a heart, may be touched ...
Or any part that yet sounds man about you ...
If you have touch of holy saints ... or heaven ...
Do me the grace to let me scape ... If not,
Be bountiful, and kill me ... You do know   245
I am a creature hither ill betrayed

247 would: *would like to.*

249 feed . . . lust: *Celia in her fear associates both Volpone's anger and his sexual desire with a gross appetite for food: even in seeking to repel him, she responds to the form of his imagination and tastes. In all his desires, Volpone is predatory and consuming.*

253–4 seducing/Your blood . . . rebellion: *tempting your passion to break out.*

257 disfavour me: *mar my beauty.*

262 Nestor's hernia: *Nestor was the oldest of the Greek kings to take part in the siege of Troy, and hence was the name for aged impotence. The Roman poet Juvenal makes matters worse by giving him a hernia.*

263 degenerate: *fall short of the qualities proper to my race.*
abuse my nation: *slander the Italian reputation for virility.*

267–275: *Bonario's melodramatic intervention and ornate rebukes are both comic and sensational in their effect. Bonario's moral rightness is undeniable, and Celia's rescue welcome, yet Bonario's pomposities and Celia's stiff virtue ensure that our laughter is directed at the whole absurd scene, not just Volpone's discomfiture.*

272 this altar . . . idol: *Volpone's first speech in the play expressed his worship of gold. Bonario correctly observes the perverted religiousness of Volpone's gold-filled den, and scorns the valuable filth ('dross') which Volpone adores as his god.*

By one whose shame I would forget it were . . .
If you will deign me neither of these graces,
Yet feed your wrath, sir, rather than your lust . . .
(It is a vice, comes nearer manliness) . . .   250
And punish that unhappy crime of nature,
Which you miscall my beauty . . . Flay my face,
Or poison it with ointments for seducing
Your blood to this rebellion . . . Rub these hands
With what may cause an eating leprosy,   255
E'en to my bones and marrow . . . anything
That may disfavour me, save in my honour . . .
And I will kneel to you, pray for you, pay down
A thousand hourly vows, sir, for your health . . .
Report, and think you virtuous –

VOLPONE   Think me cold,   260
Frozen, and impotent, and so report me?
That I had Nestor's hernia, thou wouldst think.
I do degenerate, and abuse my nation,
To play with opportunity thus long;
I should have done the act, and then have parleyed.   265
Yield, or I'll force thee.

CELIA   O! just God.

VOLPONE   In vain –

       BONARIO *leaps out from where Mosca had placed him*

BONARIO

Forbear, foul ravisher! libidinous swine!
Free the forced lady, or thou diest, impostor.
But that I am loath to snatch thy punishment
Out of the hand of justice, thou shouldst yet   270
Be made the timely sacrifice of vengeance
Before this altar, and this dross, thy idol.
Lady, let's quit the place, it is the den
Of villainy; fear naught, you have a guard;
And he, ere long, shall meet his just reward.   275

       Exeunt BONARIO, CELIA

278 unspirited: *robbed of courage.*

6 spirits: *mental powers.*
7 engagèd: *entangled.*

10 hearkened: *eavesdropped.*

14 requite you: *do the same for you.*
   like Romans: *i.e. by suicide, to avoid capture and dishonour.*
15 like Grecians: *i.e. dissolutely, and by play-acting.*

VOLPONE

    Fall on me, roof, and bury me in ruin;

    Become my grave, that wert my shelter. O!

    I am unmasked, unspirited, undone,

    Betrayed to beggary, to infamy –

(Scene eight)

Enter MOSCA, *bleeding*

MOSCA

    Where shall I run, most wretched shame of men,

    To beat out my unlucky brains?

VOLPONE   Here, here.

    What! dost thou bleed?

MOSCA   O, that his well-driven sword

    Had been so courteous to have cleft me down

    Unto the navel, ere I lived to see   5

    My life, my hopes, my spirits, my patron, all

    Thus desperately engagèd, by my error.

VOLPONE

    Woe, on thy fortune.

MOSCA   And my follies, sir.

VOLPONE

    Th'hast made me miserable.

MOSCA   And myself, sir.

    Who would have thought he would have hearkened so?   10

VOLPONE

    What shall we do?

MOSCA   I know not; if my heart

    Could expiate the mischance, I'd pluck it out.

    Will you be pleased to hang me? or cut my throat?

    And I'll requite you, sir. Let's die like Romans,

    Since we have lived like Grecians.

                         They knock without

VOLPONE   Hark, who's there?   15

16 footing: *steps.*
 'Saffi': *police.*

19 ears are boring: *probably a reference to branding of the ears as a punishment, but the reference is obscure and uncertain.*
20 Make ... however: *Keep that fortress secure, whatever happens.*
20–1 Guilty men ... still: *Guilty men always fear that what they deserve is about to happen. (After his initial panic, Mosca is recovering, and suggests that they may be exaggerating their danger).*
21 still: *always.*

2–7 Your son ... kill you: *with this brilliant piece of improvization on Mosca's part, Jonson skilfully prepares the way for several strands of the plot to be woven together.*

8 This act ... indeed: *Corbaccio has already planned to disinherit Bonario and make Volpone his beneficiary, but he then intended to restore Bonario to favour when the profits were secured. Now he plans to disinherit Bonario permanently.*

11 tendered: *cherished.*

I hear some footing – officers, the *Saffi*,
Come to apprehend us! I do feel the brand
Hissing already at my forehead; now
Mine ears are boring.

MOSCA   To your couch, sir; you
Make that place good, however. Guilty men   20
Suspect what they deserve still. Signior Corbaccio!

(*Scene nine*)

Enter CORBACCIO

CORBACCIO

Why! how now? Mosca!

Enter VOLTORE *unseen*

MOSCA   O, undone, amazed, sir.
Your son – I know not by what accident –
Acquainted with your purpose to my patron
Touching your will, and making him your heir,
Entered our house with violence, his sword drawn,   5
Sought for you, called you wretch, unnatural,
Vowed he would kill you.

CORBACCIO   Me?

MOSCA   Yes, and my patron.

CORBACCIO

This act shall disinherit him indeed;
Here is the will.

MOSCA   'Tis well, sir.

CORBACCIO   Right and well.
Be you as careful now for me.

MOSCA   My life, sir,   10
Is not more tendered; I am only yours.

CORBACCIO

How does he? will he die shortly, thinkst thou?

MOSCA   I fear
He'll outlast May.

13 Today?:   *Corbaccio is still deaf!*

14 a dram: *dose of medicine; Corbaccio, of course, means a fatal overdose.*

17–18 Scarce . . . tricks: *Voltore replies sarcastically that he can scarcely be welcome at a time when he has just overheard Mosca double-crossing him. For Mosca (and Volpone) crisis is now following ever more rapidly on crisis, so that more and more ingenuity is needed for survival. There is plenty of ingenuity left, however. Their exhilarating triumphs over mounting external threats seem gradually to create the play's final logic: in the end, we feel that they can only be defeated by each other.*

22 Put not your foists . . . scent 'em: *Don't try your trickery on me; I shall see through it.*

CORBACCIO   Today?

MOSCA   No, last out May, sir.

CORBACCCIO

  Couldst thou not gi' him a dram?

MOSCA   O, by no means, sir.

CORBACCIO

  Nay, I'll not bid you.

                                        Walks aside

VOLTORE (*Aside*)   This is a knave, I see.   15

MOSCA (*Aside*)

  How! Signior Voltore! did he hear me?

VOLTORE   Parasite!

MOSCA

  Who's that? O, sir, most timely welcome –

~~VOLPONE~~   Scarce

  To the discovery of your tricks, I fear.

  You are his, only? and mine, also? are you not?

MOSCA

  Who? I, sir!

VOLTORE   You, sir. What device is this   20

  About a will?

MOSCA   A plot for you, sir.

VOLTORE   Come,

  Put not your foists upon me, I shall scent 'em.

MOSCA

  Did you not hear it?

VOLTORE   Yes, I hear Corbaccio

  Hath made your patron there his heir.

MOSCA   'Tis true,

  By my device, drawn to it by my plot,   25

  With hope –

VOLTORE   Your patron should reciprocate?

  And you have promised?

MOSCA   For your good, I did, sir.

  Nay more, I told his son, brought, hid him here,

  Where he might hear his father pass the deed;

32   disclaiming in him: *disowning his son's legal claim on him.*
(Mosca now finds a useful variation on the lie he told to Corbaccio
concerning Bonario's supposed violent intentions.)

36   you be stated in a double hope: *with Corbaccio dead and*
Bonario imprisoned, Voltore would have hopes not only of Vol-
pone's existing wealth but the addition to it of Corbaccio's legacy.
The size of this appeal to his greed, together with Mosca's per-
suasive   fervour,   is   quite   enough   to   pacify   Voltore.
(stated: *established.*)

39   sepulchres: *tombs; i.e. the two decrepit old men, Volpone and*
Corbaccio.

41   change: *reversal of hopes.*

42   success: *outcome.*
      hapless: *unlucky.*

55   'Scrutineo':   *law court in the Senate House.*

Being persuaded to it by this thought, sir,   30
That the unnaturalness, first, of the act,
And then, his father's oft disclaiming in him –
Which I did mean t'help on – would sure enrage him
To do some violence upon his parent,
On which the law should take sufficient hold,   35
And you be stated in a double hope.
Truth be my comfort, and my conscience,
My only aim was to dig you a fortune
Out of these two, old rotten sepulchres –

VOLTORE
  I cry thee mercy, Mosca.

MOSCA   – worth your patience   40
  And your great merit, sir. And, see the change!

VOLTORE
  Why? what success?

MOSCA   Most hapless! you must help, sir.
  Whilst we expected th' old raven, in comes
  Corvino's wife, sent hither by her husband –

VOLTORE
  What, with a present?

MOSCA   No, sir, on visitation   45
  (I'll tell you how anon), and, staying long,
  The youth, he grows impatient, rushes forth,
  Seizeth the lady, wounds me, makes her swear
  (Or he would murder her, that was his vow)
  T'affirm my patron to have done her rape;   50
  Which how unlike it is, you see! and hence,
  With that pretext, he's gone, t'accuse his father,
  Defame my patron, defeat you –

VOLTORE   Where's her husband?
  Let him be sent for straight.

MOSCA   Sir, I'll go fetch him.

VOLTORE
  Bring him to the *Scrutineo*.

MOSCA   Sir, I will.   55

175

58 counsel: *judgement*.

60 clerks: *scholars*.

VOLTORE

This must be stopped.

MOSCA   O, you do nobly, sir.

Alas, 'twas laboured all, sir, for your good;
Nor was there any want of counsel in the plot;
But fortune can, at any time, o'erthrow
The projects of a hundred learned clerks, sir.   60

CORBACCIO (*Overhearing*)

What's that?

VOLTORE   Wilt please you, sir, to go along?

Exeunt CORBACCIO, VOLTORE

MOSCA

Patron, go in and pray for our success.

VOLPONE

Need makes devotion; Heaven your labour bless.

Exeunt

1-2 you see/What observation is: *you see what you can do by keeping your eyes open and your wits about you.*

2-3 You mentioned ... instructions: *You referred to me as someone who could give you some useful tips about travelling. (If Peregrine did this, it was only to provoke such idiocy as he is now about to enjoy.)*

4 height: *latitude.*

6 Only for this meridian: *with this place specially in mind.*

6-10 fit ... themes: *Sir Politic uses 'your' in this exchange to suggest his friendliness towards Peregrine and his knowledge of the subject they are talking about: it is an easy colloquialism. Peregrine pretends to misunderstand him and take the word as a personal affront.*

8 phrase: *form of expression.*

9 old: *i.e. old, familiar stuff.*

10 themes: *topics.*

11 I'll ... wit: *thinking that Sir Politic has been too stupid to see his joke, Peregrine says, 'I will never again misrepresent you by calling you witty'.*

12 garb: *demeanour.*

13 Very reserved and locked: *travellers were commonly advised to be friendly but secretive.*

14-15 scarce/A fable ... caution: *don't even tell a story without thinking carefully first.*

17 strangers: *foreigners.*

20 So as I still might be a saver in 'em: *So that I can always escape the trouble they might cause me.*

21 tricks, else, ... hourly: *Sir Politic is a most nervous and insecure traveller, for all his pompous expertise. He thinks everyone is out to deceive and swindle him.*

22-5 And then ... content you: *This is Sir Politic's second hackneyed rule for travellers: 'When in Rome, do as the Romans do'. In this case the advice amounts to a pretence of atheism, and subordination of religion to politics and law. This was a viewpoint commonly attributed to Italians.*

Act Four

Scene one

A Street
Enter SIR POLITIC WOULD-BE, PEREGRINE

SIR POLITIC
    I told you, sir, it was a plot, you see
    What observation is. You mentioned me
    For some instructions: I will tell you, sir,
    (Since we are met here in this height of Venice)
    Some few particulars I have set down   5
    Only for this meridian; fit to be known
    Of your crude traveller, and they are these.
    I will not touch, sir, at your phrase, or clothes,
    For they are old.
PEREGRINE   Sir, I have better.
SIR POLITIC   Pardon,
    I meant, as they are themes.
PEREGRINE   O, sir, proceed;   10
    I'll slander you no more of wit, good sir.
SIR POLITIC
    First, for your garb, it must be grave and serious;
    Very reserved and locked; not tell a secret
    On any term, not to your father; scarce
    A fable but with caution; make sure choice   15
    Both of your company and discourse; beware
    You never speak a truth –
PEREGRINE   How!
SIR POLITIC   Not to strangers,
    For those be they you must converse with most;
    Others I would not know, sir, but at distance,
    So as I still might be a saver in 'em;   20
    You shall have tricks, else, passed upon you hourly.
    And then, for your religion, profess none,

179

26–7 Nick Machiavel . . . Bodin . . . this mind: *in fact neither of these two great political scientists held the views which Sir Politic imposes on them. Niccolo Macchiavelli (1469–1527), author of The Prince, a guide to efficient statecraft, argued that the welfare of the state justified any means required to sustain it. He did not scorn religion, but recognized its potential for political divisiveness. Jean Bodin (1530–96) adopted some elements of Machiavelli's thought and expounded an argument for religious toleration, which caused him to be quite unfairly accused of atheism. Jonson is showing (to those who were well-informed enough to notice it) how much Sir Politic's opinions are the slaves of fashionable prejudice.*

28 fork: *the table fork was first introduced in Italy, and admired by foreigners as a mark of refined table manners.*

29 metal: *material used for glassmaking, in a molten state. Sir Politic is using a roundabout way of praising fine glassware and stressing the need to use it skilfully.*
main: *important.*

32 point of state: *question of diplomacy.*

34 Preposterous: *acting contrary to reason or convention.*
he has him straight: *he sums him up straightaway.*

40 Contarini: *Gasparo Contarini wrote a famous work on the Venetian constitution.*

41 my Jews: *Jews were safe in Venice, but strictly controlled. Cheap moneylending was one of their major roles, and the one which probably mattered to the impoverished Sir Politic.*

45 command: *insist on.*

46 projects: *Projects were schemes with some hope of winning the grant of a royal monopoly. Usually they were in the hands of speculators ('projectors') aiming to defraud the public. Sir Politic, however, is genuinely enthusiastic about his 'projects', which are only a degree more fantastic than some examples of the real thing.*

47 discover: *reveal.*

But wonder at the diversity of all;
And, for your part, protest, were there no other
But simply the laws o' th' land, you could content you;   25
Nick Machiavel and Monsieur Bodin, both
Were of this mind. Then, must you learn the use
And handling of your silver fork at meals;
The metal of your glass (these are main matters
With your Italian) and to know the hour   30
When you must eat your melons and your figs.

PEREGRINE
  Is that a point of state, too?

SIR POLITIC   Here it is.
  For your Venetian, if he see a man
  Preposterous in the least, he has him straight;
  He has, he strips him. I'll acquaint you, sir.   35
  I now have lived here ... 'tis some fourteen months;
  Within the first week of my landing here,
  All took me for a citizen of Venice,
  I knew the forms so well –

PEREGRINE (*Aside*)   And nothing else.

SIR POLITIC
  I had read Contarini, took me a house,   40
  Dealt with my Jews, to furnish it with movables ...
  Well, if I could but find one man ... one man
  To mine own heart, whom I durst trust ... I would ...

PEREGRINE
  What? what, sir?

SIR POLITIC   Make him rich; make him a fortune;
  He should not think again. I would command it.   45

PEREGRINE
  As how?

SIR POLITIC With certain projects that I have,
  Which I may not discover.

PEREGRINE (*Aside*)   If I had
  But one to wager with, I would lay odds now
  He tells me instantly.

51 red herrings: *nothing to do with the modern expression of 'red herring', meaning 'something to lay a false scent'. Red herrings were popular delicacies. However, Venice already had a good supply both of red herrings and of fish in general.*

53 correspondence: *correspondents, agents.*

54 one o' th' States: *member of the Dutch States–General.*
to that purpose: *about this matter.*

56 chandler: *candle-seller and grocer (because the paper is greasy).*

57 other: *others.*

60 I've cast it all: *I've worked it all out.*
hoy: *small coastal vessel.*

62 returns: *round trips.*

63 if there come ... I save: *if only one of the three voyages is completed safely, I shall cover my expenses.*

64 If two ... defalk: *if two come home, I can reduce my prices and still make a profit. (To 'defalk' is to allow a deduction.)*

66 draw the subtle air: *breathe the atmosphere of intrigue.*

69 considerative: *thoughtful.*

71 goods: *benefits.*

72 cautions: *precautions.*

74–5 Great Council ... Forty ... Ten: *the hierarchy of administrative bodies under the Venetian constitution.*

75 My means ... already: *My contacts with the administrative bodies are already established.*

77 he can sway: *he has influence.*

SIR POLITIC   One is (and that
  I care not greatly who knows) to serve the state   50
  Of Venice with red herrings for three years,
  And at a certain rate, from Rotterdam,
  Where I have correspondence. There's a letter,
  Sent me from one o' th' States, and to that purpose;
  He cannot write his name, but that's his mark.   55

PEREGRINE
  He is a chandler?

SIR POLITIC   No, a cheesemonger.
  There are some other too with whom I treat
  About the same negotiation;
  And I will undertake it; for, 'tis thus,
  I'll do't with ease, I've cast it all. Your hoy   60
  Carries but three men in her, and a boy;
  And she shall make me three returns a year;
  So, if there come but one of three, I save,
  If two, I can defalk. But this is now
  If my main project fail.

PEREGRINE   Then you have others?   65

SIR POLITIC
  I should be loath to draw the subtle air
  Of such a place without my thousand aims.
  I'll not dissemble, sir; where'er I come
  I love to be considerative; and 'tis true
  I have at my free hours thought upon   70
  Some certain goods unto the state of Venice,
  Which I do call my cautions; and, sir, which
  I mean, in hope of pension, to propound
  To the Great Council, then unto the Forty,
  So to the Ten. My means are made already –   75

PEREGRINE
  By whom?

SIR POLITIC Sir, one, that though his place be obscure,
  Yet, he can sway, and they will hear him. He's
  A *commandadore*

78   sergeant: *minor court official, charged with arresting offenders.*

79–80 such . . . greater: *such minor officials as this sometimes tell those in authority what to say, just as greater persons do.*

82   on your gentry: *on your honour as a gentleman.*
83   Not to anticipate: *not to try to steal any advantage.*

84   A circumstance: *any detail.*

86   tinder-boxes: *metal boxes containing the equipment for making a fire.*

89   Put case: *let's suppose.*
     ill affected: *hostile, ill-disposed.*
91   'Arsenale':   *Arsenal, the centre of maintenance for the Venetian navy.*

93   Go to, then: *very well, then.*
94   Advèrtise: *make known.*

96   suffered: *allowed.*
97   T'enjoy them: *to have the benefit of tinder-boxes.*
98   Sealed: *registered under a seal.*

101   present demonstration: *immediate test.*

PEREGRINE   What, a common sergeant?
SIR POLITIC
  Sir, such as they are, put it in their mouths,
  What they should say, sometimes, as well as greater.   80
  I think I have my notes, to show you –

Searching his pockets

PEREGRINE   Good, sir.
SIR POLITIC
  But you shall swear unto me, on your gentry,
  Not to anticipate –
PEREGRINE   I, sir?
SIR POLITIC   Nor reveal
  A circumstance – My paper is not with me.
PEREGRINE
  O, but you can remember, sir.
SIR POLITIC   My first is,   85
  Concerning tinder-boxes. You must know,
  No family is here without its box.
  Now sir, it being so portable a thing,
  Put case, that you or I were ill affected
  Unto the state; sir, with it in our pockets,   90
  Might not I go into the *Arsenale*?
  Or you? come out again? and none the wiser?
PEREGRINE
  Except yourself, sir.
SIR POLITIC   Go to, then. I, therefore,
  Advèrtise to the state, how fit it were,
  That none but such as were known patriots,   95
  Sound lovers of their country, should be suffered
  T'enjoy them in their houses; and even those
  Sealed at some office, and at such a bigness,
  As might not lurk in pockets.
PEREGRINE   Admirable!
SIR POLITIC
  My next is, how t'enquire, and be resolved   100
  By present demonstration, whether a ship,

185

102 'Soria': *Syria.*

104 where they use: *whereas the usual procedure is.*

105 lie out: *lie off shore, in quarantine.*

106 'Lazaretto': *quarantine hospital. At this period Venice had two such hospitals on outlying islands, and ships suspected of carrying the plague would be made to remain in quarantine off these islands before they were allowed to enter the city.*

for their trial: *to see whether or not they are carrying the plague.*

108 clear the doubt: *remove the uncertainty.*

109 I will lose my labour: *I'm wasting my time.*

110 conceive me: *understand me.*

onions: *peeled onions were believed to absorb into themselves any plague infection near them.*

111 'livres': *French coins.*

112 water-works: *equipment operated by water.*

114 venture: *provide the money for.*

115 strain: *stretch.*

124 By his changed colour: *Sir Politic believes that the presence of plague will change the colour of the onions.*

126 Now 'tis known, 'tis nothing: *Now that I have told you, it seems self-evident.*

Newly arrivèd from *Soria,* or from
Any suspected part of all the Levant,
Be guilty of the plague; and, where they use
To lie out forty, fifty days, sometimes,   105
About the *Lazaretto* for their trial,
I'll save that charge and loss unto the merchant,
And, in an hour, clear the doubt.

PEREGRINE   Indeed, sir?

SIR POLITIC

Or – I will lose my labour.

PEREGRINE   My faith, that's much.

SIR POLITIC

Nay, sir, conceive me. 'Twill cost me, in onions,   110
Some thirty *livres* –

PEREGRINE   Which is one pound sterling.

SIR POLITIC

Beside my water-works; for this I do, sir.
First, I bring in your ship 'twixt two brick walls
(But those the state shall venture); on the one
I strain me a fair tarpaulin; and in that   115
I stick my onions, cut in halves; the other
Is full of loopholes, out at which I thrust
The noses of my bellows; and those bellows
I keep with waterworks in perpetual motion
(Which is the easiest matter of a hundred).   120
Now, sir, your onion, which doth naturally
Attract th'infection, and your bellows blowing
The air upon him, will show – instantly –
By his changed colour, if there be contagion;
Or else, remain as fair as at the first.   125
Now 'tis known, 'tis nothing.

PEREGRINE   You are right, sir.

SIR POLITIC

I would I had my note.

PEREGRINE   Faith, so would I;
But, you ha' done well, for once, sir.

128 false: *treacherous.*

130 sell: *betray.*

138 I threw three beans over the threshold: *Sir Politic is su-*
perstitious. Some details of his precautions are drawn from Theo-
phrastus' portrait of a superstitious man. Throwing three stones
across the road was one such practice, while beans figured in vari-
ous superstitions and magical customs.

139 toothpicks: *the art of using toothpicks delicately was essential*
for the sophisticated traveller. Sir Politic, obviously waving his
about to emphasize a point in his argument, has managed to break
it straight after purchase.

141 'ragion del stato': *affairs of state.*

142 'moccenigo': *coin of little value.*

143 piecing: *mending.*

144 cheapened: *haggled over.*

145 politic: *shrewd: with a play on Sir Politic's name – 'just what*
I'd have expected of you'.
slip: *pass over.*

146 quote it: *note it down.*

1 loose: *(i) 'on the loose'; (ii) dissolute.*
housed: *i.e. indoors with his prostitute. (See Act III Scene V*
line 20.)

SIR POLITIC   Were I false,
  Or would be made so, I could show you reasons
  How I could sell this state, now, to the Turk;   130
  Spite of their galleys, or their –
                                    Examining his papers
PEREGRINE   Pray you, Sir Pol.
SIR POLITIC
  I have 'em not about me.
PEREGRINE   That I feared.
  They're there, sir?
SIR POLITIC   No, this is my diary,
  Wherein I note my actions of the day.
PEREGRINE
  Pray you, let's see, sir. What is here? '*Notandum,*   135
  A rat had gnawn my spur-leathers; notwithstanding,
  I put on new, and did go forth; but first
  I threw three beans over the threshold. *Item,*
  I went and bought two toothpicks, whereof one
  I burst immediately, in a discourse   140
  With a Dutch merchant 'bout *ragion del stato.*
  From him I went and paid a *moccenigo*
  For piecing my silk stockings; by the way
  I cheapened sprats; and at St Mark's, I urined.'
  Faith, these are politic notes!
SIR POLITIC   Sir, I do slip   145
  No action of my life, thus but I quote it.
PEREGRINE
  Believe me it is wise!
SIR POLITIC   Nay, sir, read forth.

(*Scene two*)

Enter at a distance LADY WOULD-BE, NANO, *two* WOMEN
LADY WOULD-BE
  Where should this loose knight be, trow? sure, he's housed.

2 fast: *i.e. locked safely away. A play on the expression 'fast and loose' (also the name of a game: see the note to Act I Scene II line 8).*

3 stay: *stop and rest.*

5 I do not care . . . take him: *I do not wish to hinder him from meeting his prostitute, but to catch him at his dirty work!*

7 That same's the party!:   *Lady Would-be sees Peregrine, and assumes that he is the prostitute in male disguise. She is too clever to be fooled by such a trick!*

10 demerit: *deserves blame.*

12 Were she not mine: *though it isn't for me to praise her.*

16 Being your wife, . . . miss that: *If she is your wife, she is bound to be good at talking.*

18 None?:   *Lady Would-be takes the first opportunity to show that she has seen through Peregrine's 'disguise'.*

19 Has put his face . . . world: *Has ventured abroad at so early an age.*

20 as early? but today?:   *Lady Would-be sarcastically suggests that Peregrine's venture into the world dates only from that morning, when he put on his male disguise.*

NANO

  Why, then he's fast.

LADY WOULD-BE   Ay, he plays both with me.

  I pray you, stay. This heat will do more harm

  To my complexion than his heart is worth.

  (I do not care to hinder, but to take him).   5

  How it comes off!

                                        Touching her make-up

1st WOMAN   My master's yonder.

LADY WOULD-BE   Where?

2nd WOMAN

  With a young gentleman.

LADY WOULD-BE   That same's the party!

  In man's apparel. Pray you, sir, jog my knight;

  I will be tender to his reputation,

  However he demerit.

SIR POLITIC   My lady!

PEREGRINE   Where?   10

SIR POLITIC

  'Tis she indeed, sir, you shall know her. She is,

  Were she not mine, a lady of that merit

  For fashion, and behaviour, and for beauty

  I durst compare –

PEREGRINE   It seems you are not jealous,

  That dare commend her.

SIR POLITIC   Nay, and for discourse –   15

PEREGRINE

  Being your wife, she cannot miss that.

SIR POLITIC (*As the groups meet*)   Madam,

  Here is a gentleman, pray you, use him fairly;

  He seems a youth, but he is –

LADY WOULD-BE   None?

SIR POLITIC   Yes, one,

  Has put his face as soon into the world –

LADY WOULD-BE

  You mean, as early? but today?

21 habit: *dress.*

23 odour: *reputation.*

25 massàcre: *The word could then be stressed on the second syllable, as here.*

30 humbled for an oath: *Peregrine mocks the trivial oath 'by my spurs', which Sir Politic chooses as the mark of his knighthood. Jonson is covertly poking fun at James I's profuse distribution of knighthoods.*

31 reach: *understand.*

31–2 your polity ... through thus: *your diplomatic trickery may seek to carry the affair off like this.*

35 Froward: *perverse, unseemly.*
'The Courtier': *Castiglione's classic study of courtliness,* The Courtier *(1528), is cited here by Lady Would-be as her chosen guide to behaviour. In fact Lady Would-be's conduct is virtually the opposite of that which Castiglione recommends.*

41 persèver: *persevere.*

42–3 is not warranted ... solecism: *does not escape the charge of impropriety. (Lady Would-be is pretentious, trying to speak with what she regards as tact and delicacy of feeling.)*

45 Come nearer to your aim: *speak more plainly.*

SIR POLITIC How's this! 20
LADY WOULD-BE
  Why, in this habit, sir, you apprehend me.
  Well, Master Would-be, this doth not become you;
  I had thought the odour, sir, of your good name
  Had been more precious to you; that you would not
  Have done this dire massàcre on your honour; 25
  One of your gravity and rank besides!
  But, knights, I see, care little for the oath
  They make to ladies – chiefly, their own ladies.
SIR POLITIC
  Now, by my spurs, the symbol of my knight-hood –
PEREGRINE (*Aside*)
  Lord! how his brain is humbled for an oath. 30
SIR POLITIC
  I reach you not.
LADY WOULD-BE Right, sir, your polity
  May bear it through thus. (*To* PEREGRINE) Sir, a word
    with you.
  I would be loath to contest publicly
  With any gentlewoman; or to seem
  Froward or violent (as *The Courtier* says) 35
  It comes too near rusticity in a lady,
  Which I would shun by all means; and, however
  I may deserve from Master Would-be, yet
  T'have one fair gentlewoman thus be made
  Th'unkind instrument to wrong another, 40
  And one she knows not – ay, and to persèver –
  In my poor judgement is not warranted
  From being a solecism in our sex,
  If not in manners.
PEREGRINE How is this!
SIR POLITIC Sweet Madam,
  Come nearer to your aim.
LADY WOULD-BE Marry, and will, sir. 45
  Since you provoke me with your impudence

47 light: *wanton.*

land-siren: *Sirens were figures in ancient myth who lured sailors to their deaths on a small island by the attraction of their singing. Peregrine, says Lady Would-be, has likewise lured Sir Politic to his downfall, but on land instead of water.*

48 Sporus: *Sporus was a eunuch, the favourite of Nero.*

hermaphrodite: *one who has both male and female characteristics.*

49 Poetic fury . . . storms!: *rage which takes its extravagant expression both from poetry (the Sirens) and history (Sporus).*

51 Whitefriars nation: *i.e. prostitute. Whitefriars was an area between Fleet Street and the River Thames in London. It retained rights of sanctuary dating from the times when a Carmelite priory stood there, and hence offered safety to prostitutes and other low characters. A 'nation' is a class of people.*

53 forehead: *modesty.*

55 fricatrice: *prostitute.*

57 And: *if.*

58 liquid: *open, transparent. (Sir Politic is gullible enough to believe his wife's absurd invention.)*

59 you may carry't . . . state-face!: *you can try to pass it off, with that pretence of solemn innocence.*

60 carnival concupiscence: *Lady Would-be's version of 'carnal concupiscent' or 'lecherous woman'. Jonson is also referring through Lady Would-be's linguistic errors to the riotous revelry or 'carnival' which preceded Lent in Catholic countries.*

61–2 for liberty . . . marshal: *the expression 'liberty of conscience' means 'freedom from religious persecution'. Lady Would-be sarcastically likens the profession of prostitute to a kind of religion, and suggests that Peregrine has fled from the 'persecution' of the marshal, or gaoler.*

63 disple: *discipline, whip.*

64 do you use this often?: *do you often behave like this?*

65 'gainst you have occasion: *whenever you have the opportunity.*

69 A nearer way: *without all this fuss.*

And laughter of your light land-siren here,
Your Sporus, your hermaphrodite –
PEREGRINE   What's here?
Poetic fury, and historic storms!
SIR POLITIC
The gentleman, believe it, is of worth,   50
And of our nation.
LADY WOULD-BE   Ay, your Whitefriars nation!
Come, I blush for you, Master Would-be, ay!
And am ashamed you should ha' no more forehead
Than thus to be the patron, or St George,
To a lewd harlot, a base fricatrice,   55
A female devil in a male outside.
SIR POLITIC (*To* PEREGRINE)   Nay,
And you be such a one, I must bid adieu
To your delights! The case appears too liquid.
                                                    Going

LADY WOULD-BE
Ay, you may carry 't clear, with your state-face!
But, for your carnival concupiscence,   60
Who here is fled for liberty of conscience,
From furious persecution of the marshal,
Her will I disple.
                                            Exit SIR POLITIC
PEREGRINE   This is fine, i'faith!
And do you use this often? is this part
Of your wit's exercise, 'gainst you have occasion?   65
Madam –
LADY WOULD-BE Go to, sir.
                    Snatching hold of PEREGRINE's *clothing*
PEREGRINE   Do you hear me, lady?
Why if your knight have set you to beg shirts,
Or to invite me home, you might have done it
A nearer way, by far.
LADY WOULD-BE   This cannot work you
Out of my snare.

195

73 queen-apple: *variety of apple noted for its redness. Peregrine,*
whose temper is getting the better of his amusement, rudely remarks
that Lady Would-be's nose is red on one side.

2 Right not my quest: *Doesn't do me justice in this petition.*
protest: *proclaim.*
3 no aristocracy: *not a true aristocracy (i.e. the council of state*
would not, in Lady Would-be's view, be made up of the noblest
citizens).
4 callet: *whore.*

Holding on still

PEREGRINE   Why? am I in it, then?   70

Indeed, your husband told me you were fair,
And so you are; only your nose inclines –
That side that's next the sun – to the queen-apple.

LADY WOULD-BE

This cannot be endured by any patience.

(*Scene three*)

Enter MOSCA

MOSCA

What's the matter, madam?

LADY WOULD-BE   If the Senate

Right not my quest in this, I will protest 'em,
To all the world, no aristocracy.

MOSCA

What is the injury, lady?

LADY WOULD-BE   Why, the callet

You told me of, here I have ta'en disguised.   5

MOSCA

Who? this? what means your ladyship? the creature
I mentioned to you is apprehended now,
Before the Senate; you shall see her –

LADY WOULD-BE   Where?

MOSCA

I'll bring you to her. This young gentleman,
I saw him land this morning at the port.   10

LADY WOULD-BE

Is't possible! How has my judgment wandered!
Sir, I must, blushing, say to you, I have erred,
And plead your pardon.

PEREGRINE   What! more changes yet?

16 use me: *let me do what I can for you. (The offer is not mere politeness: it implies that sexual services will be available!)*

18 conceive: *believe (but 'conceive' also continues the sexual innuendo).*

20 Sir Politic Bawd: *because of Lady Would-be's advances, Peregrine now suspects that the whole rowdy scene has been designed to instigate a sexual relationship between himself and Lady Would-be, with Sir Politic acting as her bawd, or go-between.*
22–3 practised . . . freshmanship: *plotted against my inexperience.*
23 salt: *(i) salacious, (ii) seasoned, experienced.*

1 the carriage of the business: *how the affair is to be managed. (The legacy-hunters with Mosca are gathered at the law court, where Celia and Bonario have made their accusing statements.)*
2 constancy: *(i) level-headedness; (ii) consistency in the statements you make.*
4 Safely conveyed: *circulated to ensure its consistency.*
5 burden: *refrain (hence the 'lines' of an actor's part).*

6 the advocate: *i.e. Voltore. Corvino and Corbaccio are both involved in the legal dispute. Voltore has been employed to represent them and lie on their behalf.*

LADY WOULD-BE
    I hope you ha' not the malice to remember
    A gentlewoman's passion. If you stay   15
    In Venice here, please you to use me, sir –
MOSCA
    Will you go madam?
LADY WOULD-BE   Pray you, sir, use me. In faith,
    The more you see me, the more I shall conceive,
    You have forgot our quarrel.
                    Exeunt all except PEREGRINE
PEREGRINE   This is rare!
    Sir Politic Would-be? no, Sir Politic Bawd!   20
    To bring me thus acquainted with his wife!
    Well, wise Sir Pol, since you have practised thus
    Upon my freshmanship, I'll try your salt-head,
    What proof it is against a counter-plot.   *Exit*

Scene four

The Scrutineo
Enter VOLTORE, CORBACCIO, CORVINO, MOSCA
VOLTORE
    Well, now you know the carriage of the business,
    Your constancy is all that is required
    Unto the safety of it.
MOSCA   Is the lie
    Safely conveyed amongst us? is that sure?
    Knows every man his burden?
CORVINO   Yes.
MOSCA   Then shrink not.   5
CORVINO (*Aside to* MOSCA)
    But knows the advocate the truth?
MOSCA   O, sir,
    By no means. I devised a formal tale

8   salved: *healed.*

10   make him stand for a co-heir: *cause him to win Volpone's gratitude and hence a share in the legacy.*

12   Croaker: *i.e. Corbaccio.*

14   mummia: *the flesh of Egyptian mummies was valued for its medicinal powers. Fake mummia was made from baked corpses.*

15   buffalo: *buffaloes are horned; Corvino has a cuckold's 'horns'.*

16   sport it with his head!: *Corvino, trying on Mosca's orders to be 'valiant', is holding his head high as he walks about.*

17–20: *Mosca reassures each of the suitors in turn that he will be the one to receive Volpone's legacy. His management of the multiple deception calls on all his speed and skill. At this stage each must have his confidence boosted under the very noses of the others.*

20   Much!: *That's what he thinks!*

21   Mercury: *the messenger of the gods; also the patron of those who live by their wits.*

22   French Hercules: *Hercules' tenth task was to capture the oxen of Geryon, who dwelt in the far west. On his return he fathered the founders of the Celtic race in Gaul. This 'French Hercules' was the symbol of eloquence, in which the conspirators now hope that Voltore will prove skilful. In 'French Hercules' such eloquence is an ideal quality; in Voltore, by ironic contrast, it will be used to pervert justice.*

23   club: *i.e. the weapon for which Hercules was more generally famous than his tongue.*

26   another witness: *i.e. Lady Politic Would-be.*

That salved your reputation. But be valiant, sir.

CORVINO

I fear no one but him; that this his pleading
Should make him stand for a co-heir –

MOSCA   Co-halter!   10

Hang him. We will but use his tongue, his noise,
As we do Croaker's here.

Pointing to CORBACCIO

CORVINO   Ay, what shall he do?

MOSCA

When we ha' done, you mean?

CORVINO   Yes.

MOSCA   Why, we'll think –

Sell him for mummia, he's half dust already.

(*To* VOLTORE) Do not you smile to see this buffalo,   15

(*Pointing to* CORVINO)

How he doth sport it with his head! – (*Aside*) I should,
If all were well and past.(*To* CORBACCIO) Sir, only you
Are he, that shall enjoy the crop of all,
And these not know for whom they toil.

CORBACCIO   Ay, peace.

MOSCA (*To* CORVINO)

But you shall eat it. (*Then to* VOLTORE *again*) Much!

Worshipful sir,   20

Mercury sit upon your thund'ring tongue,
Or the French Hercules, and make your language
As conquering as his club, to beat along,
As with a tempest, flat, our adversaries;
But much more yours, sir.

VOLTORE   Here they come, ha' done.   25

MOSCA

I have another witness, if you need, sir,
I can produce.

VOLTORE   Who is it?

MOSCA   Sir, I have her.

9 example: *precedent.*
And all after times!: *And will not be equalled in the future,*
either!

11 those were cited: *those who were summoned as witnesses.*

12 magnifico: *Venetian title.*

(*Scene five*)

Enter four AVOCATORI, BONARIO, CELIA, NOTARIO, COMMANDADORI, etc.

1st AVOCATORE
   The like of this the Senate never heard of.

2nd AVOCATORE
   'Twill come most strange to them when we report it.

4th AVOCATORE
   The gentlewoman has been ever held
   Of unreprovèd name.

3rd AVOCATORE   So the young man.

4th AVOCATORE
   The more unnatural part that of his father.   5

2nd AVOCATORE
   More of the husband.

1st AVOCATORE   I do not know to give
   His act a name, it is so monstrous!

4th AVOCATORE
   But the imposter, he is a thing created
   T'exceed example!

1st AVOCATORE   And all after times!

2nd AVOCATORE
   I never heard a true voluptuary   10
   Described but him.

3rd AVOCATORE   Appear yet those were cited?

NOTARIO
   All but the old magnifico, Volpone.

1st AVOCATORE
   Why is not he here?

MOSCA   Please your fatherhoods,
   Here is his advocate. Himself's so weak,
   So feeble –

4th AVOCATORE What are you?

BONARIO   His parasite,   15
   His knave, his pandar. I beseech the court

25 he may be heard in me: *I may speak on his behalf.*

27 crave it: *i.e. beg to speak as his representative.*

30 Discover: *reveal.*
31 frontless: *shameless.*

35 wants: *lacks.*
36 visor: *mask.*
37 close: (*i*) *secret;* (*ii*) *intimate.*

40 easy: *lenient.*
41 timeless: *untimely, ill judged.*

He may be forced to come, that your grave eyes
May bear strong witness of his strange impostures.

VOLTORE

Upon my faith and credit with your virtues,
He is not able to endure the air.   20

2nd AVOCATORE

Bring him, however.

3rd AVOCATORE   We will see him.

4th AVOCATORE   Fetch him.

Exeunt officers

VOLTORE

Your fatherhoods' fit pleasures be obeyed,
But sure, the sight will rather move your pities
Than indignation. May it please the court,
In the meantime, he may be heard in me.   25
I know this place most void of prejudice,
And therefore crave it, since we have no reason
To fear our truth should hurt our cause.

3rd AVOCATORE   Speak free.

VOLTORE

Then know, most honoured fathers, I must now
Discover to your strangely abusèd ears   30
The most prodigious and most frontless piece
Of solid impudence and treachery
That ever vicious nature yet brought forth
To shame the state of Venice. This lewd woman
                                        (*Pointing to* CELIA)
(That wants no artificial looks or tears   35
To help the visor she has now put on)
Hath long been known a close adulteress
To that lascivious youth there; (*Pointing to* BONARIO) not
   suspected,
I say, but known; and taken in the act
With him; and by this man, the easy husband,   40
                                        (*Pointing to* CORVINO)
Pardoned; whose timeless bounty makes him now

205

44–7 For these . . . benefit: *for Celia and Bonario, not knowing how to acknowledge the generosity of such rare forgiveness except by admitting their shame – Corvino's powers of generosity being far beyond their powers of gratitude – instead began to hate the good deed that Corvino had done for them.*

48 extirp: *root out.*

51 heart: *encouragement to further boldness.*

54 fact: *crime.*

59 turns: *i.e. turns of events.*

60 fame: *reputation.*

64 this settled purpose: *fixed determination to disinherit Bonario.*

66 the deed: *the legal act of disinheritance.*

70–1 designed/For the inheritance: *chosen to replace Bonario as the inheritor.*

Stand here, the most unhappy, innocent person
That ever man's own goodness made accused.
For these, not knowing how to owe a gift
Of that dear grace but with their shame – being placed   45
So above all powers of their gratitude –
Began to hate the benefit; and, in place
Of thanks, devise t'extirp the memory
Of such an act. Wherein, I pray your fatherhoods
To observe the malice, yea, the rage of creatures   50
Discovered in their evils; and what heart
Such take, even from their crimes. But that, anon,
Will more appear. This gentleman, the father,
                              (*Pointing to* CORBACCIO)
Hearing of this foul fact, with many others,
Which daily struck at his too tender ears,   55
And grieved in nothing more than that he could not
Preserve himself a parent (his son's ills
Growing to that strange flood) at last decreed
To disinherit him.

1st AVOCATORE   These be strange turns!

2nd AVOCATORE
    The young man's fame was ever fair and honest.   60

VOLTORE
    So much more full of danger is his vice,
    That can beguile so, under shade of virtue.
    But as I said, my honoured sires, his father
    Having this settled purpose (by what means
    To him betrayed, we know not) and this day   65
    Appointed for the deed; that parricide
    (I cannot style him better) by confederacy
    Preparing this his paramour to be there,
    Entered Volpone's house (who was the man
    Your fatherhoods must understand, designed   70
    For the inheritance), there sought his father.
    But with what purpose sought he him, my lords?
    I tremble to pronounce it, that a son

76 It was, to murder him!: *this is the key motive which the conspirators have invented to explain Bonario's actions and discredit him.*

79 Mischief . . . begins: *Crime is remorseless in carrying its purposes through.*

85 stale to his forged practice: *decoy in his deceitful plot.*

87 to note but my collections: *to take special note of my conclusions.*

89 ends: *intentions.*

89–90 discredit . . . gentleman: *show that Corbaccio was misguided in freely choosing Volpone as his heir.*

92 owe: *confess that they owe.*

97 sols: *small coins.*

Unto a father, and to such a father,
Should have so foul, felonious intent.   75
It was, to murder him! When, being prevented
By his more happy absence, what then did he?
Not check his wicked thoughts; no, now new deeds –
Mischief doth ever end where it begins –
An act of horror, fathers! He dragged forth   80
The agèd gentleman, that had there lain bed-rid
Three years and more, out off his innocent couch,
Naked, upon the floor; there left him; wounded
His servant in the face; and, with this strumpet,
The stale to his forged practice, who was glad   85
To be so active (I shall here desire
Your fatherhoods to note but my collections
As most remarkable) thought at once to stop
His father's ends, discredit his free choice
In the old gentleman, redeem themselves   90
By laying infamy upon this man,

                      (*Pointing to* CORVINO)

To whom, with blushing, they should owe their lives.
1st AVOCATORE
    What proofs have you of this?
BONARIO   Most honoured fathers,
    I humbly crave there be no credit given
    To this man's mercenary tongue.
2nd AVOCATORE   Forbear.   95
BONARIO
    His soul moves in his fee.
3rd AVOCATORE   O, sir.
BONARIO   This fellow,
    For six sols more, would plead against his Maker.
1st AVOCATORE
    You do forget yourself.
VOLTORE   Nay, nay, grave fathers,
    Let him have scope. Can any man imagine

102   creature: (*i*) *a human being (created by God, dependent upon Him, and therefore barred from seeking refuge in suicide*); (*ii*) *creature dependent on another (namely Corvino, who is largely responsible for her predicament when as her husband he should be the one to protect her from it*).

105   Speak to the knave?:   *Corbaccio has simply been asked to give evidence, but once again his deafness causes him to misunderstand.*

106–107 my heart/Abhors his knowledge: *my spirit prevents me from acknowledging him as my son.*

108   The mere portent of nature: *he is an unnatural monster, and his birth an ominous sign of disorder in nature.*

109   He is . . . loins: *I deny that I am his father.*

110   made you to this!:   *persuaded you to say this.*

112–114 Sir, I will sit down . . . father: *Bonario's passive response to Corbaccio's attack tends to link virtue with weakness, but its main effect is to demonstrate the natural relationship between parent and child (in this case, a son's patient obedience) and so to highlight the ugliness of Corbaccio's corrupted and unnatural fatherhood.*

That he will spare his accuser, that would not   100
Have spared his parent?

1st AVOCATORE   Well, produce your proofs.

CELIA

I would I could forget I were a creature.

VOLTORE

Signior Corbaccio!

4th AVOCATORE   What is he?

VOLTORE   The father.

2nd AVOCATORE

Has he had an oath?

NOTARIO   Yes.

CORBACCIO   What must I do now?

NOTARIO

Your testimony's craved.

CORBACCIO   Speak to the knave?   105

I'll ha' my mouth first stopped with earth; my heart
Abhors his knowledge. I disclaim in him.

1st AVOCATORE

But for what cause?

CORBACCIO   The mere portent of nature.

He is an utter stranger to my loins.

BONARIO

Have they made you to this!

CORBACCIO   I will not hear thee,   110

Monster of men, swine, goat, wolf, parricide,
Speak not, thou viper.

BONARIO   Sir, I will sit down,

And rather wish my innocence should suffer,
Than I resist the authority of a father.

VOLTORE

Signior Corvino!

2nd AVOCATORE   This is strange!

1st AVOCATORE   Who's this?   115

NOTARIO

The husband.

118   partridge: *bird traditionally supposed to be lustful.*

119   jennet: *high-mettled and lustful Spanish horse. (Corvino's vicious language distorts the relationship between husband and wife, just as Corbaccio's distorted that between father and son. Both men use vindictive animal imagery to degrade the innocent person they are attacking, and both reveal their own animal natures in the process.)*

124   well-timbered: *handsomely built.*
        here: *Corvino indicates his forehead, and with his fingers makes the letter 'V', the sign of the cuckold. Here and elsewhere in the play Corvino seems almost eager to degrade and humiliate himself in public, openly declaring what a normal man would most want to keep secret. He announces, as a lie, what would normally be hidden, even if true.*

125   horn: *(i) the cuckold's horns; (ii) the horn-book, a spelling primer where the 'letters' can be seen that declare him a cuckold.*

126   perfect: *complete.*

127   There is no shame . . . there?:   *Corvino's anxious and craven self-deceit could hardly go further than this. On Jonson's part the line is brutally satirical.*

128   onward: *well on the way.*

129–31   if there be . . . doubt: *if indeed there is any worse hell than to be a whore and a woman – something which a good Catholic may well doubt. (Corvino now perverts religious orthodoxy in his desperate attempt at self-conviction and injured righteousness.)*

4th AVOCATORE Is he sworn?

NOTARIO   He is.

3rd AVOCATORE   Speak then.

CORVINO

This woman, please your fatherhoods, is a whore
Of most hot exercise, more than a partridge,
Upon recòrd –

1st AVOCATORE   No more.

CORVINO   Neighs like a jennet.

NOTARIO

Preserve the honour of the court.

CORVINO   I shall,   120

And modesty of your most reverend ears.
And yet I hope that I may say, these eyes
Have seen her glued unto that piece of cedar,

(*Pointing to* BONARIO)

That fine well-timbered gallant; and that here

(*Touching his forehead*)

The letters may be read, thorough the horn,   125
That make the story perfect.

MOSCA (*Aside to* CORVINO)   Excellent! sir.

CORVINO (*To* MOSCA)

There is no shame in this now, is there?

MOSCA   None.

CORVINO

Or if I said, I hoped that she were onward
To her damnation, if there be a hell
Greater than whore, and woman – a good Catholic   130
May make the doubt.

3rd AVOCATORE   His grief hath made him frantic.

1st AVOCATORE

Remove him hence.

2nd AVOCATORE   Look to the woman.

She swoons

CORVINO   Rare!

Prettily feigned! again!

139 most laid: *carefully plotted.*

140 free: *without interruption.*

141 doubt th'imposture: *suspect that Bonario's version of events may be untrue.*

143 creature: *wretch.*
     professed: *brazen.*

145 Unsatisfied: *insatiable.*

146 take: *deceive.*
     but this day, she baited: *only today she enticed.*

147 loose eyes: *sexually provocative glances.*

151 Without: *outside.*

4th AVOCATORE   Stand from about her.

1st AVOCATORE

  Give her the air.

3rd AVOCATORE (*To* MOSCA) What can you say?

MOSCA   My wound,

  May't please your wisdoms, speaks for me, received   135

  In aid of my good patron, when he missed

                        (*Pointing to* BONARIO)

  His sought-for father, when that well-taught dame

  Had her cue given to cry out a rape.

BONARIO

  O, most laid impudence! Fathers –

3rd AVOCATORE   Sir, be silent,

  You had your hearing free, so must they theirs.   140

2nd AVOCATORE

  I do begin to doubt th'imposture here.

4th AVOCATORE

  This woman has too many moods.

VOLTORE   Grave fathers,

  She is a creature of a most professed

  And prostituted lewdness.

CORVINO   Most impetuous!

  Unsatisfied, grave fathers!

VOLTORE   May her feignings   145

  Not take your wisdoms; but this day, she baited

  A stranger, a grave knight, with her loose eyes,

  And more lascivious kisses. This man saw 'em

  Together on the water, in a gondola.

MOSCA

  Here is the lady herself, that saw 'em too,   150

  Without; who then had in the open streets

  Pursued them, but for saving her knight's honour.

1st AVOCATORE

  Produce that lady.

2nd AVOCATORE   Let her come.

                          Exit MOSCA

2   chameleon: *small lizard which can change colour to match its background; hence it was a symbol of cunning.*

3   Vie tears . . . hyena: *compete with the hyena in weeping false tears. (The hyena was a symbol of treachery.)*

4   I cry your pardons: *I beg you to excuse me.*

7   exorbitant: *exceeded the limits of propriety (in her language).*

9   or my sex's: *or my sex's honour.*

13   pertinacy: *Lady Would-be means 'pertinacity', or unmannerly insistence. This is exactly the fault she is now committing.*

4th AVOCATORE   These things,
  They strike with wonder!
3rd AVOCATORE   I am turned a stone!

(Scene six)

(*Enter* MOSCA *with* LADY WOULD-BE)
MOSCA
  Be resolute, madam.
LADY WOULD-BE   Ay, this same is she.
                             (*Pointing to* CELIA)
  Out, thou chameleon harlot! Now thine eyes
  Vie tears with the hyena! Dar'st thou look
  Upon my wrongèd face? I cry your pardons.
  I fear, I have (forgettingly) transgressed   5
  Against the dignity of the court –
2nd AVOCATORE   No, madam.
LADY WOULD-BE
  And been exorbitant –
4th AVOCATORE   You have not, lady.
1st AVOCATORE
  These proofs are strong.
LADY WOULD-BE   Surely, I had no purpose
  To scandalize your honours, or my sex's.
3rd AVOCATORE
  We do believe it.
LADY WOULD-BE   Surely, you may believe it.   10
2nd AVOCATORE
  Madam, we do.
LADY WOULD-BE   Indeed, you may; my breeding
  Is not so coarse –
4th AVOCATORE   We know it.
LADY WOULD-BE   To offend
  With pertinacy –
3rd AVOCATORE   Lady.

217

15 Let her o'ercome: *Let her have the last word.*

20 wax: *grow.*

S.D. 'impotent': *physically helpless.*
21 convince: *overpower.*

26 affect venery: *take pleasure in sexual indulgence.*
29 dissemble: *pretend. (Typically bold tactic by Voltore, to suggest sarcastically what is actually true, thus making it even less likely that the possibility will be considered.)*
30 proved: *tested.*
32 'strappado': *form of torture in which the victim's hands are tied behind his back and his body raised from the ground by a rope attached to his wrists; thus suspended, he is then dropped downwards and his arms wrenched agonizingly by a violent jerk.*
33 The rack hath cured the gout: *popular notion, referred to elsewhere in the drama of the period. The expression is a way of saying that extreme pain drives out intense but lesser pain.*
34 help him of: *cure him of.*

LADY WOULD-BE   Such a presence.
  No, surely.
1st AVOCATORE We well think it.
LADY WOULD-BE   You may think it.
1st AVOCATORE
  Let her o'ercome. (*To* BONARIO) What witnesses have you,   15
  To make good your report?
BONARIO   Our consciences.
CELIA
  And heaven, that never fails the innocent.
4th AVOCATORE
  These are no testimonies.
BONARIO   Not in your courts,
  Where multitude and clamour overcomes.
1st AVOCATORE
  Nay, then you do wax insolent.
VOLTORE   Here, here,   20
                 (VOLPONE *is brought in, as impotent*)
  The testimony comes that will convince
  And put to utter dumbness their bold tongues
  See here, grave fathers, here's the ravisher,
  The rider on men's wives, the great impostor,
  The grand voluptuary! Do you not think   25
  These limbs should affect venery? or these eyes
  Covet a concubine? Pray you, mark these hands –
  Are they not fit to stroke a lady's breasts?
  Perhaps he doth dissemble?
BONARIO   So he does.
VOLTORE
  Would you ha' him tortured?
BONARIO   I would have him proved.   30
VOLTORE
  Best try him then with goads, or burning irons;
  Put him to the *strappado;* I have heard
  The rack hath cured the gout, faith, give it him,
  And help him of a malady – be courteous.

36 as many left diseases: *as many diseases left. (Even if the rack does cure his gout!)*

37 known: *i.e. known sexually.*

38 equal: *just.*

40 May pass with sufferance: *are to be tolerated.*

40–1 what one/Citizen but owes: *is there one citizen who will not owe.*

42 traduce: *slander. Voltore argues cunningly that if Bonario and Celia escape unpunished, every respectable citizen will be at risk from slanderers.*

45 face, or colour: *appearance or likelihood.*

46 dullest: *least sensitive.*

51 hot and fleshed: *impassioned and hardened.*

52 constancy: *bold consistency.*

54 sever them: *keep them apart.*

58 creatures: *monsters.*
I have an earthquake in me!: *I am deeply shaken (by the supposed guilt of Bonario and Celia).*

61 In their discovery: *in exposing their guilt.*

I'll undertake, before these honoured fathers, 35
He shall have yet as many left diseases
As she has known adulterers, or thou strumpets.
O, my most equal hearers, if these deeds,
Acts of this bold and most exorbitant strain,
May pass with sufferance, what one citizen 40
But owes the forfeit of his life, yea fame,
To him that dares traduce him? Which of you
Are safe, my honoured fathers? I would ask
(With leave of your grave fatherhoods) if their plot
Have any face, or colour, like to truth? 45
Or if, unto the dullest nostril here,
It smell not rank and most abhorrèd slander?
I crave your care of this good gentleman,
Whose life is much endangered by their fable;
And, as for them, I will conclude with this: 50
That vicious persons when they are hot and fleshed
In impious acts, their constancy abounds;
Damned deeds are done with greatest confidence.

1st AVOCATORE
   Take 'em to custody, and sever them.

CELIA *and* BONARIO *are taken out*

2nd AVOCATORE
   'Tis pity two such prodigies should live. 55

1st AVOCATORE
   Let the old gentleman be returned with care;
   I'm sorry our credulity wronged him.

VOLPONE *is carried off*

4th AVOCATORE
   These are two creatures!

3rd AVOCATORE   I have an earthquake in me!

2nd AVOCATORE
   Their shame, even in their cradles, fled their faces.

4th AVOCATORE [*To* VOLTORE]
   You've done a worthy service to the state, sir, 60
   In their discovery.

66 The earth . . . living: *I'd prefer the earth to lack men rather than you should lack the means of earning a living.*

71 the other: *the truth (that he had tried to prostitute his wife to Volpone)*

74 doubt this advocate: *suspect this advocate (of seeking to displace him as Volpone's heir)*

1st AVOCATORE   You shall hear ere night
  What punishment the court decrees upon 'em
VOLTORE
  We thank your fatherhoods.

          (*Exeunt* AVOCATORI, NOTARIO, OFFICER)
          How like you it?
MOSCA   Rare.
  I'd ha' your tongue, sir, tipped with gold for this;
  I'd ha' you be the heir to the whole city;   65
  The earth I'd have want men, ere you want living.
  They're bound to erect your statue in St Mark's.
  Signior Corvino, I would have you go
  And show yourself, that you have conquered.
CORVINO   Yes.
MOSCA
  It was much better that you should profess   70
  Yourself a cuckold thus, than that the other
  Should have been proved.
CORVINO   Nay, I considered that;
  Now, it is her fault –
MOSCA   Then, it had been yours.
CORVINO
  True. I do doubt this advocate still.
MOSCA   I'faith,
  You need not; I dare ease you of that care.   75
CORVINO
  I trust thee, Mosca.
MOSCA   As your own soul, sir.

                      Exit CORVINO
CORBACCIO   Mosca!
MOSCA
  Now for your business, sir.
CORBACCIO   How? ha' you business?
MOSCA
  Yes, yours, sir.

79　Rest you, with both your eyes:　*Sleep easily and leave it all to me.*

81　put in:　*included in the inventory of Volpone's possessions.*

82　Curtain-rings:　*Mosca sarcastically reassures Corbaccio that even the most trivial item will not be overlooked. Corbaccio, of course, does not notice the sarcasm.*

84　too prodigal:　*too generous. Corbaccio, who owes his safety to Voltore's skilful advocacy, now begrudges him a reasonable reward for his work. Such meanness is a fitting aftermath to a court scene which has been governed throughout by scheming avarice and vicious selfishness.*

85　I must tender it:　*I must give it to him myself. (Any direct contact between the legacy-hunters is dangerous for Mosca and Volpone; Mosca must always be the one to stage-manage events by acting as a go-between.)*
　　chequeens:　*gold coins.*

89　Bountiful bones!:　*Mosca's sarcasm is no doubt caused not only by the calculated smallness of Voltore's fee but also the smallness of his own tip (at 'there's for thee').*

91　Worthy this age?:　*to make him deserve an old age like this.*

92　Unto your ends:　*in your best interests.*
　　take you no notice:　*don't seem to pay any attention to me. (Lady Would-be is nearby, and Mosca is again concerned to keep his puppets separate from each other.)*

93　the devil and all:　*the whole damned lot.*

CORBACCIO   O, none else?

MOSCA   None else, not I.

CORBACCIO

    Be careful then.

MOSCA   Rest you, with both your eyes, sir.

CORBACCIO

    Dispatch it.

MOSCA   Instantly.

CORBACCIO   And look that all   80

    Whatever be put in: jewels, plate, moneys,

    Household stuff, bedding, curtains.

MOSCA   Curtain-rings, sir –

    Only, the advocate's fee must be deducted.

CORBACCIO

    I'll pay him now – you'll be too prodigal.

MOSCA

    Sir, I must tender it.

CORBACCIO   Two chequeens is well?   85

MOSCA

    No, six, sir.

CORBACCIO   'Tis too much.

MOSCA   He talked a great while,

    You must consider that, sir.

CORBACCIO   Well, there's three –

MOSCA

    I'll give it him.

CORBACCIO   Do so, and there's for thee.

                                            Exit CORBACCIO

MOSCA

    Bountiful bones! What horrid strange offence

    Did he commit 'gainst nature in his youth,   90

    Worthy this age? you see, sir, (*To* VOLTORE) how I work

    Unto your ends; take you no notice.

VOLTORE   No,

    I'll leave you.

MOSCA   All is yours (*Exit* VOLTORE) – the devil

    and all,

                                                                    225

97 reform: *revise*.

101 sway: *persuade*.

Good advocate. – (*To* LADY WOULD-BE) Madam, I'll
  bring you home.

LADY WOULD-BE
  No, I'll go see your patron.

MOSCA   That you shall not.   95
  I'll tell you why: my purpose is to urge
  My patron to reform his will; and, for
  The zeal you've shown today, whereas before
  You were but third or fourth, you shall be now
  Put in the first; which would appear as begged   100
  If you were present. Therefore –

LADY WOULD-BE   You shall sway me.

Exeunt

1 brunt: *crisis.*

3 this fled moment: *a moment ago.*

3–4 here ... public: *this remark shows Volpone's divided impulses. On the one hand, he relishes the safety of deception in his own house, and fears the risk of public exposure. On the other hand, he cannot resist the temptation of public performances, especially when they allow him to fool or ridicule his victims. This irresistible temptation, which he knows to be misguided, will shortly ruin him. In this remark he displays an intelligent prudence which accurately defines the base of his security; only a few lines later he has abandoned it. His zeal for acting has a perverse creative energy which is also self-destructive.*

4 'Cavè': *Beware!*

6 straight: *immediately.*

7 dead palsy: *fatal paralysis.*

8 A many: *a large number.*

12 humour: *mood.*

15 possess: *fill.*

16 make me up: *make me my old self.*

17 This heat ... this time: *The warmth given me by the (red) wine is life-giving: already it is converted into blood.*

1 does the day ... again?: *This and Mosca's other questions are rhetorical. The clear answer is 'yes', and Mosca is gloating over their audacious triumph.*

2–3 wrought ... before us?: *rescued from straying into error and able to see before us the clear path of our pilgrimage. (Mosca scornfully makes use of a conventional religious image of life's journey.)*

Act Five

Scene one

VOLPONE'S *House*
Enter VOLPONE

VOLPONE

Well, I am here; and all this brunt is past.
I ne'er was in dislike with my disguise
Till this fled moment; here, 'twas good, in private,
But in your public – *Cavè*, whilst I breathe.
'Fore God, my left leg 'gan to have the cramp,   5
And I apprehended, straight, some power had struck me
With a dead palsy. Well, I must be merry,
And shake it off. A many of these fears
Would put me into some villainous disease,
Should they come thick upon me – I'll prevent 'em.   10
Give me a bowl of lusty wine, to fright
This humour from my heart. (*He drinks*) Hum, hum, hum!
'Tis almost gone, already – I shall conquer.
Any device, now, of rare, ingenious knavery,
That would possess me with a violent laughter,   15
Would make me up again! (*Drinks again*) So, so, so, so.
This heat is life; 'tis blood by this time. Mosca!

(*Scene two*)

Enter MOSCA

MOSCA

How now, sir? does the day look clear again?
Are we recovered? and wrought out of error
Into our way? to see our path before us?
Is our trade free once more?

5 carried learnedly: *carried off expertly.*

6 Good wits . . . extremities: *true statement about Volpone and even more so about Mosca himself. On the other hand, the urge to test their genius by piling extremity on extremity is their greatest weakness and danger – especially when they are no longer united in mutual support.*

9 taken: *delighted.*

10 more than if . . . wench: *the motivation of Volpone is starkly clear in this line. Neither gold nor sexual pleasure can match the joy of duping and manipulating others by consummate acting and intrigue.*

15 played thy prize: *you have played your part to the finish. (Volpone seems to accept Mosca's suggestion that the parasite has reached his climax of ingenious achievement. But he hints that he himself has not finished yet.)*

16 gull: *make fools of.*

19 borne it: *managed it.*

20 these: *i.e. the legacy-hunters.*

21 scent somewhat . . . thee: *smell something fishy, either in my behaviour or yours.*

26 Never so . . .: *No matter how . . .*

VOLPONE   Exquisite Mosca!

MOSCA

Was it not carried learnedly?

VOLPONE   And stoutly.   5

Good wits are greatest in extremities.

MOSCA

It were a folly beyond thought to trust

Any grand act unto a cowardly spirit.

You are not taken with it enough, methinks?

VOLPONE

O, more than if I had enjoyed the wench;   10

The pleasure of all womankind's not like it.

MOSCA

Why, now you speak, sir. We must here be fixed;

Here we must rest; this is our masterpiece;

We cannot think to go beyond this.

VOLPONE   True,

Thou'st played thy prize, my precious Mosca.

MOSCA   Nay, sir,   15

To gull the court –

VOLPONE   And quite divert the torrent

Upon the innocent.

MOSCA   Yes, and to make

So rare a music out of discords –

VOLPONE   Right.

That yet to me's the strangest! how thou'st borne it!

That these, being so divided 'mongst themselves,   20

Should not scent somewhat, or in me or thee,

Or doubt their own side.

MOSCA   True, they will not see't.

Too much light blinds 'em, I think. Each of 'em

Is so possessed, and stuffed with his own hopes,

That anything unto the contrary,   25

Never so true, or never so apparent,

Never so palpable, they will resist it –

31   glebe: *soil.*

32   Did not ... rare?: *Didn't the old lawyer put on a brilliant show?*

33–6 'My most honoured fathers ...': *Volpone, more and more compulsively the actor, now takes his chance to 'act' the part of Voltore.*

36–7 I had much ado ... sweat, sir: *Jonson shows a subtle break in their collusion. Volpone says he had difficulty in stopping himself from laughing. Mosca – most politely corrective – observes that he was sweating with nervousness.*

40   in a mist: *uncertain.*

41   Never but still myself: *Never losing my self-possession.*
     I think it: *I'm sure of it.*

43   out of conscience: *as my conscience dictates.*

44–6 He's taken ... richly: *Mosca is poking fun at Voltore in these lines by mimicking his language and style of advocacy in the court scene.*

47   cozened: *cheated.*

48   By that ... latter end: *judging by what I heard of the last part of his speech.*

50   Draw it ... heads: *summarize his arguments under certain headings.*
     aggravate: *expand and emphasize (his statement of the charges).*

51   vehement figures: *figures of speech, strongly worded and designed to rouse strong feelings.*

52   shift a shirt: *change his shirt. (Mosca either (i) suggests that Voltore's violent speeches made him sweat profusely or (ii) imitates Voltore's extravagant gestures with his arms, intended to reinforce his speeches but ridiculously similar to a man changing his clothes.)*

53   no hope of gain: *Mosca is being heavily ironic.*

VOLPONE

Like a temptation of the devil.

MOSCA   Right, sir.

Merchants may talk of trade, and your great signiors

Of land that yields well; but if Italy   30

Have any glebe more fruitful than these fellows,

I am deceived. Did not your advocate rare?

VOLPONE

O – 'My most honoured fathers, my grave fathers,

Under correction of your fatherhoods,

What face of truth is here? If these strange deeds   35

May pass, most honoured fathers' – I had much ado

To forbear laughing.

MOSCA   'T seemed to me, you sweat, sir.

VOLPONE

In troth, I did a little.

MOSCA   But confess, sir.

Were you not daunted?

VOLPONE   In good faith, I was

A little in a mist; but not dejected –   40

Never but still myself.

MOSCA   I think it, sir.

Now, so truth help me, I must needs say this, sir,

And, out of conscience, for your advocate:

He's taken pains, in faith, sir, and deserved,

(In my poor judgment, I speak it, under favour,   45

Not to contrary you, sir) very richly –

Well – to be cozened.

VOLPONE   Troth, and I think so too,

By that I heard him, in the latter end.

MOSCA

O, but before, sir; had you heard him first

Draw it to certain heads, then aggravate,   50

Then use his vehement figures – I looked still

When he would shift a shirt; and, doing this

Out of pure love, no hope of gain –

54 answer: *recompense*.

59 jig: *comic trick*.

61 constancy: *firmness*.
62 Sadly: *seriously*.

63 What do you mean, sir?: *What are you up to?*

66 she-wolf: *Lady Would-be. Note that Lady Would-be, though a very inept suitor by comparison with the three men, is nevertheless given a firm place amongst the animal images which direct our attitudes towards all the legacy-hunters.*
68 ravished from their mouths: *Mosca does not, of course, realize at first that Volpone's plan will make him the supposed heir. He thinks the suitors will come rushing to the house, only to find Volpone alive after all.*
70 take upon thee: *behave.*
72 blanks: *blank spaces for the names of legatees to be inserted in a will which is otherwise complete.*

234

VOLPONE   'Tis right.
I cannot answer him, Mosca, as I would,
Not yet; but, for thy sake, at thy entreaty,   55
I will begin, even now, to vex 'em all,
This very instant.

MOSCA   Good, sir.

VOLPONE   Call the dwarf
And eunuch forth.

MOSCA   Castrone, Nano!

                          Enter CASTRONE *and* NANO

NANO   Here.

VOLPONE
Shall we have a jig now?

MOSCA   What you please, sir.

VOLPONE   Go,
Straight, give out about the streets, you two,   60
That I am dead; do it with constancy,
Sadly, do you hear? Impute it to the grief
Of this late slander.

                     Exeunt CASTRONE *and* NANO

MOSCA   What do you mean, sir?

VOLPONE   O,
I shall have instantly my vulture, crow,
Raven, come flying hither on the news,   65
To peck for carrion, my she-wolf and all,
Greedy, and full of expectation –

MOSCA
And then to have it ravished from their
     mouths?

VOLPONE
'Tis true, I will ha' thee put on a gown
And take upon thee as thou wert mine heir;   70
Show 'em a will – open that chest, and reach
Forth one of those that has the blanks. I'll straight
Put in thy name.

MOSCA   It will be rare, sir.

74 e'en gape: *have their mouths open for food.* (*Food and gold are once again equated in the play's imagery.*)

77 corrupted: *decomposed* (*but the word 'corrupted' does, of course, describe Volpone's moral condition quite accurately; this is one of a number of cases where the irony is sharp and characters speak more truthfully than they realize*).

78 was fain: *I was compelled.*

81 cap: *sign of Mosca's raised status: he will wear a patrician's cap and show disrespect to the suitors by keeping it on in their presence.*
    count-book: *account book.*

83 parcels: *items.*

88 stark dull: *mentally numbed.*

89 edge: *sharp edge (a play on 'dull' meaning 'blunt').*

90 'clarissimo': *Venetian nobleman (in this case Corbaccio).*

91 crump you ... touch: *curl up like a woodlouse when it is touched.* (*The 'you' is a colloquial expression, suggesting easy familiarity between the speakers.*)

93 rope and a dagger: *the weapons of those driven mad by despair and bent on suicide or murder.*

VOLPONE   Ay,
  When they e'en gape, and find themselves deluded –
MOSCA
  Yes.
VOLPONE And thou use them scurvily. Dispatch,   75
  Get on thy gown.
MOSCA   But, what, sir, if they ask
  After the body?
VOLPONE   Say it was corrupted.
MOSCA
  I'll say it stunk, sir; and was fain t'have it
  Coffined up instantly, and sent away.
VOLPONE
  Anything, what thou wilt. Hold, here's my will.   80
  Get thee a cap, a count-book, pen and ink,
  Papers afore thee; sit as thou wert taking
  An inventory of parcels. I'll get up
  Behind the curtain on a stool, and hearken;
  Sometime, peep over; see how they do look;   85
  With what degrees their blood doth leave their faces!
  O, 'twill afford me a rare meal of laughter.
MOSCA
  Your advocate will turn stark dull upon it.
VOLPONE
  It will take off his oratory's edge.
MOSCA
  But your *clarissimo*, old round-back, he   90
  Will crump you, like a hog-louse, with the touch.
VOLPONE
  And what Corvino?
MOSCA   O, sir, look for him
  Tomorrow morning, with a rope and a dagger,
  To visit all the streets; he must run mad.
  My lady too, that came into the court   95
  To bear false witness for your worship –
VOLPONE   Yes,

98   And sweat, sir: *compare line 37. Mosca is giving Volpone a second sharp reminder of the nervousness he observed. It is another sign of Mosca's growing independent confidence and the changing balance of power between the two.*

98–105   Why, your gold . . . beauty: *having already mimicked Voltore, Mosca now imitates Lady Would-be's pretentious style.*

98–9   your gold . . . med'cine: *the idea of gold as a cure for illness is taken up again from Acts I and II. Compare, for example, with Act I Scene IV lines 71–3.*

102   strange poetical girdle: *the Cestus, or girdle of Venus, which gave beauty to the ugly and physical desire to the old.*

102–104 Jove . . . Acrisius' guards: *Acrisius was warned by oracle that his daughter, Danäe would bear a son who would kill him. Acrisius shut her up in a tower of brass, but Zeus reached her there in the form of a shower of gold. Their union led to the birth of Perseus, who accidentally killed his grandfather some years later when throwing the discus.*

103   t'himself: *for himself.*
       shroud: *disguise*

104–105 It is the thing . . . beauty: *It (i.e. gold) is responsible for all the world's grace, youth and beauty. (In the perverted values which govern the world of Volpone, the statement is a true one.)*

107   jealous of you: *devoted to your welfare.*

110   posture: *act, role.*

111   artificer: *craftsman. (Mosca must prove both a skilled actor and a skilled torturer.)*

And kissed me 'fore the fathers, when my face
Flowed all with oils.

MOSCA   And sweat, sir. Why, your gold
Is such another med'cine, it dries up
All those offensive savours! It transforms   100
The most deformèd, and restores 'em lovely,
As 'twere the strange poetical girdle. Jove
Could not invent t'himself a shroud more subtle
To pass Acrisius' guards. It is the thing
Makes all the world her grace, her youth, her beauty.   105

VOLPONE
I think she loves me.

MOSCA   Who? the lady, sir?
She's jealous of you.

VOLPONE   Dost thou say so?

Knocking without

MOSCA   Hark,
There's some already.

VOLPONE   Look.

MOSCA   It is the vulture;
He has the quickest scent.

VOLPONE   I'll to my place,

(Concealing himself)

Thou, to thy posture.

MOSCA   I am set.

VOLPONE   But Mosca,   110
Play the artificer now, torture 'em rarely.

(*Scene three*)

Enter VOLTORE

VOLTORE
How now, my Mosca?

MOSCA   Turkey carpets, nine –

3 suits . . . tissue: *sets of bed covers, in a rich cloth interwoven with gold and silver.*

6 cloth of gold: *cloth woven wholly or partly from threads of gold.*

7 several velvets: *separate velvet hangings.*

S. D. a traverse: *the meaning is not entirely certain. The traverse is probably a portable screen, which might be formed of a curtain on a rod or cord, shutting off one part of a large room. It allows Volpone to be a spectator at a scene of his own devising, and to enjoy his role as manipulator, since his victims behave exactly as he foresaw and intended.*

11 Is his thread spun?: *the three Fates were the Goddesses who spun the threads of a man's destiny. When the thread was cut, the man died. Lady Would-be, fond as ever of classical allusions and elaborate statements, means 'Is his thread spun to the end and cut?', which she regards as more elegant and sophisticated than saying 'Is he dead?'*

14 diaper . . . damask: *both were expensive fabrics.*

VOLTORE

Taking an inventory? that is well.

MOSCA

Two suits of bedding, tissue –

VOLTORE   Where's the will?

Let me read that the while.

Enter CORBACCIO *carried in a chair*

CORBACCIO   So, set me down,

And get you home.

Exeunt BEARERS

VOLTORE   Is he come, now, to trouble us?   5

MOSCA Of cloth of gold, two more –

CORBACCIO   Is it done, Mosca?

MOSCA

Of several velvets, eight –

VOLTORE   I like his care.

CORBACCIO

Dost thou not hear?

Enter CORVINO

CORVINO   Ha! is the hour come, Mosca?

VOLPONE *peeps from behind a traverse*

VOLPONE (*Aside*)

Ay, now they muster.

CORVINO   What does the advocate here?

Or this Corbaccio?

CORBACCIO   What do these here?

Enter LADY WOULD-BE

LADY WOULD-BE   Mosca!   10

Is his thread spun?

MOSCA   Eight chests of linen –

VOLPONE (*Aside*)   O,

My fine dame Would-be, too!

CORVINO   Mosca, the will,

That I may show it these, and rid 'em hence.

MOSCA

Six chests of diaper, four of damask – There.

Gives them the will

241

20 suits of hangings: *sets of tapestries and wall-hangings.*

21 i'their garters: *Volpone picks up the word 'hangings' and plays on the popular expression 'He may go hang himself in his own garters'.*

22 at the gasp: *at their last gasp.*

25 glazen-eyes: *i.e. Corbaccio, who wears spectacles. As usual he is slower than the others to catch up with events. Seeing their crest-fallen expressions, he assumes in his next remark that he is indeed the heir.*

30 I am very busy: *Mosca provokes the suitors even more by pre-tending to be so harassed and preoccupied by his new-found wealth that he can pay no attention to their questions.*

32 salt: *salt cellar.*

CORBACCIO
  Is that the will?

MOSCA   Down-beds; and bolsters –

VOLPONE (*Aside*)   Rare!   15
  Be busy still. Now they begin to flutter –
  They never think of me. Look, see, see, see!
  How their swift eyes run over the long deed
  Unto the name, and to the legacies,
  What is bequeathed them there –

MOSCA   Ten suits of hangings   20

VOLPONE (*Aside*)
  Ay, i'their garters, Mosca. Now their hopes
  Are at the gasp.

VOLTORE   Mosca the heir!

CORBACCIO   What's that?

VOLPONE (*Aside*)
  My advocate is dumb. Look to my merchant –
  He has heard of some strange storm, a ship is lost;
  He faints. My lady will swoon. Old glazen-eyes,   25
  He hath not reached his despair, yet.

CORBACCIO   All these
  Are out of hope; I am sure the man.

CORVINO   But, Mosca –

MOSCA
  Two cabinets –

CORVINO   Is this in earnest?

MOSCA   One
  Of ebony –

CORVINO   Or do you but delude me?

MOSCA
  The other, mother of pearl – I am very busy.   30
  Good faith, it is a fortune thrown upon me –
  Item, one salt of agate – not my seeking.

36   Is this my large hope's issue?:   *Is this the only outcome of all my vast expectations?*

38   fairly: *politely. (Mosca is himself apparently courteous: 'Please have the goodness to leave my house politely'. But Mosca's 'fairly' is really an insolent mockery of Lady Would-be's 'fairer', while his reference to 'my' house is a bitter irritant in itself.)*

40–5   Remember . . . riddles: *These lines complete the plot development begun at Act IV, Scene VI, lines 94–101. Lady Would-be has offered to prostitute herself to Mosca, and thus laid herself open to the blackmailed silence he now imposes on her.*

43   maintenance: *financial support.*

45   riddles: *secrets.*

48   been th'example: *led the way.*

51   fain: *willingly.*
       wittol: *man who connives at his wife's adultery.*

53   on good terms: *outspokenly.*

LADY WOULD-BE
  Do you hear, sir?

MOSCA   A perfumed box – pray you forbear,
  You see I am troubled – made of an onyx –

LADY WOULD-BE   How!

MOSCA
  Tomorrow, or next day, I shall be at leisure   35
  To talk with you all.

CORVINO   Is this my large hope's issue?

LADY WOULD-BE
  Sir, I must have a fairer answer.

MOSCA   Madam!
  Marry, and shall: pray you, fairly quit my house.
  Nay, raise no tempest with your looks; but hark you:
  Remember what your ladyship offered me   40
  To put you in an heir; go to, think on't.
  And what you said e'en your best madams did
  For maintenance, and why not you? Enough.
  Go home, and use the poor Sir Pol, your knight, well,
  For fear I tell some riddles. Go, be melancholic.   45

                                    Exit LADY WOULD-BE

VOLPONE (*Aside*)
  O, my fine devil!

CORVINO   Mosca, pray you a word.

MOSCA
  Lord! will not you take your dispatch hence yet?
  Methinks, of all, you should have been th'example.
  Why should you stay here? with what thought? what
      promise?
  Hear you, do not you know, I know you an ass?   50
  And that you would, most fain, have been a wittol,
  If fortune would have let you? that you are
  A declared cuckold, on good terms? This pearl,
  You'll say, was yours? Right. This diamond?
  I'll not deny't, but thank you. Much here else?   55
  It may be so. Why, think that these good works

58–9 extraordinary . . . title: *Corvino is a cuckold only in title, since the adultery with which Celia was branded in the court scene did not in fact occur. Corvino is a 'cuckold extraordinary', enjoying the 'honour' of the title without having deserved it. Once again Mosca's courtesies are vicious. Meanwhile he still has the black-mailing secret which he will 'not betray' – the real truth that Corvino tried to prostitute his own wife to Volpone.*

64 cozened: *tricked.*

65 Harlot: *rogue (general term of abuse, not restricted to the meaning 'prostitute').*
gulled: *duped.*

68 three legs: *Corbaccio walks with a stick. The reference is to the riddle of the Sphinx: 'What has four legs in the morning, two at noon, and three in the evening?' The answer is man, who crawls on arms and legs as a baby, walks in adult life, and uses a stick in old age. Corbaccio's age and physical decrepitude are now emphasized yet further. His deafness has been stressed throughout; we now hear of his poor sight (Volpone's reference to 'four eyes' at line 63 again refers to his spectacles), his toothlessness and his lameness.*

70–1 would have hired . . . patron: *see note to Act III Scene IX line 14.*

79 mar'l: *marvel.*

246

May help to hide your bad – I'll not betray you.
Although you be but extraordinary,
And have it only in title, it sufficeth.
Go home, be melancholic too, or mad.   60

Exit CORVINO

VOLPONE (*Aside*)
  Rare, Mosca! how his villainy becomes him!

VOLTORE
  Certain, he doth delude all these for me.

CORBACCIO
  Mosca, the heir?

VOLPONE (*Aside*) O, his four eyes have found it!

CORBACCIO
  I'm cozened, cheated, by a parasite slave;
  Harlot, thou'st gulled me.

MOSCA   Yes, sir. Stop your mouth,   65
  Or I shall draw the only tooth, is left.
  Are not you he, that filthy covetous wretch
  With the three legs, that here, in hope of prey,
  Have, any time this three year, snuffed about
  With your most grov'ling nose; and would have hired   70
  Me to the pois'ning of my patron? Sir?
  Are not you he that have, today, in court,
  Professed the disinheriting of your son?
  Perjured yourself? Go home, and die, and stink;
  If you but croak a syllable, all comes out.   75
  Away and call your porters, go, go, stink.

Exit CORBACCIO

VOLPONE (*Aside*)
  Excellent varlet!

VOLTORE   Now, my faithful Mosca,
  I find thy constancy –

MOSCA   Sir?

VOLTORE   Sincere.

MOSCA   A table
  Of porphyry – I mar'l, you'll be thus troublesome.

247

81   cry you mercy: *I beg your pardon.*

83   chance: *good luck.*

84   travails: *efforts.*

90   want: *become poor.*

91   causes: *law-suits.*

93   suits: *law-suits.*

94   Things . . . direct: *Volpone's will and affairs in general being so clear and uncomplicated.*

95   obstreperous: *bawling.* (*Compare Act I Scene II line 36 and note on that line*).

96   Conceive me, for your fee: *Understand me, I shall pay your fee and expect no favours.* (*Once again, Mosca is showing ostensible politeness in order to insult and belittle the suitors, tormenting them with his new-found superiority.*)

97   have: *know.*

99   plate: *gold-plate* (*that presented by Voltore at Act I Scene III line 10. Mosca takes special delight in facing the suitors with his inherited possession of their own gifts to Volpone*).

101   costive: *constipated.*
      purge: *take a laxative.*

102   lettuce: *lettuce was regarded as a laxative.*

105   habit of 'clarissimo': *patrician's gown. Venetian noblemen wore distinctive black gowns.*

107   We must pursue: *more than ever before, Volpone's schemes of humiliation for his victims take on a reckless impetus of their own, seizing on immediate vindictive opportunity without thought of possible consequences. The attractions of manipulation, acting, disguise, deception and over-confident risk-taking drive Volpone forward irresistibly.*

108   doubt it will lose: *fear it will cause us to lose.* (*Mosca realizes that they have dismissed not only the suitors but the chance of any further profits.*)

109   my recovery . . . all: *They will return with further offerings when they find I am still alive.*

VOLTORE
 Nay, leave off now, they are gone.

MOSCA   Why, who are you?   80
 What, who did send for you? O, cry you mercy,
 Reverend sir! good faith, I am grieved for you,
 That any chance of mine should thus defeat
 Your (I must needs say) most deserving travails.
 But, I protest, sir, it was cast upon me,   85
 And I could, almost, wish to be without it,
 But that the will o'the dead must be observed.
 Marry, my joy is, that you need it not,
 You have a gift, sir (thank your education)
 Will never let you want, while there are men,   90
 And malice, to breed causes. Would I had
 But half the like, for all my fortune, sir.
 If I have any suits (as I do hope,
 Things being so easy and direct, I shall not)
 I will make bold with your obstreperous aid –   95
 Conceive me, for your fee, sir. In meantime,
 You, that have so much law, I know ha' the conscience
 Not to be covetous of what is mine.
 Good sir, I thank you for my plate – 'twill help
 To set up a young man. Good faith, you look   100
 As you were costive; best go home and purge, sir.
             Exit VOLTORE

VOLPONE (*Coming out*)
 Bid him eat lettuce well. My witty mischief,
 Let me embrace thee. O, that I could now
 Transform thee to a Venus – Mosca, go,
 Straight, take my habit of *clarissimo*,   105
 And walk the streets; be seen, torment 'em more;
 We must pursue, as well as plot. Who would
 Have lost this feast?

MOSCA   I doubt it will lose them.

VOLPONE
 O, my recovery shall recover all.

110 That I: *if only I.*

114 'commandadori': *officers of the court.*

115 habit: *uniform.*

116 answering thy brain: *befitting your intelligence.*

119 The Fox . . . cursed: *proverb; it is appropriate here because the fox is cursed most when he escapes.*

1 warrant you: *assure you of that.*
4 Zant: *Zante, one of the Ionian islands, and at this time a Venetian possession.*
5 'Book of Voyages': *there was a current fashion for travel books, of which Hakluyt's collection,* The Principal Navigations, Voyages, Traffics and Discoveries of the English Nation *(1598–1600) was the most wide-ranging and is still the best known.*
6 his gulled . . . truth: *the story of his adventures published as the truth when in fact it was merely a deception.*

That I could now but think on some disguise   110
To meet 'em in, and ask 'em questions.
How I would vex 'em still, at every turn!

MOSCA

Sir, I can fit you.

VOLPONE   Canst thou?

MOSCA   Yes, I know
One o' the *commandadori*, sir, so like you;
Him will I straight make drunk, and bring you his
      habit.   115

VOLPONE

A rare disguise, and answering thy brain!
·O, I will be a sharp disease unto 'em.

MOSCA

Sir, you must look for curses –

VOLPONE   Till they burst;
The Fox fares ever best when he is cursed.

                                          Exeunt

Scene four

SIR POLITIC WOULD-BE'S *House*
Enter PEREGRINE *disguised, and three* MERCHANTS

PEREGRINE

Am I enough disguised?

1st MERCHANT   I warrant you.

PEREGRINE

All my ambition is to fright him only.

2nd MERCHANT

If you could ship him away, 'twere excellent.

3rd MERCHANT

To Zant, or to Aleppo?

PEREGRINE   Yes, and ha' his
Adventures put i' th' *Book of Voyages*,   5
And his gulled story registered for truth?

7   when I am in a while: *when I have been inside for some time.*
8   warm in our discourse: *involved in our conversation.*
9   Know your approaches: *get ready to enter.*

12   earnest: *urgent.*

13   Pray you: *Please do.*

16   require him whole: *require his undivided attention.*
17   possess him: *have his company.*

18   exact him: *force him out.*

21   Bolognian sausages: *the* mortadella *of Bologna was (and still is) the most famous of Italian sausages.*
     sparing: *omitting (in order to increase the profits).*
23   'tidings':   *'tidings' in Sir Politic's view is a commonplace word, which would not be used by a subtle politician or spy ('statesman'). His instruction to Peregrine that he 'wills you stay' may therefore be either (i) a polite invitation to remain, since the guest's language shows him to be unthreatening, or (ii) a demand that he should await Sir Politic's convenience, since he is clearly a person of no importance.*
24   return him: *return this reply to him.*

Well, gentlemen, when I am in a while,
And that you think us warm in our discourse,
Know your approaches.

1st MERCHANT   Trust it to our care.

Exeunt MERCHANTS

Enter WAITING WOMAN

PEREGRINE
Save you, fair lady. Is Sir Pol within?   10

WOMAN
I do not know, sir.

PEREGRINE   Pray you, say unto him,
Here is a merchant, upon earnest business,
Desires to speak with him,

WOMAN   I will see, sir.

PEREGRINE   Pray you.

(*Exit* WOMAN)

I see the family is all female here.

Enter WAITING WOMAN

WOMAN
He says, sir, he has weighty affairs of state   15
That now require him whole – some other time
You may possess him.

PEREGRINE   Pray you, say again,
If those require him whole, these will exact him,
Whereof I bring him tidings. (*Exit* WOMAN)
    What might be
His grave affair of state now? – how to make   20
Bolognian sausages here in Venice, sparing
One o' th' ingredients.

Enter WAITING WOMAN

WOMAN   Sir, he says, he knows
By your word 'tidings' that you are no statesman,
And therefore wills you stay.

PEREGRINE   Sweet, pray you
    return him:
I have not read so many proclamations,   25

35 punk: *prostitute.*

36 has made relation: *has given a report.*

37–8 a plot . . . Turk: *see Act IV Scene I line 130.*

41–2 notes/Drawn out of play-books: *when Jonson was writing, it was common for ignorant people seeking a reputation for political acumen and courtliness to borrow their conversational subject-matter from plays and playscripts. In his panic, Sir Politic betrays the source of his 'learning'.*

42 All the better: *Peregrine is not offering comfort. He says that Sir Politic's taste for plays makes it even more likely that damaging evidence will be found (since plays were commonly suspected of political sedition).*

45 if you could . . . rare: *if you could curl up, a rush basket would be just right. A 'frail' was a basket made of rushes, used for transporting raisins.*

46–7 I but talked so . . . merely: *Peregrine is achieving his aim of double revenge – to humiliate Sir Politic by making him physically ridiculous, and to make him expose his pretentious idiocy.*

And studied them for words, as he has done,
But – Here he deigns to come.

Exit WOMAN

Enter SIR POLITIC WOULD-BE

SIR POLITIC   Sir, I must crave
  Your courteous pardon. There hath chanced today
  Unkind disaster 'twixt my lady and me,
  And I was penning my apology   30
  To give her satisfaction, as you came now.

PEREGRINE
  Sir, I am grieved I bring you worse disaster;
  The gentleman you met at th' port today,
  That told you he was newly arrived –

SIR POLITIC   Ay, was
  A fugitive punk?

PEREGRINE   No, sir, a spy, set on you;   35
  And he has made relation to the Senate
  That you professed to him to have a plot
  To sell the state of Venice to the Turk.

SIR POLITIC
  O me!

PEREGRINE For which, warrants are signed by this time,
  To apprehend you, and to search your study   40
  For papers –

SIR POLITIC   Alas, sir. I have none but notes
  Drawn out of play-books –

PEREGRINE   All the better, sir.

SIR POLITIC
  And some essays. What shall I do?

PEREGRINE   Sir, best
  Convey yourself into a sugar-chest –
  Or, if you could lie round, a frail were rare –   45
  And I could send you aboard.

SIR POLITIC   Sir, I but talked so
  For discourse sake merely.

They knock without

48 a wretch: *reduced to wretchedness and misfortune.*

50 sudden: *quick.*

51 engine: *device.*

52 thought upon before time: *prepared in advance for a crisis like this.*

55 Fitted for these extremities: *designed for these emergencies.*

60 device: *contrivance.*

PEREGRINE   Hark, they are there.

SIR POLITIC

 I am a wretch, a wretch.

PEREGRINE   What will you do, sir?

 Ha' you ne'er a currant-butt to leap into?

 They'll put you to the rack, you must be sudden.   50

SIR POLITIC

 Sir, I have an engine –

3rd MERCHANT (*Off-stage*) Sir Politic Would-be!

2nd MERCHANT (*Off-stage*)

 Where is he?

SIR POLITIC – that I have thought upon before time.

PEREGRINE

 What is it?

SIR POLITIC (I shall ne'er endure the torture).

 Marry, it is, sir, of a tortoise-shell,

 Fitted for these extremities: pray you sir, help me. 55

 Here I've a place, sir, to put back my legs –

 Please you to lay it on, sir; with this cap,

 And my black gloves, I'll lie, sir, like a tortoise,

 Till they are gone.

PEREGRINE   And call you this an engine?

SIR POLITIC

 Mine own device – good sir, bid my wife's women 60

 To burn my papers.

          Exit PEREGRINE

The MERCHANTS *rush in*

1st MERCHANT   Where's he hid?

3rd MERCHANT   We must,

 And will, sure, find him.

2nd MERCHANT   Which is his study?

Re-enter PEREGRINE

1st MERCHANT   What

 Are you, sir?

PEREGRINE I'm a merchant, that came here

 To look upon this tortoise.

66 you may strike him: *Peregrine pretends to be lending support
to Sir Politic's absurd disguise. In reality he gives his fellow conspirators their cue to start beating him.*

68 Can he not go?: *Can't it walk?*

71 Forth: *Come on, move!*

74 fearful: *fearsome.*

3rd MERCHANT   How?

1st MERCHANT   St Mark!
  What beast is this?

PEREGRINE   It is a fish.

2nd MERCHANT   Come out here.   65

PEREGRINE
  Nay, you may strike him, sir, and tread upon him –
  He'll bear a cart.

1st MERCHANT   What, to run over him?

PEREGRINE   Yes.

3rd MERCHANT
  Let's jump upon him.

2nd MERCHANT   Can he not go?

PEREGRINE   He creeps, sir.

1st MERCHANT
  Let's see him creep.

Prods him with his sword

PEREGRINE   No, good sir, you will hurt him.

2nd MERCHANT
  Heart, I'll see him creep, or prick his guts.   70

3rd MERCHANT
  Come out here.

PEREGRINE (*Aside to* SIR POLITIC)
          Pray you sir, creep a little.

1st MERCHANT   Forth.

2nd MERCHANT
  Yet further.

PEREGRINE (*To* SIR POLITIC) Good sir, Creep.

2nd MERCHANT   We'll see his
  legs.

They pull off the shell and discover him

3rd MERCHANT
  God's so –, he has garters!

1st MERCHANT   Ay, and gloves!

2nd MERCHANT   Is this
  Your fearful tortoise?

74   **even:**   *i.e. Peregrine is even with Sir Politic for the embarrassment he suffered when Lady Would-be mistook him for a woman, and for the ill-usage he believes he suffered from Sir Politic's 'project' to act as bawd between Lady Would-be and himself. (See Act IV Scene II lines 32–44 and Act IV Scene III lines 16–24.) Ironically, Sir Politic, who has thought up so many absurdities, is responsible for neither of these.*

76   **funeral of your notes:**   *Sir Politic's desperate instruction (lines 60–1) has been carried out. It is likely that some device was used to show the smoke from Sir Politic's cremated documents drifting across the stage.*

77   **motion:**   *puppet play.*

78   **i' the term:**   *i.e. during law terms. Fleet Street was near the Inns of Court, and the area would be particularly busy when the lawyers were in residence and their clients in town.*
    Smithfield: *the site of the great fair held annually, starting on St Bartholomew's Day, 24 August. Puppet plays were a favourite entertainment there.*

79   **melancholic:**   *the merchant is either being sarcastic at Sir Politic's expense or (more probably) experiencing a moment of genuine sympathy.*

82   **fable of all feasts:**   *subject of gossip at every dinner table.*

83   **freight of the 'gazetti':**   *main story in the news-sheets.*

84   **talk for ordinaries:**   *chief talking-point in common taverns.*

86   **for physic:**   *as a cure.*

88–9 **Creeping . . . shell:**   *this is Sir Politic's farewell to the play. It suggests that he has learned his lesson in the tortoise-shell and will henceforth keep a 'politic shell' or prudent demeanour of humility and discretion rather than a 'politic shell' or boastful appearance of cunning and clever statecraft.*

PEREGRINE (*Removing his disguise*) Now, Sir Pol, we are
  even;
  For your next project, I shall be prepared –   75
  I am sorry for the funeral of your notes, sir.

1st MERCHANT
  'Twere a rare motion to be seen in Fleet Street!

2nd MERCHANT
  Ay, i' the term.

1st MERCHANT   Or Smithfield, in the fair.

3rd MERCHANT
  Methinks 'tis but a melancholic sight!

PEREGRINE
  Farewell, most politic tortoise.

                       Exeunt PEREGRINE, MERCHANTS

Re-enter WAITING WOMAN

SIR POLITIC   Where's my lady?   80
  Knows she of this?

WOMAN   I know not, sir.

SIR POLITIC   Enquire

                          (*Exit* WOMAN)

  O, I shall be the fable of all feasts;
  The freight of the *gazetti*; ship-boys' tale;
  And, which is worst, even talk for ordinaries.

Re-enter WAITING WOMAN

WOMAN
  My lady's come most melancholic home,   85
  And says, sir, she will straight to sea, for physic.

SIR POLITIC
  And I, to shun this place and clime for ever,
  Creeping, with house on back; and think it well,
  To shrink my poor head in my politic shell.

                              Exeunt

1 like him: *see Act V Scene III line 114.*

2 sever: *tell you apart.*

3 thou becom'st it: *the part fits you.*

4–5 If ... made one: *Mosca's public meaning is 'If I act the part well enough'. Privately, he means 'If I can keep the position, now that I've been given it'. This is the first clear hint that Mosca does not intend to give up his place as Volpone's heir without good recompense.*

6–7 My Fox ... hole: *Mosca plays on the name of the children's game 'Fox-in-the-Hole'.*

7 out on: *out of.*

8 borrowed case: *disguise.*

9 Except ... composition: *unless he strikes a bargain.*

11 abroad: *out of the house.*
    go, sport: *go out and have a good time.*

13 will needs be dead: *insists on dying.*

16 cozen him of all: *cheat him of everything.*

17 Well placed: *well deserved.*

18 Let his sport pay for't: *Let it be the price for all his entertainment.*

Scene five

VOLPONE'S *House*
Enter VOLPONE, MOSCA; *the first, in the habit of a* commandadore, *the other, of a* clarissimo.

VOLPONE
  Am I then like him?

MOSCA   O, sir, you are he;
  No man can sever you.

VOLPONE   Good.

MOSCA   But what am I?

VOLPONE
  'Fore heaven, a brave *clarissimo*, thou becom'st it!
  Pity thou wert not born one.

MOSCA   If I hold
  My made one, 'twill be well.

VOLPONE   I'll go and see   5
  What news, first, at the court.

Exit VOLPONE   *Exit* VOLPONE

MOSCA   Do so. My Fox
  Is out on his hole, and ere he shall re-enter,
  I'll make him languish in his borrowed case,
  Except he come to composition with me.
  Androgyno, Castrone, Nano!

Enter ANDROGYNO, CASTRONE, NANO

ALL   Here.   10

MOSCA
  Go, recreate yourselves abroad; go, sport.

                                    (*Exeunt the three*)

  So, now I have the keys, and am possessed.
  Since he will needs be dead afore his time,
  I'll bury him, or gain by him. I'm his heir,
  And so will keep me, till he share at least.   15
  To cozen him of all were but a cheat
  Well placed; no man would cònstrue it a sin –
  Let his sport pay for't. This is called the Fox-trap.

                                              Exit

1 set: *in session.*

5 for your will: *i.e. the will in which Corbaccio left his own
   fortune to Volpone. Mosca now possesses it.*
   come upon him: *make a claim on him (Mosca).*

13 change: *exchange.*

Scene six

Near the Scrutineo. Enter CORBACCIO *and* CORVINO

CORBACCIO

They say the court is set.

CORVINO   We must maintain

Our first tale good, for both our reputations.

CORBACCIO

Why? mine's no tale. My son would there have killed
    me.

CORVINO

That's true, I had forgot; mine is, I am sure.

But for your will, sir.

CORBACCIO   Ay, I'll come upon him   5

For that hereafter, now his patron's dead.

Enter VOLPONE *disguised*

VOLPONE

Signior Corvino! and Corbaccio! sir,

Much joy unto you.

CORVINO   Of what?

VOLPONE   The sudden good

Dropped down upon you –

CORBACCIO   Where?

VOLPONE   And none knows how –

From old Volpone, sir.

CORBACCIO   Out, arrant knave.   10

VOLPONE

Let not your too much wealth, sir, make you furious.

CORBACCIO

Away, thou varlet.

VOLPONE   Why sir?

CORBACCIO   · Dost thou mock me?

VOLPONE

You mock the world, sir; did you not change wills?

CORBACCIO

Out, harlot.

VOLPONE   O! belike you are the man,

17 over-leavened with your fortune: *puffed up (as with too much yeast) by your good fortune.*

18 You should ha' some would: *Some people would ...*
wine-fat: *wine vat.*

19 autumn: *reference to the harvest of wealth that Corvino has supposedly reaped.*

20 Avoid: *Clear off!*

21 a very woman: *a thoroughgoing woman (in her supposed unfaithfulness).*
you are well: *you have no worries.*

22–3 you have a good ... chance: *you are rich enough to put up with it, and even more so as a result of what has happened (i.e. Corvino's 'inheritance' from Volpone).*

25 be a 'known: *confess (to your good fortune).*

28 snuffing: *sniffing in indignation.*

2 make legs, for crumbs?: *bow and scrape for mere trifles?*

3 stays: *waits.*

7 I mean ... your worship: *Volpone now pretends to believe that Voltore is the heir, and begs the tenancy of a small property, part of Volpone's estate, which Voltore would have inherited.*

Signior Corvino? Faith, you carry it well;   15
You grow not mad withal; I love your spirit.
You are not over-leavened with your fortune.
You should ha' some would swell now like a wine-fat
With such an autumn – Did he gi' you all, sir?

CORVINO
  Avoid, you rascal.

VOLPONE   Troth, your wife has shown   20
Herself a very woman; but you are well,
You need not care, you have a good estate
To bear it out, sir, better by this chance.
Except Corbaccio have a share . . . ?

CORBACCIO   Hence, varlet.

VOLPONE
You will not be a'known, sir – why, 'tis wise.   25
Thus do all gamesters, at all games, dissemble.
No man will seem to win.

                          (*Exeunt* CORBACCIO, CORVINO)

             Here comes my vulture,
Heaving his beak up i' the air, and snuffing.

(*Scene seven*)

Enter VOLTORE

VOLTORE
  Outstripped thus, by a parasite? a slave?
  Would run on errands? and make legs, for crumbs?
  Well, what I'll do –

VOLPONE   The court stays for your worship.
I e'en rejoice, sir, at your worship's happiness,
And that it fell into so learned hands,   5
That understand the fingering –

VOLTORE   What do you mean?

VOLPONE
I mean to be a suitor to your worship

8 tenement: *house*.
out of reparations: *in a bad state of repair*.
10 'Piscaria': *fish-market*.

12 customed bawdy-house: *well-patronized brothel*.
13 none dispraised: *without meaning any offence to the others*.
14 But fell with him: *But fell into disrepair at the same time as Volpone fell into ill-health*.
15 prating: *chattering*.

16 give me but your hand: *just shake hands with me to confirm the agreement*.
17 ha' the refusal: *have first refusal*.
18 toy: *trifle*.
candle-rents: *rents from property which is deteriorating*.

20 God decrease it!: *petty officials were often depicted as prone to ignorant errors with words, and Voltore supposes that Volpone (the 'Mistaking knave') has said 'decrease' when he means 'increase'. In fact Volpone is enjoying the fun of an open and deliberate curse*.

22 would 'twere more: *ostensibly Volpone is saying 'I wish your wealth were greater'; in reality, 'I wish your misfortune were greater'*.
23 to my first: *to return to my first victim*.

1 in our habit: *Mosca is wearing the gown of a nobleman*.
2 That I could: *if only I could*.
gunstones: *cannonballs*.

3 of the parasite: *what is said about Mosca (being the heir)*.

268

For the small tenement, out of reparations –
That at the end of your long row of houses,
By the *Piscaria*; it was, in Volpone's time,   10
Your predecessor, ere he grew diseased,
A handsome, pretty, customed bawdy-house
As any was in Venice (none dispraised),
But fell with him; his body and that house
Decayed together.

VOLTORE   Come, sir, leave your prating.   15

VOLPONE

Why, if your worship give me but your hand,
That I may ha' the refusal, I have done.
'Tis a mere toy to you, sir – candle-rents.
As your learn'd worship knows –

VOLTORE   What do I know?

VOLPONE

Marry, no end of your wealth, sir, God decrease it!   20

VOLTORE

Mistaking knave! what, mock'st thou my misfortune?

VOLPONE

His blessing on your heart, sir, would 'twere more.

                              (*Exit* VOLTORE)

– Now, to my first again; at the next corner.

                              Stands aside

(*Scene eight*)

Enter CORBACCIO, CORVINO, (MOSCA *passant*)

CORBACCIO

See, in our habit! see the impudent varlet!

CORVINO

That I could shoot mine eyes at him, like gunstones!

VOLPONE (*Stepping forward*)

But is this true, sir, of the parasite?

6   over-reached: *outsmarted.*

      never brooked: *could never abide.*

7   methought his nose should cozen: *I thought that even the appearance of his nose seemed deceitful.*

8   still: *always.*

9   bane: *destruction.*

10   traded: *experienced.*

11–14 the fine bird ... emptiness: *Volpone refers to Aesop's fable of the fox which expressed a desire to hear the crow singing, thus tricking it into opening its mouth and dropping the piece of cheese in its beak. The fable applies very closely, since Volpone (the fox) is directly laughing at Corvino (the crow) who dropped his cheese (his presents to Volpone) when he was tricked. Corvino 'sang his shame' when he proclaimed his own cuckoldry in the court.*

12   moral emblems: *i.e. emblem books, collections of engravings accompanied by mottoes which explained their moral application; the crow was a frequent symbol in such works.*

14   emptiness: *both 'loss of wealth' and 'stupidity'.*

15   privilege of the place: *either (i) immunity you enjoy because of your position as sergeant or (ii) immunity associated with the spot near the Scrutineo where they have met.*

16–17 And your red ... chequeens: *the uniform of a com-mandadore – Volpone's disguise – consisted of a black gown and a red cap with two gilt buttons. Corvino compares the gilt buttons to the gold coins called chequeens.*

17   jolt-head: *block-head.*

18   warrant your abuses: *sanction your abuse of your office.*

23–4 I were ... Would stand: *I would be a wise man, wouldn't I, if I were to try to withstand ...?*

CORBACCIO

Again, t'afflict us? monster!

VOLPONE   In good faith, sir,
I'm heartily grieved, a beard of your grave length   5
Should be so over-reached. I never brooked
That parasite's hair, methought his nose should cozen;
There still was somewhat in his look did promise
The bane of a *clarissimo*.

CORBACCIO   Knave –

VOLPONE   Methinks
Yet you, that are so traded i' the world,   .   10
A witty merchant, the fine bird, Corvino,
That have such moral emblems on your name,
Should not have sung your shame, and dropped your
    cheese,
To let the Fox laugh at your emptiness.

CORVINO

Sirrah, you think the privilege of the place,   15
And your red, saucy cap, that seems, to me,
Nailed to your jolt-head with those two chequeens,
Can warrant your abuses; come you hither –
You shall perceive, sir, I dare beat you. Approach.

VOLPONE

No haste, sir, I do know your valour well,   20
Since you durst publish what you are, sir.

CORVINO   Tarry,
I'd speak with you.

VOLPONE   Sir, sir, another time –

CORVINO

Nay, now.

VOLPONE   O God, sir! I were a wise man,
Would stand the fury of a distracted cuckold.

                                    Mosca walks by 'em

CORBACCIO

What! come again?

VOLPONE   Upon 'em, Mosca; save me.   25

271

27 basilisk: *i.e. the cockatrice, a fabulous reptile which was said to be able to kill by its breath or even its look. The very sight of Mosca is unbearable to Corbaccio and Corvino.*

1 flesh-fly: *blow-fly. (The blow-fly lays its eggs in rotting flesh. Like the crow, the raven and the vulture, it feeds on carrion, so Voltore's image links Mosca with the legacy-hunters themselves.)*

4 'solecism': *impropriety. (See Act IV Scene II line 43: 'madam' is Lady Would-be, from whom Mosca is scornfully borrowing the word.)*

5 biggin: *lawyer's skull-cap.*

6 Would you ha' me: *Volpone pretends to take Voltore's side and be angry with Mosca.*

7 This same: *i.e. Volpone. (Voltore recognizes the mocking pretence.)*

8 familiar: *fellow from the same household (with the secondary meaning 'familiar spirit' or 'devil').*

9–11 I am mad . . . ride an advocate: *I am outraged that Mosca (a mule, hence servant and beast of burden) should get the better of a lawyer. (This emphasizes the sudden reversal of roles and status. Lawyers habitually rode on mules.)*

10 Justinian: *the code of Roman law, the Corpus Juris Civilis, was drawn up on the orders of the Emperor Justinian I.*

11 quirk: *trick.*

12 gullage: *being fooled.*

14 but confederacy, to blind the rest: *just a plot between you and Mosca to deceive the other legacy-hunters.*

CORBACCIO
    The air's infected where he breathes.
CORVINO   Let's fly him.
                            Exeunt CORBACCIO, CORVINO
VOLPONE
    Excellent basilisk! turn upon the vulture.

(*Scene nine*)

Enter VOLTORE
VOLTORE
    Well, flesh-fly, it is summer with you now;
    Your winter will come on.
MOSCA   Good advocate,
    Pray thee not rail, nor threaten out of place, thus;
    Thou'lt make a 'solecism', as madam says.
    Get you a biggin more – your brain breaks loose.   5
                                                        Exit

VOLTORE
    Well, sir.
VOLPONE   Would you ha' me beat the insolent slave?
    Throw dirt upon his first good clothes?
VOLTORE   This same
    Is doubtless some familiar!
VOLPONE   Sir, the court,
    In troth, stays for you. I am mad, a mule
    That never read Justinian should get up   10
    And ride an advocate. Had you no quirk
    To avoid gullage, sir, by such a creature?
    I hope you do but jest; he has not done't;
    This's but confederacy, to blind the rest.
    You are the heir?
VOLTORE   A strange, officious,   15
    Troublesome knave! thou dost torment me.
VOLPONE   I know –

17   cozened: *tricked.*

4   Once win upon: *for once supplant.*

8   Will he betray himself?:   *note that Voltore has less to lose than the others. He has already lost the legacy, he thinks. His dishonest advocacy in the earlier court scene could no doubt be passed off as the result of wrong briefing. When Mosca dismissed the suitors in Act V Scene III, Voltore was the only one who could not be black-mailed by the threat to reveal hidden misconduct.*

10   possessed: *i.e. possessed by a devil.*

It cannot be, sir, that you should be cozened;
'Tis not within the wit of man to do it,
You are so wise, so prudent – and 'tis fit
That wealth and wisdom still should go together.   20

Exeunt

Scene ten

The Scrutineo
Enter four AVOCATORI, NOTARIO, COMMANDADORI, BONARIO, CELIA,
CORBACCIO, CORVINO
1st AVOCATORE
    Are all the parties here?
NOTARIO   All but the advocate.
2nd AVOCATORE
    And here he comes.
Enter VOLTORE, VOLPONE
1st AVOCATORE   Then bring 'em forth to sentence.
                              BONARIO, CELIA *are led forward*
VOLTORE O, my most honoured fathers, let your mercy
    Once win upon your justice, to forgive –
    I am distracted –
VOLPONE (*Aside*)   What will he do now?
VOLTORE   O,   5
    I know not which t'address myself to first,
    Whether your fatherhoods, or these innocents –
CORVINO (*Aside*)
    Will he betray himself?
VOLTORE   – whom, equally,
    I have abused, out of most covetous ends –
CORVINO (*To* CORBACCIO)
    The man is mad!
CORBACCIO   What's that?
CORVINO   He is possessed.   10

275

14　mine own noose: *the noose is Volpone's extension of his trickery in declaring himself dead and Mosca the heir. This irresistible joke has removed the self-interest that kept Voltore quiet.*

16　passion: *frenzy.*

21　now: *just now.*

24　Dead since: *dead since the court last met.*

26　The parasite: *i.e. it is the parasite who is the deceiver.*

VOLTORE

    For which, now struck in conscience, here I prostrate

    Myself at your offended feet, for pardon.

1st and 2nd AVOCATORI

    Arise.

CELIA   O Heaven, how just thou art!

VOLPONE (*Aside*)   I'm caught

    I' mine own noose –

CORVINO (*To* CORBACCIO) Be constant, sir; naught now

    Can help but impudence.

1st AVOCATORE   Speak forward.

COMMANDADORE   Silence!   15

VOLTORE

    It is not passion in me, reverend fathers,

    But only conscience, conscience, my good sires,

    That makes me now tell truth. That parasite,

    That knave, hath been the instrument of all.

1st AVOCATORE

    Where is that knave? fetch him.

VOLPONE   I go.

                          Exit VOLPONE

CORVINO   Grave fathers,   20

    This man's distracted; he confessed it now;

    For, hoping to be old Volpone's heir,

    Who now is dead –

3rd AVOCATORE   How?

2nd AVOCATORE   Is Volpone dead?

CORVINO

    Dead since, grave fathers –

BONARIO   O, sure vengeance!

1st AVOCATORE   Stay –

    Then he was no deceiver?

VOLTORE   O no, none;   25

    The parasite, grave fathers.

CORVINO   He does speak

    Out of mere envy, 'cause the servant's made

28 The thing he gaped for: *the beneficiary he longed to be.*

29–30 I'll not justify . . . faulty: *I will not excuse Mosca, for he may be to some extent at fault. (Even in trying out of self-preservation to discredit Voltore, Corvino will lose no chance to stick some blame on the hated Mosca.)*

31 to your hopes: *at the cost of your expectations.*

32 modesty: *moderation.*

33 certain: *particular.*

but confer: *just consider.*

35 The devil has entered him: *sharp irony; like 'He is possessed', at line 10. At last one of the legacy-hunters is telling the court the truth, only to be accused of being possessed by a devil. The inversion of truth and values is apparent again.*

43 Stand you unto . . .?: *Do you still stand by . . .*

state: *estate.*

44 fame: *reputation.*

at the stake: *i.e. staked on the truth of my testimony.*

The thing he gaped for; please your fatherhoods,
This is the truth; though I'll not justify
The other, but he may be some-deal faulty.   30

VOLTORE

Ay, to your hopes, as well as mine, Corvino.
But I'll use modesty. Pleaseth your wisdoms
To view these certain notes, and but confer them;

(Gives them papers)

As I hope favour, they shall speak clear truth.

CORVINO

The devil has entered him!

BONARIO   Or bides in you.   35

4th AVOCATORE

We have done ill, by a public officer
To send for him, if he be heir.

2nd AVOCATORE   For whom?

4th AVOCATORE

Him that they call the parasite.

3rd AVOCATORE   'Tis true;

He is a man of great estate now left.

4th AVOCATORE

Go you, and learn his name; and say the court   40
Entreats his presence here, but to the clearing
Of some few doubts.

                                                        Exit NOTARIO

2nd AVOCATORE   This same's a labyrinth!

1st AVOCATORE

Stand you unto your first report?

CORVINO   My state,

My life, my fame –

BONARIO   Where is't?

CORVINO   – are at the stake.

1st AVOCATORE

Is yours so too?

CORBACCIO   The advocate's a knave,   45
And has a forkèd tongue –

                                                                        279

47 So is the parasite: *like Corvino, Corbaccio is now protecting himself against Voltore's truth-telling but also seeking to discredit Mosca in the process.*

49 credit: *believe.*
the false spirit: *i.e. the devil which has 'possessed' Voltore.*

2 with laughter: *for sheer amusement, without any sense of danger.*

4 wantonness: *impulsive recklessness. Volpone now realizes that his own foolishness in this last stage of the game, with no hope of profit and no other motive than to ridicule his victims, has led him to the brink of disaster.*
dull devil: *devil of stupidity.*

6 gave it second: *supported it.*

7 sear up: *cauterize, thus stopping the flow of blood from the wound.*

9 kitlings: *kittens.*

10 called us: *sent us.*

13 I am farther in: *I am in even deeper trouble. (Mosca's action with the keys causes Volpone to suspect for the first time that his partner may be playing a double game.)*
conceits: *schemes (i.e. 'This is where my clever schemes have got me!')*

14 I must be . . . mischief to me: *I had to have my fun, devil take me! (Volpone again takes the measure of his own recent folly.)*

2nd AVOCATORE	Speak to the point.

CORBACCIO

So is the parasite, too.

1st AVOCATORE   This is confusion.

VOLTORE

I do beseech your fatherhoods, read but those.

Indicating his notes

CORVINO

And credit nothing the false spirit hath writ.

It cannot be but he is possessed, grave fathers.   50

Exeunt

Scene eleven

A Street

Enter VOLPONE

VOLPONE

To make a snare for mine own neck! and run

My head into it wilfully! with laughter!

When I had newly scaped, was free and clear!

Out of mere wantonness! O, the dull devil

Was in this brain of mine when I devised it,   5

And Mosca gave it second; he must now

Help to sear up this vein, or we bleed dead.

(*Enter* NANO, ANDROGYNO, CASTRONE)

How now! who let you loose? whither go you now?

What, to buy ginger-bread? or to drown kitlings?

NANO

Sir, master Mosca called us out of doors,   10

And bid us all go play, and took the keys.

ANDROGYNO   Yes.

VOLPONE

Did master Mosca take the keys? why, so!

I am farther in. These are my fine conceits!

I must be merry, with a mischief to me!

281

16 crotchets: *fancies*.

17 coundrums: *whims*.

18 His meaning . . . my fear: *His intentions may be more loyal to me than I fear they are.*

21 Unscrew my advocate, upon new hopes: *Reduce Voltore's passion by giving him renewed expectations.*

1 These things can ne'er be reconciled: *Voltore in his papers has alleged (i) that Corvino forced Celia to visit Volpone, intending to prostitute her, and (ii) that Volpone could not have ravished Celia since he was impotent. Clearly the two things together do not make sense! The audience knows that the first statement is true but the second is not. Voltore, however, believes that both are true. It is typical of the play's world that a sincere attempt to tell the truth should produce apparent nonsense.*

2 gentleman: *i.e. Bonario.*

9–10 possession and obsession: *possession is control by an evil spirit which has entered the body; obsession is control by an evil spirit outside the body.*

What a vile wretch was I, that could not bear   15
My fortune soberly! I must ha' my crotchets!
And my conundrums! well, go you and seek him –
His meaning may be truer than my fear.
Bid him, he straight come to me, to the court;
Thither will I, and, if't be possible,   20
Unscrew my advocate, upon new hopes.
When I provoked him, then I lost myself.

Exeunt

Scene twelve

The Scrutineo
Four AVOCATORI, VOLTORE, BONARIO, CELIA, CORBACCIO,
CORVINO, COMMANDADORI
1st AVOCATORE
    These things can ne'er be reconciled. He, here,
                (*Indicating* VOLTORE's *papers*)
    Professeth that the gentleman was wronged;
    And that the gentlewoman was brought thither,
    Forced by her husband, and there left.
VOLTORE   Most true.
CELIA
    How ready is Heaven to those that pray!
1st AVOCATORE   But that   5
    Volpone would have ravished her, he holds
    Utterly false, knowing his impotence.
CORVINO
    Grave fathers, he is possessed; again, I say,
    Possessed; nay, if there be possession
    And obsession, he has both.
3rd AVOCATORE   Here comes our officer.   10
Enter VOLPONE

12   invent some other name: *devise a better title for him* (*than 'parasite'*). *Mosca is gathering the respect due to his new-found wealth: the court, too, is susceptible to the transforming powers of money.*

14   misty: *confused.*

17   still the man: *still the man chosen as Volpone's heir.*

19   affected: *disposed.*

20   Do I live, sir?:   *He's just as alive as I am!* (*The irony, of course, is that this conventional expression is literally true, since the disguised Volpone is speaking about himself.*)

22   fall down: *i.e. fall down as if you were having a fit.* (*Fits were one supposed effect of possession by a devil.*)

23   I'll help to make it good: *I will assist you to make your act effective.*

24   Stop your wind hard: *Hold your breath tightly.*

25   He vomits crooked pins!:   *possession by devils was something generally accepted as possible at this time. Vomiting of crooked pins is one symptom of possession quoted in documents from the period, as are those in the following lines. The subject naturally aroused much superstitious interest, which caused such symptoms to be fraudulently imitated by the assistants of quack exorcists, hoping to trade on popular credulity for profit.*

25   set: *fixed.*

26   poulter's: *poulterer's.*

27   running away: *twitching in violent spasms.*

VOLPONE
    The parasite will straight be here, grave fathers.

4th AVOCATORE
    You might invent some other name, sir varlet.

3rd AVOCATORE
    Did not the notary meet him?

VOLPONE   Not that I know.

4th AVOCATORE
    His coming will clear all.

2nd AVOCATORE   Yet, it is misty.

VOLTORE
    May't please your fatherhoods –

                    VOLPONE *whispers to the advocate*

VOLPONE   Sir, the parasite   15
    Willed me to tell you that his master lives;
    That you are still the man; your hopes, the same;
    And this was only a jest –

VOLTORE   How?

VOLPONE   Sir, to try
    If you were firm, and how you stood affected.

VOLTORE
    Art sure he lives?

VOLPONE   Do I live, sir?

VOLTORE   O me!   20
    I was too violent.

VOLPONE   Sir, you may redeem it –
    They said, you were possessed; fall down, and seem so;
    I'll help to make it good. (VOLTORE *falls*) God bless the
       man!
    (*To* VOLTORE) Stop your wind hard, and swell – See, see,
       see, see!
    He vomits crooked pins! his eyes are set,   25
    Like a dead hare's hung in a poulter's shop!
    His mouth's running away! do you see, signior?
    Now, 'tis in his belly.

35 dispossessed: *freed from devilish possession.*
    accident: *unforeseen happening.*

41 hand: *handwriting.*

42 practice: *trickery.*

43 maze: *confusion.*

CORVINO   Ay, the devil!

VOLPONE
  Now, in his throat.

CORVINO   Ay, I perceive it plain.

VOLPONE
  'Twill out, 'twill out; stand clear. See where it flies!   30
  In shape of a blue toad, with a bat's wings!
  Do not you see it, sir?

CORBACCIO   What? I think I do.

CORVINO
  'Tis too manifest.

VOLPONE   Look! he comes t'himself!

VOLTORE
  Where am I?

VOLPONE   Take good heart, the worst is past, sir.
  You are dispossessed.

1st AVOCATORE   What accident is this?   35

2nd AVOCATORE
  Sudden, and full of wonder!

3rd AVOCATORE   If he were
  Possessed, as it appears, all this is nothing.

CORVINO
  He has been often subject to these fits.

1st AVOCATORE
  Show him that writing. Do you know it, sir?

VOLPONE (*Aside to* VOLTORE)
  Deny it, sir, forswear it, know it not.   40

VOLTORE
  Yes, I do know it well, it is my hand;
  But all that it contains is false.

BONARIO   O practice!

2nd AVOCATORE
  What maze is this!

1st AVOCATORE   Is he not guilty then,
  Whom you there name the parasite?

47 subtler: *more obscure and bewildering.*

49 make him way: *make way for him.*

50 proper: *handsome.*

53 Had betrayed all: *Was just about to give everything away.*
54 o' the hinge: *restored to order.*
55 busy knave: *interfering rogue. (For the first time in the play,
Mosca spurns Volpone in public; treats Volpone in his presence as
if his 'death' were an accomplished fact, and their respective disguises were authentic; and risks allowing Volpone to realize the
split between them in circumstances which leave each of them with
little room for manoeuvre or retreat. Despite first Mosca's and then
Volpone's further whispered efforts to negotiate a settlement, this is
effectively the moment when their long and brilliant pact is shat-
tered.)*
60 quick: *alive.*
   cozen me of all: *cheat me of everything.*

VOLTORE   Grave fathers,
  No more than his good patron, old Volpone.   45
4th AVOCATORE
  Why, he is dead?
VOLTORE   O no, my honoured fathers.
  He lives –
1st AVOCATORE How! lives?
VOLTORE   Lives.
2nd AVOCATORE   This is subtler yet!
  You said he was dead!
VOLTORE   Never.
3rd AVOCATORE (*To* CORVINO) You said so!
CORVINO   I heard so.
4th AVOCATORE
  Here comes the gentleman; make him way.
Enter MOSCA
3rd AVOCATORE   A stool!
4th AVOCATORE (*Aside*)   50
  A proper man! and were Volpone dead,
  A fit match for my daughter.
3rd AVOCATORE   Give him way.
VOLPONE (*Aside to* MOSCA)
  Mosca, I was a'most lost; the advocate
  Had betrayed all; but now it is recovered.
  All's o' the hinge again – say I am living.
MOSCA
  What busy knave is this! Most reverend fathers,   55
  I sooner had attended your grave pleasures,
  But that my order for the funeral
  Of my dear patron did require me –
VOLPONE (*Aside*)   Mosca!
MOSCA
  Whom I intend to bury like a gentleman.
VOLPONE (*Aside*)
  Ay, quick, and cozen me of all.

61 come about: *the situation is reversed.*

62 It is a match: *Mosca's words have seemed finally to confirm that Volpone is dead and Mosca the heir, so the fourth of the Avocatori now firmly decides to arrange a profitable marriage between Mosca and his daughter.*

64 cry not so loud: *keep your voice down.*
    Demand: *ask.*

69–70 I cannot now ... cheap: *Mosca, at line 63, appeared ready to divide Volpone's wealth between them. Once this offer is rejected, and believing himself to have the upper hand, it is Mosca's turn to overreach himself by vindictively seizing on everything. The result is an extreme version of what we have already seen with Voltore's confession: in any such criminal conspiracy, it is fatal to leave one of the partners feeling he has nothing to lose and hence no reason for secrecy.*

73 this creature: *i.e. Mosca.*

74 good: *favourable.*

75–6 must pass/Upon me: *is allowed to be directed at me.*

2nd AVOCATORE   Still stranger!   60
  More intricate!
1st AVOCATORE   And come about again!
4th AVOCATORE (*Aside*)
  It is a match, my daughter is bestowed.
MOSCA (*Aside to* VOLPONE)
  Will you gi' me half?
VOLPONE (*Aside to* MOSCA) First, I'll be hanged.
MOSCA (*Aside to* VOLPONE)   I know
  Your voice is good; cry not so loud.
1st AVOCATORE   Demand
  The advocate. Sir, did not you affirm   65
  Volpone was alive?
VOLPONE   Yes, and he is;
  This gent'man (*Indicating* MOSCA) told me so.
  (*Aside to* MOSCA)   Thou shalt have half.
MOSCA
  Whose drunkard is this same? speak some that know
    him –
  I never saw his face. (*Aside to* VOLPONE) I cannot now
  Afford it you so cheap.
VOLPONE (*Aside to* MOSCA) No?
1st AVOCATORE   What say you?   70
VOLTORE
  The officer told me.
VOLPONE   I did, grave fathers,
  And will maintain he lives, with mine own life,
  And (*Indicating* MOSCA) that this creature told me.
  (*Aside*)   I was born
  With all good stars my enemies.
MOSCA   Most grave fathers,
  If such an insolence as this must pass   75
  Upon me, I am silent; 'twas not this
  For which you sent, I hope.
2nd AVOCATORE   Take him away.

78 whipped: *men of property could not be sentenced to a whipping; it was a punishment reserved for those without means. The punishment brings home with special force to Volpone that he has lost everything (materially, which has been his measure of judgement) and therefore has nothing left to lose by confession and exposure.*

79 to bear himself: *to show proper respect.*

81 Soft, soft: *Let me see, let me see . . .*

84 allied: *related by marriage.*

85 uncase: *remove his disguise.*
Patron!: *surprised by the shock of Volpone's grand gesture of desperation, Mosca instantly reverts to their former relationship.*

86–7 your match I'll hinder sure: *I will prevent your marriage, beyond any doubt.*

88 into a family: *into a good family through marriage.*

90 avarice's fool: *i.e. one who is fooled by his own avarice.*

91 chimera of wittol, fool and knave: *monster made up of three parts: a conniving cuckold (wittol), a fool and a villain. The chimaera was a monster in Greek myth with a lion's head, a goat's body and a serpent's tail.*

93 Naught but a sentence: *nothing more than the sentence of the court.*
despair it: *be disappointed of it.*

94 You hear me brief: *I have spoken briefly.*

VOLPONE (*Aside*)
  Mosca!
3rd AVOCATORE
      Let him be whipped –
VOLPONE (*Aside*)   Wilt thou betray me?
  Cozen me?
3rd AVOCATORE – and taught to bear himself
  Toward á person of his rank.
4th AVOCATORE   Away.   80
                              VOLPONE *is seized*

MOSCA
  I humbly thank your fatherhoods.
VOLPONE (*Aside*)   Soft, soft. Whipped?
  And lose all that I have? if I confess,
  It cannot be much more.
4th AVOCATORE (*To* MOSCA) Sir, are you married?
VOLPONE
  They'll be allied anon; I must be resolute:
                      (*He puts off his disguise*)
  The fox shall here uncase.
MOSCA (*Aside*)   Patron!
VOLPONE   Nay, now   85
  My ruins shall not come alone; your match
  I'll hinder sure; my substance shall not glue you,
  Nor screw you, into a family.
MOSCA (*Aside*)   Why, patron!
VOLPONE
  I am Volpone, and this (*Pointing to* MOSCA) is my
    knave;
  This, (*To* VOLTORE) his own knave; this, (*to* CORBACCIO)
    avarice's fool;   90
  This, (*To* CORVINO) a chimera of wittol, fool, and knave;
  And, reverend fathers, since we all can hope
  Naught but a sentence, let's not now despair it.
  You hear me brief.
CORVINO   May it please your fatherhoods –

95   knot: *complicated tangle.*

98   Heaven ... be hid: *Although we have seen that the villains have ruined themselves by their self-destructively ambitious energies, it is conventional for Bonario, as the representative of pious goodness, to attribute the outcome to divine justice.*

101–102   These possess wealth ... possess them: *for a last, powerful time in the play, wealth is directly linked to and compared with disease. The double use of the word 'possess', following so soon after Voltore's courtroom performance, also associates wealth with demonic possession.*

104   stay: *halt.*

105   And mercy: *Celia's plea for mercy to the wrongdoers is a purely formal contribution to the proceedings, as brief as it could be and clearly intended by Jonson to carry almost no dramatic weight. No humane and gentle scale of values is allowed to moderate the harshness of the play – a harshness which is now transferred to the operations of a public justice which sets out to be vindictively appropriate.*

108   minister: *agent.*

109   lewd: *base.*

111   And habit ... Venice: *And you have also abused the dress of a Venetian nobleman, by wearing it when not entitled to do so.*

112   blood: *rank.*

COMMANDADORE   Silence!

1st AVOCATORE

    The knot is now undone, by miracle!   95

2nd AVOCATORE

    Nothing can be more clear.

3rd AVOCATORE   Or can more prove

    These innocent.

1st AVOCATORE   Give 'em their liberty.

BONARIO

    Heaven could not long let such gross crimes be hid.

2nd AVOCATORE

    If this be held the highway to get riches,

    May I be poor.

3rd AVOCATORE   This's not the gain, but torment.   100

1st AVOCATORE

    These possess wealth, as sick men possess fevers,

    Which, trulier, may be said to possess them.

2nd AVOCATORE

    Disrobe that parasite.

CORVINO, MOSCA   Most honoured fathers –

1st AVOCATORE

    Can you plead aught to stay the course of justice?

    If you can, speak.

CORVINO, VOLTORE We beg favour.

CELIA   And mercy.   105

1st AVOCATORE

    You hurt your innocence, suing for the guilty.

    Stand forth; and first, the parasite. You appear

    T'have been the chiefest minister, if not plotter,

    In all these lewd impostures; and now, lastly,

    Have, with your impudence, abused the court   110

    And habit of a gentleman of Venice,

    Being a fellow of no birth or blood;

    For which, our sentence is, first thou be whipped;

    Then live perpetual prisoner in our galleys.

115 I thank you for him: *the first texts of the play give this speech to Voltore, but all modern editors agree that it must be Volpone's. It is Volpone's ironic reprisal to Mosca's 'I humbly thank your fatherhoods' at line 81.*

Bane: *destruction.*

116 'Saffi': *sergeants of the court, bailiffs.*

118 like censure: *comparable sentence.*

119 substance: *property.*

120 'Incurabili': *the Hospital of the Incurables actually existed in Venice.*

121 the most was gotten: *the greater part was obtained.*

124 Till thou be'st sick and lame indeed: *pretence of disease has been the keystone of Volpone's fraud and trickery. Actual lameness and infirmity have been apparent in one of the victims, Corbaccio. The play has been dominated by the imagery of disease. Now, at its conclusion, the reality and not the image or the acting of disease are imposed on Volpone himself.*

125 mortifying of a fox: *Volpone's final grim, sardonic line plays on several meanings of 'mortifying'. It means 'killing' (implying that he has received a death sentence, not a term of imprisonment). It means 'disciplining the body by abstinence' (a wry comment on his secular version of religious self-discipline). It means 'keeping game until it is "high", so that it will be more tender when eaten. And it means 'causing gangrene', perhaps the last and worst of the sicknesses that Volpone's imprisonment may bring. See introduction page xxxiv–xxxv.*

130 state: *estate.*

133 learned: *taught.*

136 'Grand Canale': *the Grand Canal which divides Venice.*

138 Instead of horns: *since Celia has been proved innocent, Corvino is not a cuckold. He therefore wears an ass's ears, proclaiming him a fool, instead of a cuckold's horns.*

139 'berlino': *pillory.*

VOLPONE

   I thank you for him.

MOSCA   Bane to thy wolfish nature.   115

1st AVOCATORE

   Deliver him to the *Saffi*. (MOSCA *is led aside*) Thou, Vol-
      pone,
   By blood and rank a gentleman, canst not fall
   Under like censure; but our judgment on thee
   Is, that thy substance all be straight confiscate
   To the hospital of the *Incurabili*;   120
   And, since the most was gotten by imposture,
   By feigning lame, gout, palsy, and such diseases,
   Thou art to lie in prison, cramped with irons,
   Till thou be'st sick and lame indeed. Remove him.

VOLPONE

   This is called mortifying of a fox.   125

                          VOLPONE *is led aside*

1st AVOCATORE

   Thou, Voltore, to take away the scandal
   Thou hast given all worthy men of thy profession,
   Art banished from their fellowship, and our state.
   Corbaccio! – bring him near. We here possess
   Thy son of all thy state; and confine thee   130
   To the monastery of *San' Spirito*,
   Where, since thou knew'st not how to live well here,
   Thou shalt be learned to die well.

CORBACCIO   Ha! what said he?

COMMANDADORE (*Leading him aside*)

   You shall know anon, sir.

1st AVOCATORE   Thou, Corvino, shalt
   Be straight embarked from thine own house, and rowed 135
   Round about Venice, through the *Grand Canale*,
   Wearing a cap with fair, long ass's ears
   Instead of horns; and so to mount, a paper
   Pinned on thy breast, to the *berlino* –

CORVINO   Yes,

145 judgments: *sentences.*

149–50 Let all ... love to study 'em; *a concise statement of the purpose and justification of comedy, as defined by critics and dramatists who derived their theory from classical models.*

154 no suffering due: *the actor playing Volpone hopes that the audience has no cause to punish him for the quality of his performance.*

155 fact: *crime.*

156 doubtful: *unsure of the audience's judgement.*

And have mine eyes beat out with stinking fish,   140
Bruised fruit, and rotten eggs – 'Tis well. I'm glad
I shall not see my shame yet.

1st AVOCATORE   And to expiate
Thy wrongs done to thy wife, thou art to send her
Home, to her father, with her dowry trebled.
And these are all your judgments –

ALL   Honoured fathers!   145

1st AVOCATORE
– which may not be revoked. Now you begin,
When crimes are done, and past, and to be punished,
To think what your crimes are. Away with them!
Let all that see these vices thus rewarded,
Take heart, and love to study 'em. Mischiefs feed   150
Like beasts, till they be fat, and then they bleed.

                                                         Exeunt

VOLPONE *comes forward*

VOLPONE
The seasoning of a play is the applause.
Now, though the Fox be punished by the laws,
He yet doth hope there is no suffering due
For any fact which he hath done 'gainst you.   155
If there be, censure him – here he doubtful stands.
If not, fare jovially, and clap your hands.

Study questions

1   A recent professional production of the full play took four hours to perform. If you were producing the play, what arguments would you consider both *for* and *against* omitting the sub-plot?

2   The only character who takes part in both the main plot and the sub-plot is Lady Would-be. Do you think Jonson makes her a consistent figure in both parts of the play? What does her presence add to the main plot, *either* in aiding plot development *or* in broadening its dramatic effect?

3   How far do you consider that justice is done in *Volpone*? Consider the fate of *all* the chief figures in the main plot, and also the gulling of Sir Politic Would-be.

4   It has been said that Jonson invents a special language for Mosca, skilfully blended from simultaneous politeness and insult. Examine Mosca's dramatic style and see if you agree. Then look at one or two other characters and ask yourself whether they also have a distinctive language.

5   One of *Volpone*'s strengths as a play is that its greatest recurrent images are also concrete material facts in the play. Do you agree? Consider the image and the actuality of (i) gold and material wealth and (ii) disease and physical deformity.

6   A recent production depicted Volpone as having genuinely warm and protective feelings towards his 'mascots', Nano, Androgyno and Castrone. What effect do you think this might have on our reactions to Volpone? Is there anything in the text to justify it?

7   Volpone is very useful to Mosca and Mosca to Volpone. How much more does Jonson allow us to find in their relationship, such as trust, affection, dependence or respect? What do you think causes their final split? Is it

inevitable? How early do we detect signs that it might happen? Both of them share a relish and gift for acting: is their mutual skill as actors a factor in their final break with each other?

8   'The irony of the play repeatedly involves turning pretences and imagination into reality, and this irony is most powerful in the conclusion of both the main plot and the sub-plot.' Do you agree?

9   'The things we loathe in the legacy-hunters are also the things we laugh at. This is partly what allows us to hold them at a distance and judge them accurately.' Consider the relationship between what is debased in Corvino, Corbaccio and Voltore, and what is ridiculous in them.

10   What do you think the play gains by being written in verse? Why is it necessary for Volpone's speeches as Scoto the mountebank (Act II Scene II) to be delivered in prose? Why do you think Jonson chooses an unusual four-stressed verse form for the freaks' play (Act I Scene II)?

11   It is sometimes said that Aesop's fable of the fox and the crow can be seen as a key to the whole play. (See Act I Scene II line 95; Act V Scene VIII lines 10–14 and notes.) Do you agree? Explore the range of bird and animal imagery in the play, over and above the characters' names. What do you think its main effects are?

12   'In spite of all its sordid spectacle, the effect of the play is one of magnificence.' If you think this is so, how would you account for it?

13   On the stage, Jonson's characters are often at their most effective and important either when they are talking too much or when they are silent. Look at the text carefully, and examine some important occasions (i) when characters seem to be carried away by their own language, and (ii) when they are unexpectedly silent.

14   What is your own view of the argument that *Volpone* comes close to tragedy? Make out the best case you can

both *for* and *against* this interpretation, and decide which you find most convincing.

15 The whole play is built on characters' expectations that others will behave predictably, like well-trained animals, and the major crises of the play arise at moments when they disobey the rules and behave unpredictably instead. Examine this suggestion. If it is true, what does it indicate about Jonson's Venice?

16 A modern critic (not writing specifically about Jonson) has said this: 'As the textbooks tell us, the standard theme of New Comedy or Roman Comedy, from which most modern comedy and melodrama derive, is that of the social misfit – miser or crank or misanthrope or lecher – creating a series of problems for the young lovers and, once baffled by the aid of a crafty servant who, for the sake of comedy's holiday spirit, often oversteps his rank, the misfit is re-integrated into society or expelled from it. The result is an affirmation of society's ideals and conventions.' How much of this definition applies to *Volpone*? How important to the play's special effects are the points where it does *not* fit?

17 Eric Bentley, in his book *The Life of the Drama*, wrote: 'In *Volpone* there is no one to like, and everyone is sick, not just to the point where he becomes believable, but far beyond it – to the point where you are tempted to *disbelieve*. Ben Jonson's characters are "far out". His world is a madhouse.' Discuss your reaction to this verdict on the play.